My Texas Life
IN THE (NOT SO) FAST LANE

A Memoir of a Coach, Teacher and "Down Ballot" Politician

DAN MONTGOMERY

outskirts
press

My Texas Life in the (not so) Fast Lane
A Memoir of a Coach, Teacher and "Down Ballot" Politician
All Rights Reserved.
Copyright © 2019 Dan Montgomery
v4.0

The opinions expressed in this manuscript are solely the opinions of the author and do not represent the opinions or thoughts of the publisher. The author has represented and warranted full ownership and/or legal right to publish all the materials in this book.

This book may not be reproduced, transmitted, or stored in whole or in part by any means, including graphic, electronic, or mechanical without the express written consent of the publisher except in the case of brief quotations embodied in critical articles and reviews.

Outskirts Press, Inc.
http://www.outskirtspress.com

ISBN: 978-1-9772-0874-3

Cover Photo © 2019 Dan Montgomery. All rights reserved - used with permission.

Outskirts Press and the "OP" logo are trademarks belonging to Outskirts Press, Inc.

PRINTED IN THE UNITED STATES OF AMERICA

Table of Contents

Introduction i
Chapter 1   Trains That Don't Stop, Bonnie & Clyde, and the
            "Hitler War" (Rural Navarro County) 1
Chapter 2   Whiskey, Fruit Jars, Crooked Noses, and Camp
            Meetings (Freestone County) 8
Chapter 3   James Fuller "Buddy" "Full-O-Pep" Withrow 23
Chapter 4   Aaron "Puncher" Montgomery 29
Chapter 5   "Ignorant Hill" in the City of My Birth
            (Navarro Jr. College) 33
Chapter 6   "Harvard on Highway 75" (Sam Houston State) 37
Chapter 7   Getting Started on a Long and Successful Career
            (Calvert) 42
Chapter 8   My Memorable Year in the East Texas Oil Field
            (Carlisle) 49
Chapter 9   Win Too Many "Thump-Thump" Games and
            You're Fired!!! (Wharton) 59
Chapter 10 Two Years of Heat, Sweat, Traffic, and
            Mosquitoes (Houston) 73
Chapter 11 Starting A High School Basketball Dynasty
            (Silsbee) 85
Chapter 12 Four Happy Years as a "Kerr-Vert"
            (Kerrville Tivy) 110
Chapter 13 My Time on a Hill in South Austin (St. Edward's) ... 123
Chapter 14 The Wild and Wacky World of Juco
            Basketball (Cisco) 156

Chapter 15	Living in a "Theme Park" and Life After Coaching (Fredericksburg) 169
Chapter 16	Becoming "That Other Guy" 174
Chapter 17	My Introduction to the Wild and Wacky World of the Texas State Board of Education 181
Chapter 18	Charter Schools and the "Textbook Wars" 188
Chapter 19	Redistricting, Re-Election, and (God forbid!) Terri Leo 194
Chapter 20	Liberal History Books and the Permanent School Fund 200
Chapter 21	"Strengths and Weaknesses" (The Biology Textbook Debate) 208
Chapter 22	My Final Years Dealing with Democrats and "Wing Nuts" 215
Chapter 23	The Election of 2006 (and After) 226
Chapter 24	My Nemisis, David Bradley 236
Chapter 25	Looking for a Shoulder to Cry On 242
Chapter 26	"Montgomery Hill Plantation" 244
About the Author 250

Introduction

OVER THE LAST several months, I've asked myself several times, "Why am I doing this"? Why would I choose to write a memoir about my very ordinary life and why would anybody want to read it? After all, I'm not a famous person and, while most Texans who write memoirs are identified with a particular region of the state (Hill Country, Panhandle, etc.) where they grew up, my roots are in a very nondescript part of Texas that is too far to the west to call myself an East Texan, and too far to the east to call myself a Central Texan, much less a West Texan. Hardly anyone has heard of the "Black Land Prairie" or the "Post Oak Belt", and very few people can locate Navarro or Freestone counties on a map. In addition, I didn't attend an Ivy League school or even a large state university such as the University of Texas or Texas A&M, nor did I coach or teach at a major university. I have no war stories to tell because I was too young for World War II and Korea, barely too old for Vietnam, and way too old for Iraq and Afghanistan.

But I did two things that might distinguish me from the norm in my state. First, for more than thirty years, I was a fairly successful basketball coach in a state where football is king and basketball is considered somewhat of a stepchild. I am proud to have been one of the pioneers who swam against the tide and helped to make my chosen sport respected in a football state. Second, after I retired from coaching, I served on one of the most dysfunctional bodies in state history, the Texas State Board of Education. And, although it was a struggle,

I would like to think that I made at least a small contribution toward improving education for Texas students. On the pages that follow, I will attempt to tell a story of my early life, my coaching/teaching career, and my political career for anyone who cares to know.

CHAPTER 1

Trains That Don't Stop, Bonnie & Clyde, and the "Hitler War" (Rural Navarro County)

I WAS BORN in the Corsicana Texas hospital on October 6, 1939, just more than a month after Germany invaded Poland, marking the start of World War II, or the "Hitler War", as some of the old timers during my childhood called it. My parents, Richard Whitney ("Deb") and Leona Daniel Montgomery, lived about nine miles south of town down a one lane pavement in the tiny community of Navarro where my dad had owned the cotton gin and my mother taught at the three room school that housed six grades. The gin burned down shortly before my birth and Dad was working for his brother Buck at his gin in Eureka, an equally tiny community six miles east of Navarro and twelve miles southeast of Corsicana on U.S. Highway 287. I had an older sister Mary Frances who was born in the same hospital in December, 1937.

My mother was a native of Fairfield, a small town about thirty-five miles south of Corsicana on Highway 75 (now IH 45). She was the only girl in a family of seven children. Fairfield schools had only

1

ten grades so her parents moved temporarily to Waco to allow her to graduate from Waco High School. She later graduated from Baylor University in Waco and began a long teaching career in Texas public schools. Navarro was her third teaching position and it is where she met and later married the handsome owner of the local cotton gin. It was here that I began life as Jerry Daniel Montgomery, or simply "Dan". I've always hung up the phone when the caller asks for "Jerry". My mother was the first in her family to graduate college and, several years later, I became the first college graduate from the Montgomery side of the family.

My roots are in Navarro County because of my great grandfather Prosper King Montgomery Jr. He was the son of a plantation owner in Mississippi, and later owned his own plantation in Carroll Parish, Louisiana near the Mississippi River, upstream from Vicksburg, Mississippi. He joined the Confederate Army in 1862, and was captured by Grant's army in the Battle of Vicksburg in 1864. Grant paroled all Vicksburg prisoners who signed a pledge to never again take up arms against the Union. Prosper signed but had already lost his land in Louisiana. His in-laws had already sold everything and moved to Texas, settling in northern Navarro County. Prosper and his wife Margaret joined them in Texas toward the end of the war and his father-in-law later sold him some land along Chambers Creek near Eureka. They later had three children – Walter, Whitney, and Naomi. Walter was my grandfather but he passed away before my birth.

We lived in a small frame house on the main road in Navarro. It had no running water or indoor plumbing and our toilet was an outhouse in back stocked with a few old Sears and Roebuck catalogs. We bathed in a number two wash tub on the back porch and pumped water from a well in the backyard. We had a milk cow, a few hens, and a rooster just like everyone else in the community and when the first "blue norther" blew in, most residents gathered at Sam Marsh's house and butchered a few hogs for winter meat. I suspect a few people in Navarro still follow this tradition. Every family in town relied on wood for cooking and heat. I tell people that I was eleven years old when I found out that my name wasn't "Git Wood". We didn't consider ourselves rich or poor. Everybody in town was pretty similar to the Montgomerys as far as I can recall.

Navarro had one general store with a post office inside, a school, and two churches (Methodist and Presbyterian). Baptists, if there were any, worshiped in Corsicana. If you wanted an alcoholic drink you were out of luck because Navarro County was, and still is, dry. The nearest beer joint was about thirty miles away in Mexia. Hard liquor was even farther away in Dallas, although the next county down, Freestone, was known as a haven for bootleggers. A railroad track ran right through town but the trains didn't stop. Mail came by train and was dropped by a conductor onto a platform. He then quickly picked the outgoing mailbag that was hanging from a tall steel stand. Watching this quick exchange each day was about the only entertainment that the citizens of Navarro had but it was over in a couple of seconds and sometimes the exchange wasn't successful, which caused outgoing mail to be delayed for a day. My aunt, Estelle Montgomery, became postmaster in Navarro several years after we left and was well into her nineties when she retired. And, speaking of Mexia, the Dairy Queen there is famous because it is the subject of an old Aggie joke involving the correct pronunciation of Mexia. I won't repeat the joke here because every living Texan has heard it a million times already, but the correct pronunciation is "Muh-HAY-uh" and Dairy Queen is "Day-ree-Queen".

Most of my years in Navarro were during World War II. My dad and both his brothers were not drafted because they all had high blood pressure and couldn't pass the physical. Their father died of a stroke at an early age and they all passed away because of strokes in their forties or fifties. Instead of serving in active duty, my dad was assigned as a security guard at the temporary German POW camp located at the Corsicana airport near our home. He was later sent to Port Arthur, Texas to help provide security for the oil refinery there.

During the war, while Daddy was away, my mom continued her teaching job. Because she couldn't find anyone to keep me, the school allowed her to informally enroll me in first grade even though I was not quite five years old. My sister and I were in the same room but she sat in the second grade row and I was in the first. This was a decision that negatively affected me later in life because I was two years behind my classmates physically and socially, although I suffered little academically.

With little to do in a small community like Navarro, everybody went to town on Saturdays. Town was Corsicana which, at the time, had a population of about 15,000. But it was like a large city to us and, because it was an oil boom town, it was quite bustling. There was a Sears, JC Penny, and Montgomery Ward. In addition, there was a substantial Jewish community and several Jewish owned stores downtown. There were three movie theaters within a four block area along Beaton Street, the town's main street. One of the most vivid memories of my childhood is attending the victory parade in 1945 after the Japanese surrender. To me, Corsicana was a really large city and I had no idea that Dallas even existed although it was only 55 miles to the north. Corsicana, as far as I know, is famous for only two things: fruit cake from Collin Street Bakery and Wolf Brand Chili. I understand that nobody has ever eaten a fruit cake but, for some reason, people still send it in the mail to friends at Christmastime. As for Wolf Brand, my apologies to its founder Lyman Davis, but I can't imagine a true Texan ever eating a bowl of chili that originated from a can. That would be a sin right up there with eating chili with beans and ketchup on a hot dog.

Shortly after the end of the war, my parents announced that we were leaving our home in Navarro and moving six miles away to Eureka, which was home to most of my father's relatives. I was too young to understand the reason for the move but I assume it was because it was six miles closer to my father's work at Uncle Buck's cotton gin. Even though we were Methodists, we rented the Presbyterian parsonage which was vacant because the Presbyterians couldn't find a replacement for their pastor. The Methodist Church was located next door and my grandmother lived across the dirt road behind the churches. There was no Baptist church, which probably explains why dancing was allowed in Eureka.

Eureka was, and is, a relatively nondescript community, not unlike most small Texas communities. But it has produced a few notable people. Probably the most notable one was my great uncle, and fill-in grandfather, Whitney Maxwell Montgomery. Although his formal education ended with the eighth grade, he acquired a love of poetry from his father and was contributing verse to magazines at the age of nineteen. He remained on the family farm until age fifty, but continued to write. He later married fellow poet Vaida Stewart. They published a poetry magazine for many years and both won many honors. He had four books of poetry published, and Southern Methodist University conferred on him an honorary doctorate in 1956. "Uncle Whit" married late in life, never had children of his own, and was proud to sit in as grandfather for me, my sister, and our three Montgomery cousins. He passed away in 1966, and is remembered by a state historical marker on Highway 287 across a pasture from the white columned home that he and my grandfather purchased long ago. The inscription on the marker wrongly states that he was born there and it also includes one of his poems, "I Own a Home with a Rose at the Gate". I loved and am very proud of my "Uncle Whit" who was the paternal grandfather that I never had.

Another notable person who spent time as a boy in Eureka is Clyde Barrow, the notorious outlaw of Bonnie & Clyde fame. Although raised in Dallas, his parents sent him to live for a while with his uncle who owned property adjoining the Montgomery property along Chambers Creek. He and my father and uncles were boyhood friends and attended school together in Eureka. My father even had a photo of himself and Clyde sitting at a double desk at school, and my cousin Carolyn Montgomery Taylor has a photo posted on the internet of Bonnie and Clyde on the Montgomery property while they were on the run. My father was even allowed to attend Clyde Barrow's funeral in Dallas. I am sure that some of the stories told about Clyde to us were somewhat embellished as the Montgomery boys were known to do, but what the heck. I enjoy repeating them anyway. Besides, there are two pictures for proof.

Bonnie & Clyde on Montgomery property in Navarro County, early thirties

Prosper King Montgomery Jr.'s land holdings in the Eureka area were fairly substantial. When he died, he left almost 2000 acres in five different parcels to his two sons, Walter and Whitney. His daughter Naomi Davidson received another 1000 acres, also along Chambers Creek. When my grandfather Walter passed away, my grandmother Fannie (we called her "Granny") became joint owner with Uncle Whit of the almost 2000 acres scattered across the area. This included the large two-story home just off of Highway 287 in Eureka proper. My cousins, Margaret and Carolyn, grew up in that house and Margaret and her husband Gene Thomas still live nearby. Their dad was my uncle, Aaron "Puncher" Montgomery, one of the all-time great characters of Navarro County. I'll have more on him later.

Our time in Eureka didn't last long, just a little more than a year. Things were slow at Uncle Buck's gin because cotton was on the decline in Navarro County after the war even though the area was in the rich black land region of Texas. A tenant farmer raised cotton on a 150 acre parcel owned by my grandmother and her brother-in-law. My dad and his brothers owned no land of their own but were allowed keep cattle on Montgomery property. But they were all stubborn and had a hard time making good decisions together. So our lives were about to change forever. We were moving to the big city – Fairfield, 35 miles south, population 1084. This was 1946, and I had just entered third grade at age six. Most of my classmates had already turned eight.

CHAPTER **2**

Whiskey, Fruit Jars, Crooked Noses, and Camp Meetings (Freestone County)

MY PARENTS NEVER owned a house during their entire marriage. I'm sure there was no money for a down payment. Our first rent house in Fairfield was on the outskirts of town near Highway 75, the main route between Dallas and Houston. Dallas was 90 miles north and Houston was 160 miles south. Mother went to work teaching sixth grade and Dad went to work for Brian Daniel, my mother's oldest brother, at his auto and farm implement dealership. He sold Hudson cars and International Harvester tractors. This was the beginning of a relationship that never went very well.

Uncle Brian had struck it rich a few years back in the Wortham Oil Field, northwest of Fairfield. As a young man, he had a quite a reputation as a playboy. But, after suffering a near fatal car accident (he probably had been drinking), he turned his life around, accepted Jesus Christ, and became very outwardly religious. Raised a Methodist by his parents, he joined the Assembly of God Church and became a leader of the local congregation. My grandparents and one of my other uncles and his family also joined the church. In fact, my grandmother Mam-maw Daniel became one of the most devoutly religious people I've ever known. She thought almost everything outside of going to church was a sin and could quote scripture to back it up. She wouldn't even accept a ride to church without the assurance that gas for the car wasn't purchased on Sunday. We grandkids liked to say that Mam-maw wrote more scripture than the Apostle Paul.

Although my dad was not known to attend church regularly, if at all, he insisted that his kids did. In Fairfield, we continued worshiping at the Methodist Church. Mary Frances and I were actively involved in all youth church activities and our mother never missed a church service, including summer revivals. We loved the songs in the old brown Cokesbury Hymnal and I can still tell you what page most of the songs are on. ("The Old Rugged Cross is on page 30 and "Dwelling in Beulah Land" is on Page 95) My friends and I loved to sit on the back pew and substitute the word "sheets" during the singing of "Bringing in the Sheaves" (Page 65). One of our many pastors during that time, Rev. Harold Spann, had a great influence on my life. His wife taught me to read music and actually had me singing bass in the children's choir. My sister needed no music instruction. Outside of our cousin Edward Daniel she was the most natural musician that I've ever known.

In general, life was good for me in Fairfield. Although I was in a larger small school, I adjusted well and had lots of friends. All our cousins on the Daniel side lived in town and we spent lots of time with them. We continued to spend time in Eureka and my dad kept cattle on the property there. We also often went to Corsicana or Waco on Saturday. But I never felt that my dad was very happy in Fairfield. He didn't like working for his brother-in-law so he quit and held a number of different jobs thereafter. I doubt that any of them paid much money, but I never got the feeling that we were poor. He developed a love for fox hunting and he was an ardent quail and dove hunter. I cherish the many nights I spent with him and his old friends out listening to the dogs chase foxes, usually arguing about which one was leading the pack even though some of the "leaders" were sleeping under a pickup truck nearby.

My mom's family, unlike the Montgomery's, were "tee-totalers" so alcohol was allowed in the house only for "medicinal purposes". Maybe that is why my dad complained a lot about feeling bad. Both Navarro and Freestone were dry counties but Freestone had a history for bootlegging and it was not uncommon for several "moonshine" stills to be displayed outside the jail on the courthouse square. The old joke is that almost everybody reared in Freestone County has a crooked nose from drinking whiskey from a fruit jar.

Although my dad was still a part-time rancher, we lived within the city limits while most the boys in my class lived out in the country on family farms or small ranches. They were more inclined to be cowboys while I became more interested in sports. But Fairfield had no youth sports in those days. There was no organized little league baseball, basketball, or football and we didn't even know that soccer existed. As a result, the town kids played games on empty lots and had no formal adult coaching. Fairfield High School didn't even have a gymnasium at the time and I don't remember any outdoor basketball goals in the community. There was a softball field behind the school where the adult town team played, as well as the high school football field, but that was about it.

Even for junior high and high school students, opportunities for sports participation were limited. There were no team sports in junior high and football was the only high school sport until I was in sixth grade. Girls were completely out of luck if they were interested in sports participation. We didn't even have a band in Fairfield Schools until about 1950. The entire school system employed only one coach until after I graduated from high school in 1956 although the high school principal, who was not a paid coach, started baseball and a girls basketball team before I graduated. All of this resulted from the fact that there was very little equalization of property taxes in Texas school districts at the time. Schools located in areas where there were oil fields, refineries, or chemical plants had most of the money, leaving the others (called minimum foundation school districts) to divide the crumbs among themselves. It's gotten a little better over the years but there are still inequities in school funding in Texas. As a member of the State Board of Education a few years back, I tried to call attention to this problem only to be informed that the Board has no power where school finance is concerned. We were tasked with managing the $25 billion Permanent School Fund but, other than for textbooks, we had no say as to how the money is spent. Go Figure!!!

My dad and mom (standing), my sister in front, mid-1950's

With such limited opportunities for sports participation, I became an avid follower of college football and major league baseball. There was no television in our town as of yet so we followed our favorite Southwest Conference football teams on radio broadcasts sponsored by the Humble Oil Company. Everybody's favorite announcer was a guy named Kern Tips. Texas University and Texas A&M had their followers but most Baptists in town supported Baylor, and Methodists, with the exception of my Baylor graduate mother, were SMU fans. I was hooked on the Mustangs because of their All-American halfbacks, Doak Walker and Kyle Rote. The "Doaker" was especially a hero of mine. SMU dominated the Southwest Conference in the late forties and had one really big win over Notre Dame. As for baseball, the closest major league team was in St. Louis so lots of kids in town were Cardinal fans. But I became a diehard fan of the Cleveland Indians because you could listen to their games almost every day on KLIF radio in Dallas. The "Old Scotchman" Gordon McLendon, from a studio in Dallas, re-created the games from wire reports. His broadcasts used sounds simulating the crack of a bat and crowd noises to make it appear that he was actually at the game. But I didn't care. The Indians won the World Series against the Boston Braves in 1948 and their star pitcher Bob Feller joined Doak Walker as one of my heroes. I continued to support the Indians throughout my school days. They lost almost every year to the Yankees, but finally won the pennant again in 1954 only to be swept in four games in the World Series by Willie Mays and the New York Giants. I still support the Indians today unless they are playing my beloved Houston Astros. Only recently, my son Adam and I met in Cleveland to watch the Astros finish off the Indians in the American League playoffs.

My early school years in Fairfield were pretty uneventful. My third grade class had about twenty-five students and we hardly ever had anyone drop out or move in until I entered sixth grade. This was the year that brought new enrollees from Streetman, a small town fifteen miles to the north. The school there had closed at the end of the previous school year and the students were transferred to Fairfield.

Three generations of Astros fans at Astros-Angels game in Anaheim, Aug.,, 2018

We were excited to get some new blood in our class. New desks had to be added to our classroom as there were six or eight new students. Two of them had the last name of Carroll which meant that we now had four Carrolls in our class. Our class enrollment swelled to thirty three students and it stayed about the same until we graduated in 1956. One good thing about the Streetman transfers was that the boys were mostly baseball players, which gave Fairfield High School a reason to add baseball to its competitive sports program. Streetman was the birthplace of Fred "Firpo" Marberry, the first full-time relief pitcher in the major leagues. Firpo played mainly for the Washington Senators in the 1920's and had retired to the area a few years later. I guess the Streetman kids got their love of baseball from this famous player. One of the best baseball players ever at Fairfield was a pitcher from Streetman named Frankie Rouse. Frankie, however, transferred to Corsicana for his senior year and led them to the state baseball tournament in Austin. They won their first game with Frankie on the mound and his coach decided to start him the next day in the championship game. Sadly, Frankie blew out his arm and was never again the same. Too bad there was no rule in those days limiting the number of innings pitched. Frankie's sister Marjorie was a classmate of mine from sixth grade through graduation in 1956. Thinking back, I don't remember ever having a teammate from Streetman on our football or basketball teams during my high school playing days. They were all baseball players.

An even bigger thing that changed the sports scene in Fairfield during my sixth grade year was the opening of a new gymnasium on campus. It was a typical gym for those days with spectator stands on one side, a stage on the opposite side, and a basketball and volleyball court in the middle. Never mind that it had wooden backboards, kids in our town could now play basketball indoors. Up until that time, football was the only competitive sport, and the Eagles were pretty good on the gridiron. They competed in University Interscholastic League Class B and, during my childhood days, were almost unbeatable. Class B schools at that time could not advance past the regional championship game but we won our share of district, bi-district, and even regional titles. One of the local heroes of kids at the time was Hayward Guyton, a big and fast running back who wore number 79. Another was Dickey Cole, whose parents owned Cole Cleaners on the town square. We eventually moved up to Class A and continued to win against bigger schools through my freshman year in high school. The team that year had three great senior athletes – Leighton Steward, David Lott, and Glendale Black. Leighton was the real All-American boy. Not only was he a great athlete, he was also valedictorian of his graduating class. He later played end at SMU. After graduation, he became a geologist for a large oil company in Louisiana, but is better known today as the lead author for "The Sugar Busters Diet". David, my next door neighbor, played football at Tyler Jr. College and North Texas State. This team won the district football championship and the same three players, along with junior Don Emmons, led the basketball team to the finals of the regional tournament in College Station.

For many years after, basketball was a bigger sport than football at Fairfield High School. It was also the beginning of a long time love affair with the sport for me.

I may have been an average small school athlete had I not been two years younger than my classmates. Because I had started school at age four, I was only twelve when I started ninth grade so I was far behind my peers, both physically and socially. Compared with students in seventh grade who were my age, I'm sure I was at least average in every way. I had a leg up on my classmates in baseball however, having honed my skills in the summer time while most of them toiled on their farms. I was a starter on the baseball team as a sophomore and the only game in any sport that I was ever the hero in was that year. We were playing tiny Oakwood in a non-district game and there was a runner on either second or third base with the score tied in the last inning when I came up to bat. I had good bat discipline but with very slow bat speed which meant that, as a right handed hitter, most my bat contacts resulted in hits to the right side of the field. Sure enough, I swung late and popped a "Texas Leaguer" to short right field, scoring the runner for the win. This was a meaningless non-district game and I doubt any of my teammates remember it. But it remains my only claim to fame as an athlete at Fairfield High School. I was only fourteen at the time and should have been an eighth grader.

A long standing tradition at Fairfield High School was the "belt line" where, on the first day of school, all freshman boys were forced to line up at one goal post on the football field and run, one at a time, to the goal post at the other end of the field. Stationed about five yards apart on the field on each side, were upperclassmen boys with their belts in their hands. The freshmen were patted down beforehand to make sure they had no padding in the seat of their pants. You can imagine the whelps on our behinds when we reached the other goal post, but a sense of relief came over us knowing that we would be swinging instead of receiving the next three years. Although there were never any school personnel present at this event, someone must have complained my freshman year because I never got to stand in line and swing my belt in future years. A long standing tradition had come to an end.

Aside from our principal Mervil Wood, who volunteered to coach baseball and girls basketball, there was only one coach for the whole school system. During my first two years in high school the coach was Leland Willis. Coach Willis was a really good guy and a good coach. But he had no assistants in any sport and there was no junior high program. In spite of this, Fairfield won district in both football and basketball during his first year. And because star players Don Emmons, Wayne Daniel, and Joe Ed Lane were returning, there were big expectations for the basketball team the following year. Many fans expected a trip to the state tournament which was, and still is, the ultimate goal for high school basketball teams in Texas. Don, despite losing a finger in a farm accident, was a great athlete and later played basketball at Sam Houston State. Wayne, my third cousin, was 6'5" and the first person I ever saw dunk a basketball. Joe Ed was 6'4" and a great shooter and later played at the University of Houston. As far as I know, Joe is still the only FHS graduate who has ever played Division I basketball. We (I say "we" because I was at least a seldom used substitute on the B team) marched through the district schedule unscathed, and faced Thorndale, a school east of Austin, in the bi-district game. Nobody expected the Eagles to lose a first round game, but there was a problem. Coach Willis was a strong proponent of the zone defense and almost never switched to a man to man because we were almost never behind. But Thorndale got out to an early lead, and then went into a stall which lasted almost the entire game. At one point, the Thorndale players actually sat down on the court. When Coach Willis finally decided to come out and force the action it was too late. We lost by a score of something like 26-22. Many fans, upset that they had already made their reservations in Austin, called for the school board to fire Coach Willis. But, instead, he later resigned and was hired as the football and basketball coach and Henderson County Jr. College in Athens. He later came back to Fairfield as middle school principal and eventually went on to coach at Cisco Jr. College, where he later became president. Several years later I became the basketball coach at Cisco. But this is a story for a later chapter.

Before our stunning defeat to Thorndale, my mother had arranged to visit her cousin in Austin during the state basketball tournament in March. In spite of our loss, we went anyway and my life was changed forever. The games were played at old Gregory Gym on the Texas University campus. All seating was general admission so lines gathered hours before the doors opened. Teams were from all over the state in classes B through 4A. Cayuga, a Class B team 25 miles east of Fairfield, won the state championship over Big Sandy, an Indian reservation school from southeast Texas. Ned Duncan was their star player and he later starred at SMU. Russell Boone played for Class A Sweeney and scored 50 points in the championship game. Russell became an all American at Tyler Jr. College and later was a great player at The University of Houston. Both Ned and Russell became friends of mine during my coaching career – Ned as a sporting goods salesman and Russell as a coach in southeast Texas. Because of that trip to the state tournament, I became hooked on basketball but I knew my future was as a coach, not as a player. This was in the spring of 1954 and I was a fourteen year old high school sophomore. It would be sixty years later before I missed a state high school basketball tournament in Austin. While I was a member of the State Board of Education I was appointed to chair an advisory committee for the University Interscholastic League (UIL). I think we met one time to discuss implementing drug testing for high school athletes. This short stint, however, entitles me to receive free tickets forever to UIL championship events. I hardly ever use them anymore but my phone rings off the wall before big events. My old coaching friends have to stand in line to get my free tickets. The only other thing I ever got from my six years on the State Board was the chair that I'm sitting in as I write this. It's a replica of the one that I sat in during meetings in Austin and has the seal of the State of Texas on it. I've got one more free thing coming though – a burial plot in the state cemetery in Austin. But this is a freebie that I never intend to use because, last time I checked, ashes have no need for burial plots.

Coach Willis was replaced by Lawrence Baggett for my junior and senior years in high school. The two could have not been more different. Coach Baggett was probably in his forties but had already coached at several schools, and it was obvious as to why shortly after he arrived. He was a native of rural Louisiana, very profane, and didn't care what anyone thought of him. He gave almost every student a nickname, some of which were not repeatable in a mixed crowd. In fact, he even gave some of our parents and other faculty members nicknames. Animal names were his favorite such as "Mouse", "Monkey","Fishface" and "Birdlegs". I was "Frog" because he said I looked like a frog in my football stance. He was an extremely tough taskmaster and never allowed water at practice sessions even during two-a-day practices in the dog days of August. But he was a good coach and, if he had some assistants, better players, and a junior high program, we would have probably been more successful. But we didn't win more than a couple of football games in either of my last two years of high school, and these were against Class B schools in non-district play. Most our district opponents pinned the flower on their homecoming queen at halftime when they played us, and we did the same when we played Buffalo or Centerville, the two Class B schools on our non-district schedule that we almost always beat. I was the center on offense for Coach Baggett and hardly ever played on defense. Trivia question: Who was the first platoon football player at Fairfield High School? Answer: "Frog" Montgomery. Of course, if I was the first offensive specialist, then there had to be a defensive one. Maybe Winfree "Jughead" Tate? I don't remember after all these years. I just remember that almost everyone associated with Fairfield schools, and their next of kin, was a victim of "nickname abuse" at the hands of Coach Lawrence Baggett.

The last four words of our school song are "Eagles Will Always Fly", but there were few wings flying on the gridiron in 1954 and 1955. Our team was so bad that Coach Baggett cut practice short the last couple of weeks in the season and started basketball practice. Joe Ed Lane was returning for his senior season and that alone meant that we had a good chance to succeed in 1954-55. I hardly played at all my junior year and was only a part-time starter as a senior. To say that I was a mediocre athlete in high school would be a gross overstatement and would be giving me too much credit. Because of my age, I was simply too far behind my peers physically to compete. However, I worked hard at it and became an excellent shooter, scoring a few points every now and then. I almost never missed a free throw in games or in practice. But Coach Baggett was a very good coach and I believe he was more interested in basketball than football. We competed well in basketball my last two years in high school but failed to advance to the playoffs both years.

I think Coach Baggett was planning to stay for a while because he was determined to start a sports program for junior high boys. There was no way that could happen in football without more coaches and expensive equipment. But he recognized my interest in coaching strategy and set me up as coach of the first junior high basketball team in the history of our school. He had my schedule arranged so I could coach the seventh and eighth grade team during their recess period. I worked them hard and used the same drills that Coach had taught us. He made sure that I ran only a man-to-man defense, and insisted that I run the same offense that he used. We played mostly in tournaments on January and February Saturdays, and finished the season undefeated!! That was due largely to the fact that Johnny Cole, who later became one of best athletes in FHS history, was a seventh grader at the time. He had broken his arm before the season started and played most games with one arm in a sling. He was our leading scorer even though he used only one hand for much of the season. Johnny later was a two-sport athlete in college and our paths crossed often later in life when he became a coach himself. It always makes me proud when Johnny refers to me as his first coach ever. He was largely responsible for my only undefeated season in a 32-year coaching career. I was sixteen and he was thirteen. I knew at that time what I planned to do for most of the rest of my life.

Baseball was my best sport in high school and I continued to play first base on our team. We didn't play many games simply because most Class A schools didn't field teams. The UIL placed us in a district with larger 2A schools such as Mexia and Marlin. I had played baseball in the summer on various semi-organized teams in the area and had attended a baseball camp in College Station one summer conducted by future major league star Wally Moon while my mother was taking a graduate course at Texas A&M. So I had a slight advantage over some of my peers in the sport. Because of my slow foot speed and weak arm, Mervil Wood, our coach/principal, made a first baseman out of me. I purchased a huge mitt for five bucks from another student who had received it from his older brother who was in stationed in Korea. It was bright maroon and the largest baseball glove or mitt I've ever seen, before or since. I'm not even sure that it would have been legal in the major leagues. It was almost impossible to miss a throw from across the scraggly diamond with it, so I was a pretty good first baseman and a decent hitter as long as you didn't throw me a good curve ball or even a fast ball traveling more than seventy miles per hour. Firpo Marberry had settled in Mexia by that time and his son, Fred Jr., was a pitcher on their team. He had a real hard fast ball, and not much control. I spent most of my time when I faced him bailing out of the batter's box, as did most of my teammates. Suffice it to say that, compared to the other sports, I was at least a decent small school baseball player who was smart enough to know that there was no future in the game for me.

As for Coach Baggett, he was fired during the spring of my senior year. Fairfield was a "Bible belt" town, and his profanity and general demeanor finally got the best of him. Although I agreed with this decision, I still give credit to him for recognizing my potential as a future coach. I don't know how he ended his career but he eventually retired somewhere in his native rural Louisiana. When I later coached at two different schools in East Texas, he attended several of my playoff basketball games and I always made sure that he sat right behind our bench. Like my Uncle Puncher Montgomery, he was one of the most colorful characters that I've ever known and he had a great impact on my life. Never mind that he called a school bus a "school truck". If you've ever seen one of my favorite movies, "The Last Picture Show", Coach Popper could have been playing Coach Baggett. Come to think of it, the entire movie closely resembles Fairfield, Texas during the 1950's.

My sister Mary Frances was twenty-one months my senior and was a grade ahead of me in school. She was extremely talented in music and could play many instruments "by ear". I don't know if she ever learned to read music, but I guess she did. She played clarinet in the school band and also became a baton twirler of some renown. She was drum major of the band during her high school years and received a music scholarship to Texas Christian University when she graduated in 1955. But, as a young teenager, she became obsessed about gaining weight and developed a severe case of anorexia, causing lots of pain for our parents. Thankfully, she finally overcame this condition and graduated as valedictorian of her class. She was also voted "Most Likely to Succeed" by her classmates but she spent most of her adult life as a waitress in our Uncle Sam's restaurant in Fairfield. Joe Ed Lane, the basketball star, was salutatorian of this class, finishing less than a percentage point behind her.

Mary stayed at TCU only one year and I never knew why. The Horned Frogs played Ole Miss in the Cotton Bowl that year and my father and I traveled to Dallas for the game which TCU lost to Ole Miss 14-13. Their quarterback Chuck Curtis was injured on the first play and never returned to the game. Their All-American halfback Jim Swink rushed for two touchdowns but a missed extra point after the first one gave Ole Miss the win. But we got to see Mary march with the band which is why we went in the first place. Little did I know at the time that my world would come crashing down in just more than two months when my father suffered a sudden stroke and passed away. He was only 46 years old. I was absolutely crushed, and I still think about him every day. He didn't even live to see his only son receive his high school diploma, an event that was less than two months away. He didn't accomplish a lot in his life, and wouldn't have boasted about it even if he had. One of his physical features was a perpetual smile on his face so his Lawrence Baggett nickname was "Sunny Smile". We buried him in the Eureka Cemetery under the rich black soil that the loved. He probably had a little of it caked between his toes.

I didn't set the world on fire academically in high school but I was probably a little above average in my class, finishing with either an A- or B+ average. My best subjects were history and civics and I followed all the elections – local, state, and national. I minored in history in college and usually taught history or civics during my public school teaching and coaching career. My love of politics came from my dad who was a small time political operative who worked for Beauford Jester, a Corsicana native, in his successful campaign for governor in 1946. His nickname "Deb" (No one ever called him Richard or Whitney) came from Eugene Debs, a five time Socialist Party Candidate for President during my dad's childhood. Don't ask me why because Richard Whitney Montgomery didn't have a socialist bone in his body. He was a conservative Democrat like almost everyone else in Texas at the time. Later in life I became involved a little in politics myself as a Republican. But I'll have a lot more on that later.

CHAPTER 3

James Fuller "Buddy" "Full-O-Pep" Withrow

BEFORE LEAVING MY childhood days in the rearview mirror, I must mention my best childhood friend, James Fuller "Buddy" Withrow, sometimes known as "Full-O-Pep". Anybody who attended school in Fairfield during the early to mid-fifties would surely agree that he was one of the most colorful and mischievous characters to have ever walked the halls of Fairfield High School. He lived several miles out of town but his grandfather Fuller Huckaby, a fox hunting friend of my father's, lived in town in an old farm house up a country lane right behind our house. Buddy spent much of his time at his grandfather's house and we became very close friends. He was a grade ahead of me in school and was two years older. I had other friends such as Warren Awalt, Buddy Kitchens, and Curtis "Monkey" Carroll, but Buddy Withrow and I were almost inseparable during our childhoods. We roamed the streets of Fairfield almost on a daily basis, especially during the summer months. I could write volumes about our adventures during those years. Fairfield was a typical "Courthouse Square" town with a courthouse in the center and businesses on all four sides. The courthouse lawn, with old Confederate cannons displayed (and occasional confiscated moonshine stills), was a hangout for people of all ages. I've lost count of the number of times an older kid pulled my pants down and drug me across that courthouse lawn. Kids today think they're bullied, they have no clue!!! We took it all in stride and had our secret ways of getting even. We must have played a thousand games of ping pong in the basement of the Methodist Church two blocks off the square. Buddy, like I, was a Methodist and led the singing of "Bringing in the Sheets" (Sheaves) from the back pew. He could really belt it out!!! In those days, the movie theater was located on the east side of the square and I'm almost certain Buddy Withrow never missed a movie. He would sneak a slingshot inside, buy a box of milk duds, and shoot them at the screen when the projector stopped, as it often did, in the middle of a movie. Our friend Larry Folk was not permitted by his devout Pentecostal mother to attend movies. She worked the counter at Cole Cleaners across the square with a good view of the movie theater and on Saturdays, when all the kids watched Tom Mix, Roy Rogers, Gene Autry, Lash Larue, or Hopalong Cassidy ride across the silver screen, we would serve as human body shields to block her view of Larry entering the "picture show", as everybody called it in those days.

    Other than maybe a few watermelons from Sheriff Henry Brown's patch on Highway 75, I'm sure that Buddy Withrow never stole anything in his life. But he owned a secret key that would open any Master lock on the globe and everything in Freestone County in those days was secured by a Master lock. This key was used mainly to open the gymnasium for pickup basketball games on weekends or summer days, but also to open school lockers of older kids with habits of throwing younger kids into the locker room shower with their clothes on, or dragging them across the courthouse lawn with their pants pulled down. Freestone County had its share of "unsuccessful road crossers" (possums, armadillos, skunks, etc.) whose carcasses were excellent for stinking up school lockers and for making algebra and biology books unfit for classroom use. Other than Buddy Withrow himself, I may have been the only soul who knew the identity of the owner of this special key. Didn't I say earlier that we had our ways of getting even? Oh, I almost forgot – sometimes the carcasses were accompanied by a dried cow patty or two, or even maybe a live garter snake now and then.

Major League Baseball was really big during the post war years, and kids all over the country fell in love with baseball cards that you could buy with pictures of all the players on them inside a package that contained an unchewable plank of bubblegum. There were only two companies at the time that made the cards, Topp's and Bowman's. Newman's Variety Store on our town square sold Topp's, and the closest place to buy Bowman's was at a drug store in Mexia, twenty-three miles away. The candy man that brought the cards came to our town on Tuesdays and the Bowman's guy came to Mexia on Wednesdays. My friend Buddy and I bought all that we could afford on Tuesdays, and hitched a ride with a rancher going to the cattle auction in Mexia the next day. We eventually collected all the cards in each set plus multiple cards of the same player. While most kids in town were also collectors, nobody could match our collections. Sadly to say, when my mother cleaned out her attic several years later, she threw mine away. But Buddy protected his and sixty plus years later he has all his cards in perfect condition, including multiple rookie cards of Mickey Mantle, Willie Mays, Roberto Clemente, and other stars too numerous to list. They must be worth a fortune.

My favorite adventure with Buddy was a spring Saturday in 1955, when we hitched a ride to Dallas to watch an exhibition game between the Cleveland Indians and the New York Giants. These two teams had met in the 1954 World Series with the Giants sweeping my Indians in four straight games. For several years, after breaking camp, they made a trip across the south playing exhibition games in different cities before starting the regular season. They always played one game at Burnett Field, the minor league park in Dallas. We saved our money for weeks and, when the big day came, we strolled out to Highway 75 and began sticking out our thumbs to the north. Lo and behold, the first car to stop was driven by Beacie Lott, our next door neighbor, who was on her way for some shopping in Big D. In those days, Highway 75 became South Lamar Street in Dallas and I knew there was a big Sears store on that street and that the ballpark was somewhere across the Trinity River behind the store. Ms. Lott let us out at Sears and we quickly found the Jefferson Street viaduct, walked across it, and found the ballpark on the other side. Burnett Field held only about 10,500 people and the stands overflowed. We were allowed to stand behind a rope down the right field line with hundreds of other people. Within a few minutes, one of the most memorable things in my young life happened. The Cleveland pitchers were running conditioning drills in front of us, jogging from the right field line to the left-centerfield wall and back when Herb Score, their rookie pitching sensation, dropped his glove on the field ahead of us and didn't stop to pick it up. My mischievous friend quickly darted under the rope, picked the glove up, and returned back into the crowd. Of course, a policeman came over and demanded that he hand the glove over to him. At first, Buddy refused and the crowd of over 15,000 was cheering him on. But the cop eventually won out and boos rained down on the poor guy for several minutes. I still feel sorry for that poor cop who was just doing his job. At least Herb Score got his glove back and went on become Rookie of the Year that season. He would have been a lock for the Hall of Fame had he not suffered an injury to the eye on a line drive in 1957, which cut his career short.

Nobody cares who wins exhibition games and I have no memory of who won this one. Most of the top players never leave the dugout or bullpen. So, after the game, we walked to the parking lot to locate the Cleveland bus and wait for the players to come out of the locker room. We could afford only one game program and Buddy had it. He got a few autographs from players outside the bus, then snuck onboard and got even more. He still has that program with all the autographs today. I did some research recently and discovered that nine future Hall of Famers were on the rosters of those two teams that day, which could be a record for all I know. They are: Bob Feller, Bob Lemon, Early Wynn, Larry Doby, Ralph Kiner, Hal Newhouser, Willie Mays, Monte Irvin, and Hoyt Wilhelm. Herb Score was also there and so was Rocky Colavito who, for some reason that I've never understood, is not yet in the Hall.

After the game, we made our way back across the viaduct over the Trinity River to the Sears store and put our thumbs out to the south hoping to catch a ride back home ninety miles away. Soon a Trailways bus came along and we waved it down. Between us, we had enough money for one ticket but we talked the driver in to letting both of us board the bus. Sometimes I think the driver may have relented because he somehow knew about the secret Master lock key. But, then again, I doubt that bus drivers kept lockers in the halls of Fairfield High School in the spring of 1955. We arrived home after dark which is about the same time that we always got home from whatever we did on Saturdays. Our parents never knew we were gone. I guess that our neighbor Ms. Lott never said a word even though she and my mother were very close friends. Buddy graduated from Fairfield High School that spring. Soon after that, he moved with his family to Orange in deep southeast Texas near the Louisiana state line. His father and older brother worked in the DuPont Chemical plant there, and he joined them at DuPont shortly after graduation. All three of them eventually retired from there. His younger sister Lila later married former Minnesota Twins player and manager Frank Quilici. I sometimes wonder if Buddy has his brother-in-law's baseball card and autograph. I bet that he does and he's not giving it up. I've had some great friends in my lifetime but James Fuller "Buddy" "Full-O-Pep" Withrow is right up there at the top.

This has nothing to do with my friend Buddy Withrow but I would be remiss, before leaving my growing up days, if I didn't mention a Fairfield landmark, Sam's Original restaurant, on IH-45, a few blocks west of the town square. It would be almost impossible to find anyone who has ever traveled between Dallas and Houston who has not had at least one meal at this famous place. I'm proud to say that Sam is Sam Daniel, my uncle "Sammy", who along with my aunt Doris, owned numerous restaurants in Fairfield before opening this place many decades ago before his death in the 1960's. It is still run by his son, my first cousin "Ponty", and is a famous stopping place for travelers on this busy interstate. My sister Mary Frances worked as a waitress at Sam's for most of her adult life before passing away in 2009. A few years ago, I visited the Sam's Original website and read a review from a person who had dined there and had praised a waitress named "Mary" for giving $100 to a family who needed money to continue on to their destination. There is no doubt in my mind that "Mary" was my sister, a meek and loving soul, who never had much herself but would never turn down an opportunity to help someone else.

CHAPTER 4

Aaron "Puncher" Montgomery

AFTER MY HIGH school graduation in May 1956, I planned to enroll at Sam Houston State Teachers College (Sam Houston State University now), major in physical education, and start a career as a public school teacher and coach. But my plans were put on hold that summer with some bad news on two fronts. First, I learned that my dad and his younger brother "Puncher" had borrowed money to buy cattle and were behind on their payments to the Corsicana State Bank. Then I also learned that my Uncle Bryan Daniel was declaring bankruptcy and was losing everything except his homestead where he and his family lived. Since he also owned my grandmother's small home across the street, it would be auctioned to the highest bidder on the steps of the courthouse. My mother, in order to allow her mother to live out her years in the house she had lived in forever, stepped up to the plate and became the highest bidder. We were renters, my father had just passed away, and there was no way she could afford both rent and a house payment, to say nothing of paying tuition for two college students (My sister was transferring from TCU to Sam Houston and would have no scholarship). We had no choice but to move into my grandmother's little house on the corner of South Hall and Reunion streets in Fairfield. I was just sixteen years old, and very immature, but I got started on the road to manhood real soon largely due to the help of my dad's younger brother, Aaron "Puncher" Montgomery, a truly unique character and one of the heroes in my life.

DAN MONTGOMERY

Aunt Bessie and Uncle "Puncher" Montgomery

I have lived in the Texas Hill Country for over thirty years of my life, and have crossed paths with several hill country legends, or "characters", such as Hondo Crouch who founded Lukenbach, Ace Ried of "Cowpokes" cartoon fame, and the Texas Jewboy Kinky Friedman. But they are all professional Texans who made pretty good livings just being Texas characters. My uncle Puncher was a true Texas character who never made a dime playing a role as one. Maybe he lived in the wrong part of the state. The nickname "Puncher" came from his unique expertise with cattle. He could visit a rancher's pasture, take a quick glimpse at maybe ten or twelve cows, and then judge within just a few pounds their total combined weight. He would offer a fair amount based on the price per pound of cattle that day, load them up in is pickup and trailer, then haul them to the stockyards in Fort Worth. He always sold them for a fair profit for himself. I doubt that he ever took advantage of a local rancher. He didn't deal exclusively with cattle as he was a "wheeler dealer" in almost anything with four legs, especially bird dogs. He, like his brothers before him, didn't have more than a ninth grade education but he somehow managed to marry a graduate of the University of Texas, Bessie Miles. Aunt Bessie was one of the smartest people I've ever known. She recognized my interest in history and politics and was always eager to discuss them with me. I owe her a lot for what little success that I later had in teaching and in the political arena. Puncher and Bessie raised two daughters, Margaret and Carolyn. Margaret is more reserved like her mother while Carolyn is definitely more the "wheeler-dealer" type like her father.

During that summer of 1956, I spent lots of time with Uncle Puncher hauling cattle to the Fort Worth stockyards in an effort to pay off the cattle loans. Growing up, I had worked with my dad on the Montgomery property a little bit but I was more of a "town kid" that was in to sports instead of farm chores. I took vocational agriculture and was in the FFA in high school. But, in those days in small towns, any boy not in FFA was somewhat "suspect" if you know what I mean. In other words, we weren't "too sure" about him. Besides, FFA members got to ride the bus with the Future Homemakers to the State Fair on FFA-FHA Saturday in October. That alone was reason enough to join the Future Farmers of America. But regardless of the expertise, or lack thereof, that I gained in vocational agriculture, Uncle Puncher would have been just as successful paying off the loans had I not rode in the pickup truck with him. But the loans eventually got paid off and I learned a lot that summer. A few short years later, Uncle Puncher died of a stroke, just like his father and two older brothers ahead of him. The church in Eureka was not nearly big enough to hold all the people that came to pay their respects. A few years later I learned that he had interceded on my family's behalf to persuade Uncle Whit not to leave our side of the family out of his will because of the perceived transgressions of my former brother-in-law. I owe a lot to my Uncle Puncher Montgomery and not a day goes by that I don't think of him and all that he did for me.

CHAPTER 5

"Ignorant Hill" in the City of My Birth (Navarro Jr. College)

WITH ALL THESE financial problems, my mother and I decided it would be best for me to live at home and commute to Navarro Junior College in Corsicana for two years. There was no financial aid such as grants or student loans at that time and my sister was already planning to transfer to Sam Houston. We simply couldn't afford tuition plus room and board for two college students. In fact, I needed to fast track my college graduation and get a full-time job as soon as I could. Navarro furnished a van at that time to transport students to the school each day from Teague (a town ten miles west) and Fairfield. They paid tuition for a student driver and I was that student my sophomore year. My first car was a 1951 Oldsmobile that I bought with a loan from the United Methodist Church organization, but that was after I had completed my first two years at Navarro. So I rode the van seventy round trip miles to school five days a week for two years and I could write an entire book about that experience alone. It was not uncommon for some students to finish classes earlier than others on some days and then wait several hours later for the van to leave campus. Many times we would get a ride out to Highway 75 and try to hitch a ride home earlier. An unwritten rule said that the van does not stop for any students still on the highway when the van comes by.

The rule did not prevent honking, waving, or hollering by the van's driver and passengers at the poor soul standing alone on the side the road. It also didn't forbid one middle finger salutes and there were plenty of them from both inside and outside the van, especially from the outside. On days that I left campus early, I made sure to locate my roadside position near an accessible culvert so I had a chance to avoid unnecessary humiliation from my fellow students. On more than one occasion, I had the pleasure of catching a ride later, then passing the van on the way home. That was especially exhilarating.

Academically, I was ready for some, but not all, subjects at the college level. I had really good English and math teachers in high school and, although the instruction was lacking, I was always a good social studies student because that's where my interests lay. But science was another story. Fairfield, as best I can recall, didn't even offer chemistry, and biology was taught by Coach Baggett (enough said). I don't believe we had any access at all to a science lab. The first class I attended in college was biology, taught by Dr. Roy Reese who had been at Navarro for many years. Although I didn't realize it at the time, something he said that first day ended up affecting my thinking on a very controversial subject that I would come face to face with much later in my life. Dr. Reese said that he was a lifelong Baptist and was taught to believe strictly in the Biblical story of Creation, and that evolution could not possibly be true. But he said that, over the years, he came to realize that "It takes just as great a God to create man from an amoeba as from a mold of clay". In other words, his belief that God is our Creator is not inconsistent at all with the scientific theory of evolution. Since I had hardly any instruction in biology, I really didn't know much about evolution and was not aware that there was much of a controversy. But now I know that there is no way you can teach a biology class without teaching evolution, even though I'm sure many teachers skip over it anyway. Little did I know at the time that I would later become a member of the Texas State Board of Education and would have to confront this issue since the Board approves textbooks and adopts curricula for the public schools. I don't know that the "amoeba" statement is all that scientific but, just the same, Dr. Reese made his point which made a lot of sense to me on my first day in a college classroom. I'm not sure about this, and I don't want to take too much credit, but I would like to think that Dr. Reese's statement that day in a nondescript junior college freshman biology class had some impact on the way that biology is taught in Texas public schools today.

My two years at Navarro Jr. College were pretty uneventful. Almost all my classmates were graduates of small high schools in the immediate area. Many were Korean War veterans attending school on the GI Bill, and were in their mid-twenties. I made money for my college expenses by becoming a football and basketball referee and a baseball umpire. I refereed my first high school football game at age sixteen, a year or two younger than most of the players. A friend of the Montgomery family, Maco Stewart, took me under his wing and made me a part of his officiating crew. Maco had played football at SMU in the thirties and owned a car dealership in Corsicana. He was already a Southwest Conference official but also called high school games in the area. My basketball officiating partner was Ernest Joel (E.J.) Lane in Fairfield, the father of our high school star Joe Ed Lane and his younger brother David. E.J. and I refereed games all over the area those two years, both boys and girls. Some Saturdays we may call six tournament games without a break. The three Lanes were lifetime friends of mine. Dave later became a TV personality and rose in the ranks at WFAA TV in Dallas to station manager, a position he held when he developed a brain tumor and passed away while still in his forties. He's right up there with Buddy Withrow as one of my best friends ever. His Coach Baggett assigned nickname was "Mouse" because of his high pitched voice as a young quarterback signal caller. Dave's mother Marie was a staunch "church going" Pentecostal lady who was right up there with Mam-maw Daniel and the Apostle Paul in the scripture writing department. One of her commandments, among many, was "Thou Shalt Not Wear Short Pants No Matter What", which prevented her from attending any basketball games that her husband refereed or that her sons played in. But Marie was a great lady and I considered her a second mother.

Since Navarro was largely a commuter school, there was not much of a social life on campus, but I had almost no social skills anyway. Social life consisted largely of students hanging out in the Student Union Building between class periods or while waiting for the van to leave for home for the day. About the only memory that I have was watching the World Series of 1956 on the television in the SUB. This was the series between the Yankees and Dodgers when Yankee pitcher Don Larsen pitched the only perfect game in World Series history. I remember Yankee catcher Yogi Berra celebrating by running to the mound after the last out and jumping up into Larsen's arms. Later it was reported that Yogi told him, "That may be one of the best games you've ever pitched". That may have been the biggest understatement of all time, and is one of my favorite "Yogi-isms" ever. So much for my social life in junior college, and it wouldn't get much better at Sam Houston.

In May, 1958, I walked across the stage and received my diploma from "Ignorant Hill" (that's what we called Navarro at the time), and I don't remember ever setting foot on the campus again. Within a couple of weeks, I drove my newly acquired black 1951 Oldsmobile eighty-five miles down Highway 75 to Huntsville, Texas and enrolled in summer classes at Sam Houston State Teachers College (SHSTC). Legend has it that it was named Sam Houston Institute of Technology at one time, but the name changed when college bumper stickers came along. Can you imagine one that says "My daughter goes to S.H.I.T"?

CHAPTER **6**

"Harvard on Highway 75" (Sam Houston State)

WHILE MOST JUNIOR colleges are commuter schools, regional state colleges tend to be "suitcase" schools which Sam Houston was, and probably still is. Most of the students live within 100 miles of campus and go home almost every weekend. Houston is only about seventy miles to the south down IH 45 (US 75 back then) and a great majority of the students graduated from high schools in the Houston Metro area. This is how Sam Houston State became lovingly known in Houston as "Harvard on IH- 45 north". So, if there wasn't much going on at Navarro, it was only slightly better in Huntsville. But I didn't really care because I was on a fast track to get a full-time job as soon as possible.

I majored in physical education (they call it kinesiology now) and minored in history. I had already completed my required English, math, and science requirements so I had very little problem with keeping my GPA up. I guess you could get a business degree at Sam Houston but almost everybody was there for a teaching certificate or a degree in Criminal Justice since Huntsville is headquarters for the Texas Prison System. All my courses at Sam Houston were in physical education, education, or social studies. Most students called the physical education department "The Joe Kirk School of Physical

Education" after Dr. Joe Kirk who was the department head. Coaching courses in the department were taught by the head coach of each sport and Dr. Kirk taught the others himself. He was a crusty old codger who had been at Sam Houston for many years. His teaching method was to stand up and talk for the whole hour about things that hardly ever had anything to do with physical education. Whether the course was titled "Principles of P.E.", "Teaching Methods of P.E.", or "Tests and Measurements in P.E.", it was all the same. I'm not sure he even knew which of the courses he was teaching on any given day. On more than one occasion, a poor soul (usually an athlete) would discover that he had taken the same course under Dr. Kirk twice. I have no idea how he determined a grade for his classes since there were no exams. But the only way to fail was to almost never show up. He always checked roll.

Since I was always interested in anything relating to history, government, or politics, I breezed through those subjects with no trouble. I hated the education courses but it was almost impossible to fail them. An old joke is: "What do you get when you drive your car slowly across the Sam Houston campus with the windows rolled down?" Answer: "A college diploma and a teaching certificate". But that's not really true. You've actually got to bring your car to a stop first.

During my short time in Huntsville, I continued to make spending money by officiating football and basketball games. Most nights were spent at a small town football stadium or at some small gymnasium in the Huntsville area. And, like most other students, I drove home almost every weekend. I was at Sam Houston for only two summers and one regular college year. Nine weeks of one semester were spent in Bryan, where I did my student teaching at Anson Jones Junior High School. Just before the summer of my graduation, I discovered that I would short of graduating by one class hour so I quickly found a 1-hr. course in Library Science that met once a week. It was in this class that I thought I fell in love with a beautiful girl from Rosenberg named Myrna. As it turns out, she wasn't as smitten with me as I was with her. It may have been the '51 Olds that I drove, about which my friends said was more suitable for a little old lady going to church on Sunday morning then to the bootlegger's place on Sunday afternoon. But I got one hour credit anyway which was all I needed to graduate in August, 1959.

I had already secured a coaching job and was not able to attend the graduation ceremony because of two-a-day football practices at Calvert High School. I was only nineteen years old, but the people at Calvert, probably because they couldn't find anyone else, hired me anyway. My salary was to be the minimum pay for teachers at $3204 per year plus $400 for coaching. The superintendent at Valley Mills, a small school northwest of Waco, offered me more money but his school board wouldn't approve my hiring because of my age. I wouldn't have approved me either.

During my last summer session at Sam Houston, I took a class that counted toward my Physical Education degree called "Driver Education and Safety". Successful completion of this course would qualify me to teach driver education courses in public schools, thus making me some much needed money on the side in the summer months during my teaching/coaching career. It was one of the few non-coaching courses in the department not taught by Dr. Joe Kirk, which meant that there may actually be some instruction that was at least remotely related to the subject matter. Also enrolled this this class was a Sam Houston alumnus, Marshall "Cotton" Robinson, the basketball coaching legend at Buna High School in deep Southeast Texas. I recognized Cotton because of my frequent trips to the state high school basketball tournament in Austin, where he had already won four state championships, and would add three more in the future. Although he was one of the most successful high school basketball coaches in Texas, Cotton was a very modest man and was always willing to share his knowledge and experience with young coaches like myself. His specialty was a full-court man-to-man defense and he advised others to copy it rather than his "Buna Offense" which was a double post set with low post moves, spot shooting, and very little motion. He got the offense from the Buna girls coach R. C. Hyden, who was also the superintendent of schools. Cotton said he ran this simple no motion offense in order to spend more time on defense. Slow to brag about his success, he always reminded those seeking his secrets for success that he had an advantage over other Class A or AA schools in that Buna was one of the few schools in those classifications that didn't field a football team. Buna was a Class B school during Cotton's first few years there and most Class B schools at the time, especially in east Texas, didn't field football teams. All seven of his championships were at the higher Class A or AA levels. But he scheduled several top Class 4A teams in non-district play and won more than his share of games against them. One year, he even beat Class 4A state champion Port Arthur twice, and Class 3A champion Smiley once. Needless to say, Cotton Robinson was one of the greatest, if not THE greatest, high school basketball coaches in Texas history regardless of classification. He retired at age 38 in 1963, saying that he was putting too much pressure on himself to win championships. But I suspect that it may have also had something to do with the fact that Buna had started a football program.

Along with receiving my certification to teach driver education, I learned a lot from Cotton about coaching during breaks in class that summer of 1959 and, unlike many others, I took his advice and never adopted his offense. But one of his former assistants Jimmy Horn, running the Buna offense and defense, won multiple state championships at tiny Class B Snook and developed a dynasty of his own that continued for many years after he left. I would later coach at Silsbee, twenty miles from Buna, from 1966 until 1975. Cotton had been retired by then for a few years and was selling insurance. But he was a familiar face at high school basketball games during that time and still willing to share his vast knowledge. Several of his former players such as Melvin Ellison, Jimmy Burke, and Billy Kirkpatrick were coaching in the area by then and I played their teams many times. They all, as well as many other coaches in the area, still ran the Buna defense and offense. Little did they know that the knowledge I gained from their former coach several summers before would help me have very successful records against them. On one occasion, while coaching at Silsbee, I suspected one of my players was smoking cigarettes and sought his advice about proper punishment. Cotton's sly answer was "I'd first want to know if he was a main player".

CHAPTER 7

Getting Started on a Long and Successful Career (Calvert)

CALVERT, WHEN I arrived in August 1959, was a town of about 2000 people. It is located on State Highway 6, midway between Waco and Bryan-College Station, in the Brazos River Valley. Because of the rich fertile soil of the Brazos bottoms, the major crop was cotton. At one time, Calvert boasted the largest cotton gin in the world. Although the town didn't look like much driving through on Highway 6, there were several nice old white-columned homes located in the main residential area east of the railroad tracks that were occupied by wealthy descendants of plantation owners. Like most other towns in the Brazos Valley such as Marlin, Hearne, and Navasota, Calvert had a large African-American population. And Jim Crow was alive and well in the area at the time. Although the U.S. Supreme Court had ruled school segregation laws unconstitutional in 1954, most southern school boards ignored the ruling for many years. It would be 1966 before I taught or coached my first African-American student. So, because of the large African-American population of Calvert, the high school where I started my career had an enrollment of only sixty students in four grades. On nights that we played Lott, Chilton, or Coolidge, the school across the tracks was playing Waco, Temple, or Bryan.

The kids at Calvert were great and I already knew it since I had refereed several of their basketball games, both boys and girls. Their parents were great people who insisted that they always do right thing and I hardly ever had a problem with any of them. I was only nineteen when I arrived but I turned twenty in October. Since there were only six seniors in high school, I was at least three years older than most of the students and they showed me just as much respect as they did for the older teachers. Despite my young age and the fact that I was single, I don't remember any of the girls expressing any romantic interest in me, or I in them. Maybe it was the "Granny" car that I drove. Several years later, I would marry one of these students, but all our contact came after I left town. I was never accused of any improper contact with any of my students.

Calvert was such a small school that the head coach was also the principal and math teacher. The previous principal/coach had resigned during the summer months and a great guy named Herb Busse was hired in his place. Herb, who was probably twenty years my senior, and I both rented rooms in the same house owned by an older widow lady just a few blocks from the school. Herb was a military veteran and ran football practices like a boot camp. Our pre-practice calisthenics session must have lasted at least thirty minutes with about 250 jumping jacks alone. The rest of practice consisted of full contact drills and scrimmages with lots of winds sprints at the end. Although nearly every boy in high school played football, we still had a maximum of 25 players and many of them were too banged up to play on Friday night. Herb's theory was, regardless of your coaching knowledge or strategies, the team with the toughest kids would usually win. His idea of offense was to snap the ball to your best player and let him pick a hole to run through. That first year that best player was a tough Hispanic kid named Moses Mata or a smart, but equally tough kid named Charles Ford. We still lost every game but one because there were very few holes to run through.

Herb Busse and me, the entire Calvert coaching staff

My coaching assignment was to have been assistant football coach, head boys basketball coach, and junior high football coach. Herb was to be head football and track coach and girls' basketball coach. But, near the end of football season, he asked me to agree to coach girls instead of boys. I was disappointed but I agreed anyway. After all, he was my boss plus, I don't think he had ever seen a girls' basketball game and probably didn't know that they played with three girls on the offensive end of the court and three other girls on the defensive end. My junior high football team fared a little better than the high school team. We only had sixteen or eighteen players. I installed the split-t offense right out of Oklahoma Coach Bud Wilkinson's book, and we actually looked pretty good running it. I had a really good quarterback named Ruben Bonilla. Ruben's older brothers, William and Tony, had been great players for Calvert several years before and Tony had later played at the University of Houston. Their parents owned a little store in Calvert and were rock solid citizens of the community who made sure that their kids would succeed. Their youngest was Mary Helen, who was a fourth grader at the time. Both William and Tony had, by this time, finished law school and had established law practices in Corpus Christi. After Ruben's eighth grade year in Calvert, the Bonillas closed their store and moved to Corpus where Ruben became a star player for Ray High School. Both Ruben and Mary Helen also became attorneys in Corpus. Mary Helen Berlanga, formerly Bonilla, was elected to the State Board of Education in the 1990's and I became a colleague of hers on the Board for six years, starting in 2001. When Ruben learned that I was a candidate for the State Board, he was one of the first donors to my campaign although he was a Democrat and I was a Republican. But he didn't care a bit and neither did I. I will always cherish my relationship with Ruben, Mary Helen, and the entire Bonilla family.

My girls' basketball team at Calvert that first year was mediocre at best. I installed Buna coach R.C. Hyden's offense which was guaranteed to produce points provided you had a post player who could score down low, one point guard who could dribble and shoot, and one wing player who could shoot extremely well. This was because, with just three players, there was no "help" defense on the opposite side to provide extra help on a good post player. I actually had three players who fit the bill but I had one big problem. My defensive players were tenacious on defense but couldn't get the ball back to the offensive end when the other team scored, or when they didn't score for that matter. Most of the time was spent with the ball on our defensive end of the court. But I had lots of fun with these kids who worked hard and never complained. Besides, we won about as many games as we lost mainly because the opposition had many of the same problems.

My teaching assignment at Calvert consisted of one class each of World History, American History, General Science, and Biology as well as supervision of a study hall. I had no idea that I was certified to teach science classes but Superintendent Howard Pearson pulled out my college transcript which showed a class in Anatomy and Physiology that I completed as a requirement for a Physical Education major. I know I did a good job in the history courses but I'm not sure about the others. I think I survived because of the small class sizes as well as the fact that the kids, and their parents, were so good to me. All I know is that I was worn out at the end of every day but that I enjoyed almost every minute of it.

At the end of my first year, I looked for other jobs in larger schools that would pay more than $3604 per year and possibly give me a lighter teaching load. But Coach Busse was returning for a second year and he had promised to let me coach boys' basketball as long as I would continue to coach the girls' team. Besides, my salary would increase by a whopping $56 per year to $3660. That summer, I returned to Sam Houston to begin work on my Master's Degree in the Joe Kirk School of Physical Education.

My second year at Calvert, 1960-61, was almost an exact replica of the first except I started my first year in a long and successful career as a boys' basketball coach. Coach Busse did not change his coaching methods so our football team won only one or two games. It was obvious after the season that he would not be back so he concentrated on his principal's duties and teaching, leaving most of the coaching duties to me. He coached track in the spring but didn't really put his heart into it. He was looking for another job and I felt for him. He was a really good guy and I considered him my good friend. My girls' team that year was a little better, but we still had trouble getting the ball to the offensive end of the court and didn't win many games. I never coached girls' basketball again.

My first year coaching the boys' team was not bad but it ended up being the only losing season that I ever had as a high school head coach. It was always my goal to win district and advance to the playoffs so I scheduled larger schools for non-district play. So, entering district play in January, we had a losing record but had gained some much needed experience against good teams. We were in a Class B district with Lott, Chilton, Coolidge, Prairie Hill, and Riesel. Lott and Chilton had always dominated the district and were predicted to do so again. Our first district game was at Lott and I was well prepared. I had scouted them a couple of times and noticed a weakness in their guard play. I decided to use a 1-2-1-1 zone press that UCLA Coach John Wooden outlined in his book "They Call Me Coach". As far as I know, no one else had ever used the defense before in my neck of the woods. As usual, my players were not very talented but played very hard and had no problem following coaching instructions. I had a pretty good athlete in Charles Ford and a 6'4" skinny post player, Calvin Wiese. Using the press, we quickly caused turnovers that were converted into layups and jumped out to a 26-5 lead midway through the second quarter. Lott had a very good coach though and they cut the lead to about 15 points at halftime. But it was too late and they were too far behind so we won by about five points. My players were overjoyed. They had done nothing but lose during their high school careers and thought they had finally turned things around. I must admit that I thought I may have started a basketball dynasty at lowly Calvert.

My first basketball team ever, 1961-62 Calvert Trojans

We went undefeated in the first round of district play by also upsetting Chilton at home. But the second round of district play was a different story. I used the same pressing defense against Lott at home but was soundly outcoached in a horrible loss. We later lost to Chilton on the road while Lott went undefeated after their loss to us in the first district game. In those days, only one team in district advanced to the playoffs. We finished second and my first season as a head boys basketball coach was over with a 12-16 season record. I would never again have a losing record as a high school basketball coach.

During the spring of 1961, I began looking for another job. The kids in Calvert were great but I needed a higher salary, a lighter teaching and coaching load, and, preferably, a job at a school with a larger enrollment. Plus, my friend Herb Busse had been fired and the school board hired a new principal/head coach that had a reputation for disliking basketball. Those kinds of coaches in those days had a habit of referring to basketball as "thump-thump". So I began my search for a head boys' basketball coaching job that would fit my requirements. Since it was almost impossible to move up in the basketball coaching profession without coaching football in some capacity, I eliminated schools that didn't field a football team. Almost without exception in Texas high schools, the head football coach also serves as athletic director which justifies a higher salary as well as freedom from a teaching assignment. These dual role coaches wield supreme power over the other sports, and many use this power to keep the other sports from succeeding. They usually have power to hire and fire coaches at will. Football was, and still is, king in Texas.

CHAPTER **8**

My Memorable Year in the East Texas Oil Field (Carlisle)

I HAD TWO job offers that spring that fit my job requirements. One was the head basketball and assistant football coaching job at Valley Mills, the same school that had turned me down two years before because of my age. The other was the same position at Carlisle High School, located in the southern tip of the East Texas oilfield about twenty miles south of Kilgore and nine miles west of Henderson. Both were Class B schools with reputations for successful sports teams, both had larger enrollments than Calvert, and both would require me to teach just two different subjects. I was making four hundred dollars per year above the state minimum pay at Calvert. Valley Mills offered me nine hundred, so I accepted Carlisle's offer of $1000. Six hundred dollars doesn't sound like much but fifty dollars more a month was a lot when you were making only three hundred a month before. I would now be making a whopping $4312 per year!!! That was more than my mother's teaching salary at the time in Fairfield, although she had been teaching for more than thirty years.

Carlisle was the name of the school district located in Price, Texas. Price was not a really a town. It had one store, a post office, and maybe two or three churches. But there were oil derricks and pumping jacks as far as the eye could see, and several were located on the school campus. The store was owned by an older couple named Barron and it was attached to their house. I rented a room from them there and they treated me as if I was their son. The school superintendent, high school principal, and athletic director/head football coach all lived on campus in school district provided housing. In spite of all the producing oil wells, there were few wealthy families because most of the mineral rights were in the possession of absentee landowners. Almost everybody worked blue collar jobs in the oilfield and provided a decent living for their families. My favorite bumper sticker read "If you think I'm oilfield trash, you ought to see my pay stub".

Price was located at the junction of State Highway 42 and FM 13 at the southern end of the East Texas oilfield, which was a narrow stretch of real estate about forty-five miles long north to south, but only five miles wide east to west. At that time it contained the second largest deposit of oil in the continental United States. There were schools scattered all over the oilfield just a few miles apart. Five different high schools, all in separate school districts, were located on a twenty mile stretch of highway from Price to Kilgore. Since schools in Texas get most of their money from local property taxes, those located within the oilfield had high tax bases and, under school finance laws at that time, were considered "self-supporting", meaning that they got very little money from the state. But because of their property wealth, they didn't need extra funding, plus they didn't have to help support the poorer districts. As a result of all of this, there was a wide financial disparity between school districts, especially in East Texas. I was one of the lucky ones fortunate to be going to work for a "self-supporting" school district. As a result of these financial disparities, all Class B schools located the oilfield played football and most of the others, lacking the resources for a football team, concentrated on basketball. This could be a problem but, compared with Calvert, my new school was superior in every way except maybe for the quality of the kids. I couldn't wait to get started. The football coach/athletic director at Carlisle, Earl Meyer, was a really nice guy and the most laid back football coach I've ever known. We didn't even have two-a-day practices in August and he didn't seem to mind if players didn't show up for the one practice that we had. Most practices began with a casual drill in which all players, regardless of position, lined up and ran out for passes thrown by the quarterback. We would then break down into drills with Earl supervising the backs while I ran drills with the linemen. He never dictated to me what drills to run. Most of his time at practice was spent observing while kneeled down on one knee. But, when it came to strategy, he knew his stuff. He ran an offense featuring an unbalanced line and a unique "split six" defense that featured our two best athletes at middle linebacker. We never worked on team defense until Thursdays when we practiced without pads. Probably the reason for his laid back attitude that year was the fact that Carlisle was not only undefeated the previous year, but had not had a close game against a Class B team, and had the bulk of its players returning. One of these was Mickey Don Thompson, a 6'3", 225 pound sprinter who may have been the best athlete in the history of Class B football in Texas. Coach Meyer loved to show the film of a game against Winona in which Carlisle scored 106 points and Mickey Don was not tackled a single time the whole game while carrying the ball on at least every other play.

In those days, Class B football teams could advance only to the regional finals, which meant only two playoff games. Carlisle had won regional the previous year and its only close game was a win over arch-rival Gaston, a Class A school just four miles up the road. We lost to Gaston in a close game in 1961, but still had no problem winning our Class B district. There were only three football districts in our region at the time and this was the year that we got a bye in bi-district play. We had soundly beaten the two other district winners in non-district play and didn't even bother to scout the game. In fact, we didn't even practice during the bye week and Coach Meyer told me to go ahead and start basketball practice. That may have been the only time that ever happened in the history of Texas high school sports, before or since. We won the regional football championship anyway and it wasn't even close. We resumed basketball practice the following Monday and I was pleasantly surprised at what I saw.

Before my arrival, Carlisle had fielded decent basketball teams but, compared to the basketball-only Class B schools in the area, they were pretty far behind because of the late start each year. The UIL allowed those schools to practice year round and to start playing games on October 15, right in the middle of football season. As a result, it was unusual for a Class B oilfield school that played football to advance in the state playoffs. There were tons of schools in east Texas at the time with rich basketball traditions and the Class B State champion almost always came from the area. Carlisle, though, had a few ways to overcome this huge advantage. First, our enrollment was almost enough for Class A, giving us an advantage over smaller schools. Second, there was no girls' team with which to share the gym. Third, our junior high coach Armour Hays was a former head high school coach who was very knowledgeable about the game and had taught the kids well. But the most important equalizer was that we had great athletes who loved winning no matter the sport. They all played football but at least three of them were more talented in basketball.

Our starters that year were Billy Childress at point guard, Sammy Hamilton at shooting guard, Jerry Chamberlain and Bobby Spence at forward, and Mickey Don Thompson at center. With the exception of Chamberlain, they were all seniors. Childress was a hard-nosed little football halfback who loved basketball and was an excellent ball handler who could really attack the rim. Hamilton was from a long line of Hamilton's who were known for their prowess on the basketball court. He was a great shooter and was our leading scorer. Chamberlain, our only junior, was probably the purest basketball player on the team. He was about 6'3" and a good rebounder and scorer. Spence was a quiet, somewhat sullen 6'4" kid who could rebound and defend. He never backed down or took any flak from anybody, including his coach. And Mickey Don Thompson was just Mickey Don Thompson, one of the best Class B athletes ever. He was somewhat of a "bull in the china closet" on the basketball court but you could depend on him to grab at least twenty rebounds almost every game. Mickey Don later played football at the University of Houston, where he started at fullback in Coach Bill Yoeman's vaunted "veer" offensive attack. You may wonder why I always refer to him by both his first and middle names. The answer is that's just the way East Texans have always done it. Many years ago when Princess Di was pregnant with her first child, one of the newspapers in East Texas had a contest for readers to suggest a name for the baby, which was to be a boy. The winner in a landslide was "Billy Wayne". "Jim Bob" finished a distant second.

The late start after a long football season resulted in a shortened non-district schedule. I don't even remember what our won-loss record was when we began district play in January. Since I didn't have time to fully install the offense I had used at Calvert, Coach Hays suggested that I use the one that he had taught the players in junior high. I took his suggestion and it turned out to be one of the best coaching decisions I ever made. I didn't have to make a decision on defense because I was a strong advocate of man-to-man with a lot of full court zone press thrown in. The UIL was kind enough to allow football-playing schools to play in the same district that we had in football, allowing us some time to catch up with the others in case we won district. We quickly marched through district undefeated and got better with every game. Sammy Hamilton was one of the leading scorers in East Texas, much to the delight of his tribe of older brothers who were at every game, both at home and on the road.

Because of our fortunate financial situation at Carlisle, I had to get used to not doing a lot of things that I had done in Calvert. We had a janitor, John Ross Martin, assigned strictly to the athletic department. John Ross was pure East Texas to the core. If Webster had made "easttexas" a word in the dictionary, he would have put John Ross's picture next to it. Not only did he keep the athletic facilities clean and in good working order, he also washed all the uniforms and practice equipment. He was the team bus driver for every sport in addition to a regular route that he drove every day. So when an opposing fan would holler at me to "Sit down bus driver" when I stood to give instructions to a player or to jump on a referee, he was talking to the wrong person because our bus driver was sitting behind the bench. When our teams played on the road, the school provided us with a good sit down meal at a nice restaurant, and John Ross always blessed the food, uttering the same exact words each time. One night, with all heads bowed, John went silent in the middle of his prayer. Mickey Don looked up and said "I think he forgot it Coach", then proceeded to finish it for him without missing a word that John Ross always used.

After winning district, we learned that our bi-district opponent would be Bullard, a town about twenty miles south of Tyler. Bullard was one of those feared basketball only schools that had a rich winning tradition in the sport. Their coach was Leonard Roper, an older guy who always wore a nice suit and a felt hat when he coached. He was a Bullard native, married to the town doctor, and was highly respected both as a coach and as a person. As a young coach, I was honored to have the chance to compete against him. I don't remember where the game was played but, since Class B basketball was so big in the area, most playoff games were played in large gyms, usually in Tyler, Kilgore, or Jacksonville. All these towns had junior colleges with nice basketball facilities. I don't remember much about the game except that we won and would be advancing to the regional tournament in Kilgore the following weekend. This would be Carlisle's first trip ever to this eight team tournament, the winner of which would advance to state tournament in Austin. Needless to say, I was very excited, as were the players and fans.

Carlisle Indians, 1962 bi-district champs (Mickey Don Thompson is #32)

    The Kilgore regional tournament was played on the campus of Kilgore Junior College each year, and the winner of this region almost always went on to win the state championship. The winner had to win three games in two days against some of the state's best Class B teams. I'm not sure who did the seeding for the tournament that year, but we were seeded eighth, or last, and had to play the number one seed, Spring Hill, a school just outside of Longview. They had been ranked number one in the state for most of the year. Their coach was J.D. Menasco, a proponent of Cotton Robinson's "Buna offense". Our paths would cross several times in later years when both of us were college coaches. You didn't see this offense much in upper east Texas but J.D. and his former teammate at East Texas State, Jerry Matthews, both ran it almost to perfection. Jerry was the coach at Gaston at the time and later in his career was head coach at East Texas State.

Without becoming too technical, the offense was a very patient one with the defense allowed to dictate its options. Its success was based on getting the ball inside for a one-on-one scoring opportunity for a post man, or if he was double-teamed, a player would take an open shot from his favorite spot on the floor. Each player spent hours practicing shots from his spot, and the post players were almost perfect on their one-on-one moves. At least at Buna they were. I had studied this offense thoroughly and, with the help of others, I used an unorthodox 1-1-3 zone against it. We practiced it all week before the tournament started on Friday.

The Class B regional in Kilgore was always a big event and every game was always sold out. There were four games on Friday and our game against Spring Hill was the last one on Friday night. We started out hot and stayed that way almost the entire game. Sammy Hamilton couldn't miss, scoring a game high 31 points. My big guys played tough defense on their post men all night and Mickey Don was, as usual, dominant on the boards. Our crazy 1-1-3 zone confused their players although they kept it decently close the whole game. I knew we would win when Spring Hill tried to zone press because Billy Childress never had any problem dribbling through double teams. I don't even remember the score but I knew we would be facing Huntington the next day in the semi-final game and needed to eat our post-game meal, then get home and get some sleep. I've never seen a happier group of young men. I was a pretty happy twenty-two year old coach myself. And John Ross's prayer before our meal was perfect this time. The next day the Kilgore paper reported that our win was the first by a football playing school in the history of the tournament. I didn't have any empirical evidence to support that, but I accepted it as fact anyway and I still do today.

We would have to win two games the next day in order to punch our ticket to the state tournament, but so would our opponent Huntington. I understood our eight seed at regional, but I couldn't understand Huntington's four seed. After all, they had been ranked second in the state behind Spring Hill all year yet Cayuga, who was not even ranked in the top ten, was awarded the two seed. I suspect that Joe Turner, the coach at Kilgore Jr. College where the tournament was played, may have had something to do with it. Coach Turner had won three state championships at Cayuga in the early fifties, and one of his former players was now the coach. Huntington, a school in the Lufkin area, had won back-to-back Class A state championships in 1959 and 1960 but they were now in Class B. They jumped on us early in the semi-final game and never let up, beating us 79-48. My players had given their all the night before and had nothing left in them. Plus, I was soundly outcoached by Lloyd Dickens. Huntington beat Cayuga in the finals that night and went on to win the state championship in Austin for the third time. But I was a still a proud coach. I never expected to do this well in only my second year as a head coach. I would start my very short career as a baseball coach on Monday.

During the spring of 1962, I had a lot of time to ponder my future. Hardly any small schools in the area at that time fielded a baseball team so we played just a few games. All I remember is that Sammy Hamilton was a very good pitcher so we won most of them. Coach Meyer's track team won the state championship and his starting football backfield won both the 440 and mile relays, with Mickey Don Thompson anchoring both. There may have never been a greater assemblage of athletes in a Class B school in Texas until integration began a few years later. But most of them were seniors and only one of my basketball starters was returning. So I began a search for a new job. My job requirements included a larger school in a larger town, a head basketball job, and an athletic director who would be supportive of a well-rounded athletic program. I understood that I would probably have to help with football but I had no problem with that. In fact, the success of our football team at Carlisle was probably the deciding factor in the job that was offered to me. It was at Wharton, a Class 3A school about sixty miles southwest of Houston. I was jumping from Class B to 3A and I was still only twenty-two years old.

As I left my little room at Barron's store in late May that year, I thought that I would never see Price, Texas again. After all, not many people are headed anywhere that would require passage through such an out-of-the-way place. But forty years later, in 2002, I attended a school reunion there that honored the championship teams of 1961-62. Almost every living player on those teams was there, and only a handful had ever left the area. Most had good paying oilfield jobs, were proud of their families, and were happy as could be. Mickey Don Thompson even reminded me of the time that he had to finish our bus driver's prayer. As I left the parking lot to return to my home in the Texas Hill Country, I saw a bumper sticker that said "Oilfield trash, and damn proud of it". I drove home feeling pretty damn proud myself that I had spent that one memorable year amongst these proud hard working people in the southern tip of the East Texas oilfield forty years before.

CHAPTER 9

Win Too Many "Thump-Thump" Games and You're Fired!!! (Wharton)

BEFORE RELOCATING TO Wharton, I stopped over in Huntsville and took a couple of classes at Sam Houston that would count towards my Master's degree in Physical Education. They were both taught by Joe Kirk so I made sure that they were not courses for which I had already received credit. There's no way that anyone would know had they not made the extra effort to find out before the classes started. After clearing that hurdle, I completed both classes and received an A in one and a C in the other. I never learned how Joe came up with grades in any of his classes but I suspect that he flipped a coin.

In 1962, Wharton was a thriving town of about 6000 people on Highway 59 in the middle of the coastal prairie region of Texas. The Colorado River wound its way through town on its way to the Gulf of Mexico at Matagorda Bay. There was a sizable Czech population in the area that resided mostly in small farm hamlets in the county outside of town. Like my hometown of Fairfield, it had a courthouse square with businesses on all four sides and Highway 59, a few blocks off the square, was bustling with traffic and businesses of all kinds. My favorite was a seafood restaurant called Peterson's. There was even a junior college that participated in football, basketball, and baseball. In a nutshell, Wharton was a big difference from Calvert and Price. I would be living in a town where there was at least a little something to do, and just an hour away from the big city of Houston. I rented a room in a house just off the square and prepared for my new adventure. I would be the head boys basketball coach, assistant junior varsity football coach, and general science teacher. Although Wharton was not a particularly wealthy school district, my salary was still a little more than I was making at Carlisle. I may have even reached the $5000 per year mark. And, even better, a brand new high school was opening in the fall.

    The athletic teams at Wharton competed in a Class 3A district with El Campo, Bay City, Port Lavaca, Angleton, Lamar Consolidated, and West Columbia. In football, it was sometimes called "The Little Southwest Conference". Angleton and Port Lavaca had won recent state championships and El Campo, Bay City, and Lamar Consolidated were all powers in the area. Enrollment numbers are very important in football, and only West Columbia was a smaller school than Wharton. As a result, the Tigers had suffered several down years in football and hadn't done much better in the other sports. The basketball team had suffered through a losing season in 1961-62, and the coach had left to pursue better opportunities as a football coach. But, before I accepted the job, I had done some research and discovered that there were two big Czech kids looming on the horizon. One was a 6'9" sophomore named Jimmy Hubenak and the other was a 6'11 freshman named Alvin Ginzler. Jimmy was a starter on the varsity as a freshman and Alvin was a project that would really need some work. Neither of these kids played football. It seemed to me that things were really looking good for the Tigers, at least in basketball.

    My boss, the athletic director/head football coach, was Ed Lechler, who many years later would become the proud grandfather of Shane Lechler, the future hall of fame punter for the Texas Aggies, Oakland Raiders, and Houston Texans. Ed was both a good guy and a good coach who was fighting an uphill battle trying to build a winning football program at Wharton. He was best at molding a strong coaching staff that worked hard and got along remarkably well. For the first time in my short coaching career I had young single guys, like Jerry Mallory and Jackie Robinson, on the coaching staff that I could socialize with. I had never been happier. But where football was concerned, it was not to be. We would always start out strong against smaller schools in non-district play only to lose to the larger schools in our district. The same was true at the sub-varsity and middle school levels. In my two years at Wharton, we had identical 4-6 records, winning against the same four schools and losing to the same six schools. Our only district win each year was against West Columbia, the only school in the district with a smaller enrollment. The fans in Wharton were very supportive but were hungry for a winner, no matter the sport.

Most high schools in Texas, with the exception of small Class B schools and some larger 4A schools, did not start basketball practice until football season was over. The rules allowed an October 15 start date but athletic directors usually had their own rules. It made little difference to me because I was also coaching football and almost all my basketball team members played football as well. Plus, I had never coached anywhere that didn't have the same rule. But I was looking forward to getting started when the football season ended in mid-November.

A large number of the kids enrolled in Wharton schools lived in small farm communities, such as Egypt and Pierce, which had once had schools themselves. During the fifties, most of these schools were closed and consolidated with those in larger towns in the county such as Wharton and El Campo. The abandoned school buildings often became community centers where all kinds of events occurred, a common tradition in German, Polish, and Czech areas of the state. Many of the schools had gymnasiums that were still in good shape, and pickup basketball games were played almost every night and on weekends. This was particularly true in the Pierce community, between Wharton and El Campo, where many of our athletes lived. Some even had a key to the gym as did one of our junior high coaches from Pierce, Jackie Robinson. Although I visited the Pierce gym on occasion, I made sure to stay away during football season so as not to be accused of starting basketball practice too early.

DAN MONTGOMERY

After a few days of practice that first year, I had a pretty good idea of what my basketball team would look like. There wasn't much depth but I had three pretty good veteran players plus a couple of young prospects. My starting lineup included two seniors, one junior, and one sophomore. Three of these guys were returning starters from the previous year. Charles Holezal was a senior who was a good athlete, a hard worker, and a solid rebounder. Ronald Kielman, the junior, was about 6'2" and could both shoot and rebound. Jimmy Hubenak was a 6'9" sophomore who had started as a freshman and was already a pretty polished big man. He had a key to the Pierce gym and could have had a key to my car if he had asked. Robert Watson was a 6'4" sophomore, a really good athlete, and probably our best ball handler. Our point guard was Ben Sanchez who was also our best football running back and, while he was a tough competitor, may have been our weakest link. But I had a freshman guard lurking on the horizon named Trinidad (Trini) Rivera, who I decided to keep on the junior varsity to get more game experience.

TOP ROW: Student Trainer Maury Salinger, Trinie Rivera, Malcolm Rugeley, Philip Holesovsky, Duke Wilson,

Wharton Tigers, 1963 district champs (Jimmy Hubenak is #42)

62

I was always a believer in a strong non-district schedule. I was more interested in using these games as preparation for the district schedule in January. I don't remember what our non-district record was that year, but I do remember splitting home-and-home games with Alvin, and that their best player was a sophomore named Nolan Ryan. Nolan says in his autobiography that his best high school sport was basketball. I beg to differ with him a bit on that as I witnessed him mow down batter after batter when our baseball team faced him. I never saw him play basketball as a junior or senior, but he was pretty decent as a sophomore.

Although not known as a strong basketball district, both El Campo and Lamar Consolidated in Rosenberg had pretty solid programs. The others were better known as football schools so Wharton had been about average in years past. I was determined to do the best I could to change that. Like every other basketball coach in the state, my ultimate goal was to reach the state tournament and maybe even win it all. That would be a pretty tall task because our Class 3A region contained Clear Creek, one of the purest basketball programs in the state, and all roads to Austin had to pass through them. A basketball coaching legend named George Carlisle had started the program several years before in the small town of Webster, located between Houston and Galveston. As the area grew, several small schools merged and formed the Clear Creek School District, and they continued to dominate basketball in the area. By the time I arrived in Wharton, Coach Carlisle was head coach at Rice University and Henry "Hank" Bauerschlag, a legend to be, was the coach.

Although we didn't win district that year, we finished second with a 10-2 record. Our only losses were to district champion El Campo. We had this solid record although we had to play Port Lavaca twice on the road because they, with a very small African American population, had already integrated and had one African American player on their team. He was also on the football team, but our school board ruled that, while we could play them at home in football, we couldn't in basketball. Their reasoning was that it was okay for Blacks to play outdoors in Wharton, but not indoors. And this was 1963, nine years AFTER the Supreme Court ruling in "Brown vs. Board of Education of Topeka"! By the way, Port Lavaca's coach was A.B. Menasco, brother of J.D. Menasco, the coach of the team that my Carlisle team had defeated in the Class B regionals the year before. And A.B., like J.D., ran the "Buna" offense with which I never had a problem. Also, I have no idea what either J.D. or A.B. stand for, but I'm pretty sure that they grew up in East Texas. So a good guess for one of them is Jimmy Don. I don't know about the A in A.B., but a good guess for the B would be "Bubba". There is an old joke about a deputy sheriff in East Texas whose name was "Sonny Bubba" but I can't repeat the joke on these pages.

At any rate, I was looking forward to next year with the core of my team returning plus some great young prospects such as Trini Rivera, Gary Segrest, and the tall freshman project, Alvin Ginzler. We almost lost Alvin that year though. He was on the junior varsity team and the coach was Bobby Wright, a former quarterback at Rice University. Bobby took the team to a tournament somewhere and, when they got back, I asked him how it went. He replied "We won the game but I had to kick Alvin off the team because he forgot to take his shoes". My reply was "What do you mean you kicked him off the team? For crying out loud, he's 6'11" so you should have had his shoes in your hands". Needless to say, Alvin was back on the team very soon. Coach Wright was my good friend and he was merely doing what he thought I would do since he knew I didn't put up with much at all. But sometimes you have to ask yourself, as Cotton Robinson advised me many years later, "Is he one of your main players?" As of yet, Alvin wasn't a main player but he certainly had the potential to be. A year later, Bobby Wright and his wife Shirley would stand up for me in a way that I would never forget.

During the spring of 1963, I had no coaching duties and, as usual, I attended the state high school basketball tournament in Austin. The previous summer while I was taking classes at Sam Houston, I drove over to Calvert to visit friends and ran into one of my former basketball players, Patricia Dick. After graduation, Pat had attended business school in Austin and was now working in an office job there. She had been one of my tenacious defensive players who couldn't handle the ball well enough to consistently get it back to our offensive players at the other end of the court. But I never had a player, boy or girl, who worked any harder. Our meeting that summer in would eventually lead to our marriage. I was glad to see her during my trip to Austin that spring. She would eventually become a coach herself.

When the school year ended in Wharton that year, I again journeyed to Huntsville to complete my Master of Education degree and get started on obtaining an administrator's certificate. A Master's degree would automatically entitle me to a four or five hundred dollar a year pay increase, which was a pretty big deal in those days. My suite mate that summer was a teacher in Baytown who had grown up in Indiana and had coached high school basketball there for a few years. At the time, I was still using the offense that I had copied from our junior high coach at Carlisle, but I was looking for something different that would better fit my personnel at Wharton. I knew that we were due to be really good the next year, and even better the next, but I needed all the help I could get. He and I drew up a lot of plays that summer in our suite and even spent time in the gymnasium walking through them. I don't remember the guy's name, and I never ever saw him again, but I installed most of the offense and used it almost exclusively the following season.

Almost any coach will tell you that school enrollment numbers play a big part in the success of athletic teams. That's why the UIL, at the time, divided the schools into five separate classifications based on enrollment. (There are six now and each one has two divisions for football.) But numbers make a much bigger difference in football than in the other sports simply because more players are needed for football. As a result, it can be difficult to have a winning football team if you coach in a school that is one of the smaller ones in your classification. This is also somewhat true in basketball but to a much lesser extent. "Hoosiers", my favorite sports movie ever, tells the true story of a small school in Indiana beating one of the largest schools for the state basketball championship in 1954, when all schools there were in just one classification. In Texas, it is still not unusual for small schools to win games against much larger schools in basketball. In the case of Wharton High School in the 1960's, we were one of the smaller schools in our Class 3A district so it was easier for us to compete in basketball than in football. It had little to do with the quality of coaching. But, as I would later find out, it can cause some ugly conflicts between coaches of the two sports. And the eventual winner of these conflicts in Texas is almost always the football coach because he is almost always the athletic director.

In sixteen of my twenty years as a high school coach, I was involved with football in some way. In the larger schools, I was usually an assistant with the junior varsity or freshman teams. With the exception of the last game of the season, I hardly ever saw a varsity football game because I was usually scouting a future opponent. On November 22, 1963, I was going to our last game of the football season that night and would start basketball practice the next day. But, as I was teaching my general science class just after noon that day, Principal Joe Urbanovsky came on the speaker and announced that President Kennedy had been shot from a window in the Texas School Book Depository above Dealey Plaza in Dallas. In a one in a million coincidence, I looked down at my desk and saw an envelope addressed to the Texas School Book Depository. I was sending an order in that day for some science workbooks. A few hours later, it was announced that police had arrested a man whose address was that of a rooming house on North Beckley Avenue in the Oak Cliff section of Dallas. My heart sank because I knew that my sister and her husband lived in a boarding house on that street. Could it be that my brother-in-law had shot the president? Surely not, but I hardly knew him and also knew that my mother didn't care much for him. I was relieved when I heard that the arrested man was named Lee Harvey Oswald. It turned out that he lived at 1026 North Beckley, my sister's address was next door at 1028, and she had never seen him before. Because of the president's death, there was talk of canceling the football game at West Columbia. Wharton really needed to play because we were 0-5 in district play and West Columbia was the weakest team in the league. The game was played so our record became 4-6 for the season and 1-5 in district, the same as the year before. I decided to postpone the start of basketball practice until the following Monday, and I was excited to be starting what I expected to be a banner year.

The most exciting happening in Wharton in the fall of 1963 was the filming of "Baby the Rain Must Fall" starring Steve McQueen, Lee Remick, and Don Murray. Horton Foote, famous for writing the screenplay for "To Kill a Mockingbird", was a Wharton native who also had written the screenplay for this movie. McQueen and Murray, along with other cast and crew members, were given permission to use our gym for pickup basketball games a few nights during their stay in Wharton. Ms. Rector, the mother of one of our athletes, was local casting director and picked me as an extra to occupy a bus seat in the opening scene. Unfortunately, my seat was too far back in the bus for me to be seen, ending my acting career before it got off the ground. In addition to Horton Foote, Wharton's other notable native is Dan Rather, the former CBS News anchor. He and I have something in common in that we are both graduates of Sam Houston State Teachers College. I never met him, but if I ever do, I'll ask him if he is also a graduate of the Joe Kirk School of Physical Education.

As usual, I had scheduled tough teams for non-district play. In those days, my alma mater, Sam Houston State, hosted one of the best high school tournaments in the state, and invited sixteen of the best teams in the area. Because of our strong finish the previous year, we were invited and I gladly accepted the invitation. Our first game in the tournament was against Jesse Jones High School of Houston, one of the many Class 4A basketball powers in the Houston Independent School District. But my kids didn't back down and we stayed close through the first three quarters, before losing by eleven points. Their coach, Bunky Bradford, congratulated us on our play and told me that they were lucky to win. Little did I know at that time that Coach

Bradford, just a few months later, would play a huge part in salvaging my young coaching career.

When we started district play in January, it became evident to me that something special was happening. Jimmy Hubenak, our 6'9" junior center, had matured into a really great player. Ron Kielman, our only senior, provided leadership and was our leading scorer. And Robert Watson, a 6'4" red haired junior, could play both guard and forward. We had no trouble with the pure football schools in the district, and won fairly close games against Lamar Consolidated and El Campo, the two schools who actually made an effort to compete in basketball. Our gym, although new, had seats on only one side. The people of Wharton were so hungry for a winner that the stands were overflowing for every game. We finished the district season with a perfect 12-0 record. Nobody in Wharton could recall the last time that Wharton had won a district championship in basketball. But I looked it up. It was 1947.

The biggest happening in my life up to that point had nothing to do with basketball. Although Pat lived in Austin, we stayed in touch a lot for a couple of years and talked about eventually getting married. But, as time passed, we slowly grew apart and I had begun dating others. I was still only twenty-four and really wasn't sure that I was ready for married life just yet. But one day in early January, Pat called and said that she was ready and that I was the one. A couple of weeks later, we were married in a simple ceremony at the First Methodist Church in Wharton. Our attendants were my boss Ed Lechler and his wife Dottie. We took a quick honeymoon to Corpus Christi and were back by Monday before basketball practice started. We immediately moved into a small rent house on Foote Street, just a few blocks from the high school.

After winning our district that year, I was not at all surprised that our bi-district opponent would be Clear Creek, the defending Class 3A state champion. They were one of the most dominant Class 3A teams in the state, and one of their top players seemed to always be named Lenox. This year it was Jimmy Dale, who had been all-state the previous year. Coach Bauerschlag was, like Coach Carlisle before him, a former player at Southwest Texas State under Coach Milton Jowers. Coach Jowers was known for his tandem post offense and a 1-3-1 zone defense. In fact, all the coaches that I ever knew who played for Coach Jowers ran the same offense and defense. The tandem post was a 1-3-1 offensive set with a point guard, two wings, a high post, and a low post. I never cared for it myself because it featured a lot of cross court dribbling. But I must admit that I had a tough time defending it. Clear Creek, it seemed, always ran it to perfection. Coach Bauerschlag looked more like a college professor than a coach but he sure as heck won a lot of basketball games.

Our game against Clear Creek was played at Autry Court at Rice University in Houston. Clear Creek fans always turned out big for basketball, but Wharton fans, excited to finally be following a winner, also turned out in big numbers. I knew that we may have a tough time winning against such a storied program with an experienced team, and I was right. Although we never had much trouble against zone defenses, most zone coaches prefer a 2-3 defensive set, so I doubt that we had played against a 1-3-1 zone all year. As a result, our offense got off to a slow start and we could never catch up. I don't remember the final score, but I'm sure we lost by at least ten or twelve points. My message to the team in the locker room after the game was upbeat. We were beaten by a better team but things would be different next year. I was disappointed for Ron Kielman, our only senior, but we would undoubtedly be good next year. Besides, Jimmy Dale Lenox would be gone and I think he may have been the last Lenox in Clear Creek. When we dressed and left the locker room that night, I was overwhelmed to see that tons of Wharton fans were waiting in the parking lot near our bus. Some had already made signs reading "Wait 'til Next Year". This may have had something to do with what transpired the next day.

In all my days as a high school coach, I never once encouraged one of my players to quit another sport to concentrate on basketball. In my view, sports should be for the enjoyment of the student, not to advance the career of any one coach. In my first two coaching jobs, both at small schools, all my players also played football. I was a three sport athlete myself in high school. My first year at Wharton, which was a much larger school than where I had played and coached, only three kids in our entire program specialized in basketball, and all three had not played football before I arrived. Besides, one was 6'9" and another was 6'11". But shortly before our playoff game, I got word from another coach that one of my little used reserves, who was also a little used football player, had announced to Coach Lechler that he was quitting the team to improve his chances of starting in basketball his senior year. He also said that Coach Lechler threw a fit and blamed it on me, the "thump- thump" coach. But neither the player nor Coach Lechler had said a word to me about it. So I simply ignored it and forgot about it. I was too busy preparing for the state playoffs.

When the athletic period began on the day after our playoff loss, Coach Lechler called for all non-football athletes, excluding seniors, to meet with him in his office. Other coaches were not invited. After the meeting ended, Jimmy Hubenak, Trini Rivera, and Alvin Ginzler, walked into my office and delivered the news. Beginning the in the fall of the next school year, only football players would be allowed to be enrolled in the athletic period. This meant that, if you didn't play football, you would have to wait until after school to practice your chosen sport even during the season. I interpreted this as jealously on the part of Coach Lechler of the success of the basketball program. In my view, he was clearly using this success as an excuse for his football team's losing seasons. The timing of the meeting, one day after our successful season had ended, gave support to my point of view. I immediately marched into his office and respectfully voiced my opinion. His response was "If you don't like it, you can resign. If you don't resign, I can always recommend that your contract not be renewed". I thought that, since my principal had praised me for my teaching abilities, he would step in and prevent my firing. But I was wrong. He sided with the athletic director and let him have his way. In effect, Ed Lechler, who less than a month before had stood in for my wedding, had essentially fired me. Most coaches get fired for losing too many games. For me, however, the opposite was true.

Although I was allowed to complete the school year and receive a salary through August, I was a newlywed without a job. If I wanted to continue coaching basketball, I was in dire straits because no football coach/athletic director would be looking to hire a coach who had just been fired by one of his own. Plus, I vowed to never accept another job without first getting assurance from the boss that he wanted a successful all around athletic program. That left me with few choices so, in desperation, I called Bunky Bradford, the coach at Jones High School in Houston. Luckily for me, his assistant/junior varsity coach was leaving and he urged me to call Horace Elrod who was then the athletic director of Houston ISD. Mr. Elrod invited me in for an interview, was impressed with my coaching resume, and recommended to Jones principal Coy Mills that I be hired if he could approve me as a history teacher. I will always be indebted to Bunky Bradford, Horace Elrod, and Coy Mills for helping to resurrect my career as a coach and educator.

It was going to be tough for me to leave Wharton. I loved everything about it and could have probably lived there for a lifetime. The other members of the coaching staff and their families were close friends and accepted my new wife as one of their own. The basketball coach at Wharton Jr. College, Gene Bahnsen, had become a very good friend of mine. The town was small, but not too small. But I had no choice but to move on. To say the least, I was somewhat apprehensive about the move to Houston. Wharton and Huntsville had been the largest towns that I had ever lived in and I was not sure that I could adjust to big city life. Pat was especially nervous about the move for she had also been a small town girl. My vision of an inner city high school was shaped by the movie "Blackboard Jungle" that I had seen during my high school days. But we moved on. Our best friends, Bobby and Shirley Wright, did too. Bobby, in addition to being my JV coach, was Coach Lechler's backfield coach and Shirley was a high school English teacher. They both resigned, partly in protest for my firing, and accepted jobs at Tuloso-Midway High School near Corpus Christi. They remained our good friends during the entire time of our marriage.

CHAPTER **10**

Two Years of Heat, Sweat, Traffic, and Mosquitoes (Houston)

PAT AND I had been renting in Wharton, but rent payments would be much higher in Houston and I would be making about the same salary. Jones High School is located in the southern part of the city off South Park Blvd. (now MLK), a few miles south of the University of Houston campus. At the time, the neighborhood was white middle class and there were lots of new housing developments all over the area, especially to the south of the high school. Although we didn't have money for a down payment, we looked at some brand new houses that were under construction in what would be called a track home neighborhood today. We walked into a model home that also served as the builder's sales office and met the home builder, George Cox Sr., the father of a football player at Jones High School. Mr. Cox immediately took a liking to us and offered to let us move into a brand new home without a down payment. In return, I agreed to show houses for a few weeks on weekends. The total price of our first house was $10,400. I can't get my driveway paved for that today.

Although my coaching assignment at Jones was basketball only, I knew that if I wanted to be a head basketball coach again outside of Houston, I would probably need to stay involved with football in some way. When I was hired, Mr. Elrod let me know that the road to a head basketball coaching position in Houston ISD would be long because there was a policy at the time of moving up coaches from the ranks, starting in junior high. As a result, I volunteered to help coach the sophomore football team. Jones was a large high school with an enrollment of 2700 in three grades. Our athletic program had varsity, junior varsity, and sophomore teams. The head coach, W.C. Treadway, was glad to have me and offered me $75 for the entire season. My pay would come from profits from the locker room coke machine. I coached for a few days in the hot August sun until I realized that I could make more than that by officiating a couple of football games. I quit, but not before helping to discover a future college All-American and NFL player named Bill Atessis. At the time, all equipment for athletics in the Houston ISD was issued from the central office and sometimes there was not enough to share with non-varsity teams, especially sophomores. Since there were no helmets to fit Bill's head, he had to sit out contact drills and I noticed him chomping at the bit for some action. I called over Coach Treadway from the varsity practice field, showed him this big good looking kid moping on the sideline, and there was a helmet to fit Bill's head the next day. Within a couple of weeks, he was starting at defensive end on the varsity team. Bill later became an All –American at the University of Texas, played a few years in the NFL, and was later named to the Texas High School Football Hall of Fame. He also played for me on the Jones junior varsity basketball team. I doubt that he even remembers my name. Two other future All-Americans, Bobby Wuensch (Texas) and Tommy Maxwell (Texas A&M), were on the Jones team that year. Tommy, like Bill, played for a few years in the NFL. Although it was unusual for a Houston ISD football team to get past the opening round of the playoffs, Jones advanced to the state quarterfinals in both 1964 and 1965.

When school started in September, it didn't take me long to discover that my fears about teaching in a large inner city school were misguided. Jones had been open for about eight years and there was already a new high school (Sterling) under construction to relieve the crowding. But a "Blackboard Jungle" it was not. This was due to the principal, Mr. Coy Mills, who was already in his sixties and had spent his entire career in Houston ISD. Mr. Mills ruled with an iron hand and demanded excellence from students, teachers, coaches, and staff. There were no athletic coordinators or department heads. He was head of everything and wanted Jones to excel in both academics and extra-curricular activities. Student discipline problems were almost non-existent. I taught and coached at six different high schools during my career, and Jesse Jones High School was the best organized one by far. Mr. Mills was big on professionalism on the part of teachers. Male teachers were required to wear coats and ties in the classroom while P.E. teachers had to wear white shirts and long white pants. I noticed that this made a big difference in classroom management and, after I left Jones, I never walked into a public school or college classroom without wearing a coat and tie. In my view, if all public schools today were modeled after Jesse H. Jones High School of the mid-sixties, there would be no need for all the "hand wringing" from education policy makers about how to solve the problems in public education.

Where basketball was concerned, there was a big difference between Wharton and Jones. At Jones, basketball had its own athletic period in which players were enrolled the entire school year. UIL rules allowed practice all year during this period and full scale practice could start October 15. It was unusual for a kid to play both football and basketball, especially at the varsity level. Two junior high schools, Cullen and Hartman, fed into Jones with Cullen being known for football and Hartman for basketball. The kids at Hartman, under Coach Tommy Tyson, had already been well schooled in basketball before entering high school. So Jones was already known as a basketball power before I got there. However, several other schools in Houston were tough in basketball. Almost every year, the southeast Texas Class 4A region was represented at the state basketball tournament by a Houston ISD school. The same was true for the Dallas ISD in the northeast region. Basketball in the larger schools was a city game even before integration. Stephen F. Austin High School, just a few miles away from Jones, had won the state championship the previous year and they were in the same district as Jones, as was Milby, another traditional basketball power. But Jones had also had a good year the previous season and had four starters returning. They also had a great coach and an even greater person, Robert "Bunky" Bradford.

Bunky was a tall, quiet, and modest man who had grown up in Arp, a tiny town just outside the East Texas oilfield, less than ten miles from where I had coached at Carlisle. Arp must have had good basketball teams back then because it produced both Bunky Bradford and Guy Lewis, who both went on to play at the University of Houston before Guy became the long-time coach there. After graduating from "Cougar High", as many people called it back then, Bunky took a junior high school coaching job in Houston and did his time before accepting the head basketball job at Jones when it first opened eight years earlier. He had helped rescue my coaching career and I was looking forward to working with him as his assistant and junior varsity coach. Bragg Stockton, the new head baseball coach, coached the sophomore team. Bragg later was head baseball coach at San Jacinto Jr. College, the University of Houston, and TCU.

My Wharton team had been defeated by Jones in a tournament game the year before and I was aware that they would be real good the following year because most their players were juniors. Those juniors were Ronnie Arrow, Lynn Phillips, Barry Lewis, and Arthur "Killer" Coburn. Ronnie was a little 5'10" cocky Jewish kid who could really handle the ball and shot an almost two-handed jump shot. Lynn was a big 6'7" inside player who was from an extremely athletic family. Barry was a 6'5" tough and muscular kid who looked more like an offensive lineman than a basketball player. "Killer" was about 6'3", with square jaws, and a perfect flat-top that could have served as a landing strip for a small plane. He was the oldest of the group and the team leader. As seniors in 1964-65, they were joined in the starting lineup by a pretty fair shooting junior guard named Robert McFadden. The sixth man was Lynn's younger brother Gene, a wiry 6'4" sophomore. Gene would later become one of the best scorers in the history of Texas high school basketball.

For many years, Houston ISD had a unique policy of allowing kids to enroll in first grade when they were six years old, regardless of the month of their birthday. As a result, about a third of the kids became first graders in January instead of in September. This meant that they would graduate in December of their senior year instead of in May. Unfortunately for us, we would lose "Killer" Coburn in December but, fortunately for us, Stephen F. Austin High School would lose their great seven foot center Ken Spain as well. But, back to the 'unfortunate for us side' of things, we were scheduled to play Austin in December, before Ken Spain graduated. We lost that game and several other teams in the district were also pretty good. Things, at that point, didn't look too cool for the Jones Falcons! After all, our goal was a state championship in the spring.

Eventually, all of this mid-term graduation stuff actually worked out in our favor. Although we lost our team leader "Killer" Coburn, it gave Coach Bradford an opportunity to give more playing time to Gene Phillips and, as a result, we became a better team. In fact, we never lost another game. Meanwhile, Stephen F. Austin, without Ken Spain, fell back to the middle of the pack. But the road to Austin wouldn't be easy. In bi-district we had to face Sam Houston, coached by Bunky's best friend and former UH teammate John "Skinny" Davis. We barely got by them and then squared off against Spring Branch Memorial with their great player Jerry Kroll and equally great coach Don Coleman. That one was close but we won by eight points and our final game before state was against French High School of Beaumont. We had beaten French pretty soundly in a tournament in Beaumont earlier in the season, but they had some top-notch players, a strong basketball tradition, and somewhat of a home court advantage. They won the toss to determine location and chose Lamar University in Beaumont, the same location as our game with them earlier. Phil Endicott, a 6'9" center, and a tough Polish kid named Pudgie Koslowski were really good that night and kept French in it until the end. We eventually prevailed 59-58, and were on our way to the "big house" (Gregory Gym) in Austin.

My main basketball coaching assignment at Jones was the junior varsity team. We had a pretty good year also and my top player was a 6'5" kid named David Sibley. I lost David in the middle of the season because he became a senior at mid-term and was moved up to the varsity to replace "Killer" Coburn who was graduating. David played sparingly on the varsity that semester but he at least got to be on the state tournament roster. The following year, he blossomed into a top-notch player, although he had only one semester of eligibility left. He eventually got a basketball scholarship at Baylor and was a pretty solid player there. After graduation, he went to dental school and became a dentist in Waco. He later went to law school, changed professions, and was eventually elected Mayor of Waco. Still later, he was elected to represent that area in the Texas State Senate. In 2000, David would play a big role in my own entrance into the political arena although, by then, he had probably forgotten his old JV coach's name.

Jesse H. Jones Falcons, 1965 Class 4A state champs
(David Sibley is #45 standing next to me and Gene Phillips is #23)

Coach Bradford was a very good coach who, because he had played at a high level, had a great "feel" for the game of basketball. He realized that he had some great high school talent and didn't tie them down with a lot of complicated offenses and defenses. He used a high-low post set with a point guard, two wings, a high post, and a low post. Ronnie Arrow was the point guard and he would come off a screen from the high post, usually Lynn Phillips, then attack the rim himself, pass off to Lynn on the pick-and-roll, take the jump shot himself, or pass off into to corner to Gene Phillips for the shot. His decision was based entirely on the way that the defense reacted. Bunky also believed in getting the ball down inside to the low post man, and he worked hard on the fundamentals with his inside players. I learned a lot from him that helped me be successful later in my coaching career.

The athletic equipment at Houston ISD was distributed to the schools from the central district athletic department headed by Horace Elrod. It was sufficient but very basic and great care was made to ensure that one school was not favored over another. Every team wore the same uniforms, the only difference being the colors. There was one set of game pants and two sets of different colored jerseys. The pants had one stripe down each side and the jerseys were plain white or dark with no piping at all. The only thing on them was a number on front and back. Schools were allowed to upgrade with money from local fundraising but Mr. Mills felt that was unnecessary. Our colors at Jones were light gold and white and it was difficult see a light gold number on a white jersey, or vice versa. Plus, most schools at the state tournament wanted to proudly display their school name, such as "Jones", on the front of their uniforms. Mr. Mills relented and put in a special order for new uniforms for the playoffs. When they arrived, they were orange instead of gold, but they had the school name in big letters on the front. The Jones basketball team was going state wearing uniforms that were not even the school colors, and they were worn for a few years afterward.

For our first game at the state tournament, we were matched

up against Kingsville, a team that would have been winless in our Houston district. Sure enough, we had no problem against them. We won 106-71, becoming the first team in history to score 100 points in a state tournament game. We would now face Thomas Jefferson of Dallas, who had soundly defeated El Paso High School in the semi-final game. Thomas Jefferson was not new to championship play. They had been to the tournament in 1959, and had won it all in 1962 under Coach Archie Porter, who was now the head coach at my alma mater Sam Houston State. Barry Dowd, who would later become a successful college coach, was now in charge at Jefferson. Coach Dowd did a good job in defending against the Phillips brothers, Lynn and Gene. But our other post man, Barry Lewis, stepped up and had a great game. Ronnie Arrow had one of his best games ever, and Jones eventually prevailed in a nip-and-tuck game by a score of 54-49. Jesse H. Jones High School was now the Class 4A state basketball champion and both Barry and Ronnie were named to the all-tournament team. Our season record was 37-3.

Of the nine Jones players on the state tournament roster, five eventually played college basketball. Another one, Robert McFadden, didn't get a chance as he was killed in a tragic plane crash the following summer, just prior to his senior year. Ronnie Arrow later became a very successful college coach, winning three national championships at San Jacinto Jr. College. He also was a head coach at both South Alabama and Texas A&M-Corpus Christi. Lynn and Gene Phillips both starred at SMU, and Gene later played for the Dallas Chapparals of the old ABA before they became the San Antonio Spurs. Their older brother, Larry, also played at Jones and later played at Rice University. Their father, Herman, was the head football coach at Bellaire High School. I don't think any of his three sons ever played football. During his senior season, Gene Phillips broke a state record by scoring eighty-one points in a single game, a record that still stands today. Had the three point shot been in effect at the time he would have probably scored 125.

That same year I was naturally interested in how my old Wharton team was doing. As it turns out, they beat Clear Creek in bi-district but were upset by West Orange in the regional final. Jimmy Hubenak was named all state and later had a solid career at Rice University. My successor at Wharton was Jack Worthington. He left after only one season and became an assistant to Bill Krueger at Clear Creek. Many years later, Jack was diagnosed with a rare genetic disease and passed away at a relatively young age. His son, Jack Jr., made headlines when he reported that, when he considered testing for himself and his kids to determine if they may be at risk, his mother told him that he had nothing to fear because he was actually the son of former president John F. Kennedy. The issue was never resolved, as far as I know, because of problems in obtaining DNA samples.

Coach Bradford had been named assistant principal at Jones at the beginning of the school year but stayed on as coach in order to see his dreams of winning a state championship come true. I was aware that I wouldn't be a candidate for the head coaching job when I accepted the job as assistant. After the season ended, I began searching for a head coaching job but didn't find anything that I would be interested in. I even interviewed for a superintendent's job at a tiny town, Avalon, in the middle of a black land cotton field south of Waxahachie. I already had a secondary school principal's certificate, and was taking classes at the University of Houston to obtain superintendent certification. The job at Avalon would also include coaching basketball and, since superintendents in Texas had a much higher minimum pay than teachers, I would get a substantial pay raise. On my way back home to Houston after the interview, I was scared to death that they might call and offer me the job. But I didn't want to move back to such a tiny community so early in my career. I got up early the next morning and called the school board president to tell him that I wasn't interested. And I'm glad that I did.

Back in those days, almost all teachers and coaches looked for part time employment to supplement their relatively low salaries. It just so happened that the Astrodome was opening that spring, and a basketball official in town was hired as a supervisor over ushers, ticket takers, etc. He naturally recruited underpaid coaches in the area. One of the perks of a ticket taker was that you could watch every game for free after the second inning. So when the Astrodome opened on April 9, 1965 with an exhibition game between the Houston Astros and the New York Yankees, I was a ticket taker at the main gate. We were required to wear space suits and silly looking space helmets. President Johnson even attended the game. Unfortunately for me, there was such disorganization that night at the turnstiles that I didn't get inside to see the game until it was almost over. I can tell people now that I saw Mickey Mantle hit the first home run in the Astrodome, but I would not be telling the truth. I hated those space outfits and I quit after only a few games.

The new head basketball coach at Jones in 1965-66 was Ken Laird, and he deserved it. He had spent a few years as a junior high coach and was moved up to coach at Furr High School, the only Class 3A school in Houston ISD. Ken and I became fast friends and I respected his abilities as a coach. We should have had two starters returning but had lost Robert McFadden in the plane crash. David Sibley, a reserve, was back but he had only one semester of eligibility left. Gene Phillips was the best player in Houston but did not have a great supporting cast. Things were changing rapidly. Sterling High School was opening and would take lots of students from the Jones attendance zone. Integration had been postponed for way to long but it was on the horizon and most people were apprehensive about what changes would come as a result. The biggest change that was coming, at least in my view, was that Mr. Mills would soon retire. I would no doubt be leaving at the end of the school year. I was itching to have a head coaching job and, like most people who grew up in small towns, I never really liked Houston anyway. My wife literally hated it.

In the spring of 1966, I continued work toward my superintendent certification at the University of Houston, and happened to be enrolled in a class with Ed Lechler, the first guy to ever fire me (he wouldn't be the last). He was retiring as a coach and was becoming an assistant principal. Thankfully, he and I had a chance to "kiss and make up" and became friends once again. He admitted that there was some jealously on his part and I admitted that I acted like the brash young coach that I was. Who knows? I may have fired me too. I don't think that he ever gave me a bad recommendation when I applied for other jobs. For that, I am grateful because I soon found one that fit me perfectly.

I was looking to leave Houston and get a head basketball job in a smaller town with one high school, similar to Wharton. But I had no interest in a job where there was no interest in having a winning basketball program. I heard from some source that Silsbee, a Class 3A school twenty miles north of Beaumont, was looking for a new coach and that the school board had ordered the athletic director to set up an off-season program for basketball. The current coach was the football line coach who had asked to coach basketball instead of track so he wouldn't miss the crappie spawning season at Dam B Lake in the spring. Two of the board members had sons on the basketball team and were upset that basketball had been treated like a stepchild. I applied, was interviewed by the school board and athletic director, and was hired right away. Both my wife and I were happy to be leaving Houston. We were even able to buy a house in a nice neighborhood and moved to Silsbee as soon as school was out in May.

Not long after I left Houston, the schools there were gradually integrated and the sports scene changed dramatically in Houston ISD. The predominantly Black high schools remained that way and were admitted into the University Interscholastic League for sports competition. As a result, schools such as Wheatley, Kashmere, and Yates started a long period of domination in basketball. Eventually, Jesse Jones lost students and was no longer dominant. However, almost forty years later in 2004, they won the state 4A basketball championship again. A few years later, Jones became a magnet school and no longer has athletic teams. Lawrence Allen, the Jones principal, joined me on the State Board of Education in 2005 and we served together for a couple of years.

Several years back, the Geelinslaws, a country music comedy

group from Austin, recorded a song with the line "Your Daddy don't live in heaven, he's in Houston, and Houston is a far from heaven as it can be". I agree with that line. In my view, other than my beautiful wife Jo and the Astros, the only good things that ever came out of Houston are I-10 east and west and I-45 north and south. I was glad to be leaving town on I-10 east.

CHAPTER 11

Starting A High School Basketball Dynasty (Silsbee)

SILSBEE, IN 1966, was a blue collar town of about 8000 people in the heart of the Big Thicket in Southeast Texas. Kirby Lumber Company had a saw mill in town and Temple Inland operated a paper mill about seven miles east, across the Neches River in Evadale. Beaumont was only about twenty miles south and many Silsbee residents worked there at the Bethlehem Shipyard or at the Mobil Oil Refinery. Partial school integration was just beginning but, when I arrived, the Black high school (Waldo Matthews) was still operating. Silsbee High School was already one of the largest Class 3A schools in the area and full school integration had been postponed at least until a new high school could open in 1967-68. As a result, only a few Black students were enrolled at Silsbee High School during my first year there. That number increased gradually until Waldo Matthews finally closed after the 1967-68 school year.

Texas, east of the IH-35 corridor, is culturally like the Deep South states while west of the corridor it is more like the Southwest. Growing up in Navarro and Freestone counties, I had never known anything but segregation of the races in everything from public schools and churches to restroom facilities. The courthouse in Fairfield had separate restrooms and water fountains for Whites and Blacks, and all the

Silsbee Tigers, 1972 Class 3A state semi-finalists

stores on the town square had back entrances for Black people. I never had any association at all with Black kids my age. This continued during my college years and through my first five years as a teacher and coach. Therefore, it was only natural for me to experience some apprehension about teaching and coaching African American students.

Any apprehension that I may have had completely vanished shortly after we moved to Silsbee. My first assignment during the summer prior to my first school year was to direct a recreation program, along with my wife, jointly funded by the school district and the city. A majority of the kids that attended every day were Black. Although we had a variety of activities, the most popular one by far was basketball. I knew that I had come to the right place and, also, that I didn't have to treat the kids differently because of their race. One kid in particular that caught my attention that summer was a rail-thin future eighth grader named Joe Willie Price. Joe came every day just to show the new basketball coach what he could do although, at the time, it wasn't much. This was the beginning of a long friendship between Joe and me. After starring in high school, he played basketball at Schreiner Junior College and at Texas Lutheran before coaching with me for three years at Tivy High School in Kerrville. He later had a great career as a coach at Houston Smiley, Port Arthur Lincoln, Baytown Sterling, and Galena Park North Shore. He even won a state championship at Lincoln in 1985. Joe and I have remained close friends over the years and we still talk by phone fairly often. I am proud to have played a small part his very successful career as both a player and coach. Joe's younger brother Dwain didn't play basketball but he served as student manager/statistician during his high school days in Silsbee. He later became a sports writer and covered the Dallas Mavericks for the "Fort Worth Star-Telegram" for several years.

My coaching assignment in Silsbee was head basketball coach and assistant junior varsity football coach. My football duties were minimal in that I joined practice after school and was released entirely on October 15, when UIL rules allowed after school basketball practice to begin. I was allowed to hold basketball practice year round during an athletic period for basketball only athletes. This was an incredible advantage for a Class 3A school in that most schools below the Class 4A level didn't allow any basketball at all except during the playing season. My boss for athletics was Ray "Stud" McGallion, a Silsbee native, who was also the head football coach. I'm not sure that he was happy with the new basketball situation but the school board had demanded it and he went along. After all, he got another assistant football coach out of the deal. I must say that I liked Coach McGallion, respected him, and we got along reasonably well during my nine years there. He was certainly a very good football coach and a very good guy as well. After he passed away a few years back, I made the trip back to Silsbee to pay my respects.

The athletics program at Silsbee had been centered almost entirely around football. There was no girl's athletics program at all, baseball and basketball were afterthoughts, and track was used mainly as an off season program for football. Although there may have been a basketball team in junior high, very few games were scheduled and the coaches were strictly hired to coach football. In spite of all this emphasis on football, the high school team had not won a district championship in several years. A lot of this was because several teams in the area were very strong. Bridge City, for example, was one of the most successful Class 3A teams in the state and Steve Worster, a future UT All-American, was returning for his senior year. Needless to say, Silsbee lost to Bridge City in 1966 even though we had a very good football team. Coach McGallion's assistant coaches that first year were Sidney "Chief" Dauphin, Herbert Muckelroy, Pat Day, and Wayne Riley. They were all good coaches but, most of all, they each had a great sense of humor that rubbed off on me. Pat, on two different occasions, was my junior varsity basketball coach and was one of the best coaches in any sport that I ever worked with.

My first basketball team in Silsbee, benefitting from the new off-season practices, was much better than I expected. Our only senior starter was a 6'3" kid named Danny Bass who had started the year before and could "jump out of the gym". The other starters were Eugene Patillo, Mike Shuff, Manuel Tyler, and Ralph Davenport. Manuel and Ralph were the first Black kids that I ever coached and both were good athletes. Manuel was a 6'2" point guard, and Ralph was a 6'3" inside player who also played football. Our season record that year was 20-11 and we finished second in district play behind West Orange. Both West Orange and Beaumont Forest Park had good basketball programs with highly respected coaches. The coach at West Orange, Adolph Hyrhorchuk, was also the athletic director and won district almost every year. They had advanced to the state tournament two years earlier by beating my former Wharton team. Forest Park was coached by Jerry Mallett, a former All-American at Baylor, who later became the superintendent of schools in Beaumont. We finished district play at 7-3, losing twice to West Orange and once to Forest Park. Danny Bass received a scholarship to Jacksonville Baptist, a junior college, and later played at East Texas Baptist in Marshall. I was very pleased with our first year and looked forward to next season with four starters returning. Also, a new high school, with a larger gym, would be opening in 1967-68.

Buna, one of the most storied programs in Texas high school basketball history, was located about fifteen miles east of Silsbee. When I arrived, Cotton Robinson had been retired for a few years but he had left quite a footprint on the Southeast Texas basketball scene. Several of his former players were coaching in the area and, along with many others, had adopted his system of play. Coach Hyrhorchuk at West Orange, although he was not a Buna graduate, was one of these. The "Buna" defense was a full court man-to-man press for the entire game and players were taught to take charges by falling backward, or "flopping", onto the floor at the slightest contact. Rumor had it that that they used mats during practice to break their falls. The "Buna" offense was a slow and patient inside oriented attack and the post players were taught a special move that resulted in a fade away jump shot that they had perfected during hours of practice. Coach Robinson advised against adopting his offense unless his defense was copied also because he said he used this simple offense simply to be able to spend more time on defense. He said his players were just "resting" on offense. I had coached against the "Buna" system a few times in the past and had never lost against it. But this was different in that at least half the teams in the area employed it. I coached at Silsbee for nine years and lost only three or four times to "Buna" teams. Two of those losses were to West Orange in district play my first year.

After one year there, both Pat and I really liked Silsbee. We made several friends and even joined the Silsbee Country Club, the hub of the town's social activities. Almost everybody in town hunted and fished, and there were plenty of opportunities for both. After a couple of years, I even bought a boat and we spent lots of time on the area's lakes, such as Dam B and Sam Rayburn. Pat decided she wanted to be a teacher also, and began commuting to Lamar University in Beaumont. The one thing that I had to get used to was not having Mr. Mills as my principal. I taught history and, although it wasn't too bad, things were not quite as organized as what I had been used to at Jones High School. But, overall, I was very happy.

My second year, 1967-68, was a good one for the Silsbee Tigers in both football and basketball. The football team won the district championship and advanced to the quarterfinals by beating Conroe in bi-district. They were finally defeated by Alvin in the quarterfinal game. Although my best player from the year before had graduated, I had four good starters returning in Eugene Patillo, Mike Shuff, Ralph Davenport, and Manuel Tyler. They were joined in the starting lineup by a tough little sophomore named Grady Walters. As a high school coach, I believed in a tough non-district schedule to prepare my teams for district play. We scheduled mostly Class 4A schools and entered the top tournaments in the area. As a result, we lost eight games that regular season, all before district play began. We then marched through district play undefeated with a 12-0 record. All four of our seniors made the all-district team and they all averaged in double figures per game. Eugene Patillo was our leading scorer with 17.1 points per game. We, like the football team, played Conroe in bi-district but, unlike the football team, we lost. Conroe was a good team and eventually advanced to the state tournament. Both Silsbee and Conroe won district championships in both football and basketball that year which should prove that high school teams can win in both sports if they make an effort in both.

I was pleased at the progress that I was making to build a winning basketball program in Silsbee. But I knew that the next year may be a challenge. I was losing my top four players to graduation but we had some pretty good players on the junior varsity team. I didn't mind that they were all football players as long as they continued to play basketball. A plus was the fact that Waldo Matthews was closing for good and I would be inheriting the Garrett twins, Raliegh and Reggie. Reggie, in particular, would probably be one of the best athletes in the history of Silsbee High School. As it turns out, our football team advanced all the way to the state semifinals and all of the players that I was counting on, including Reggie Garrett, said that they were too worn out to play basketball. Raliegh was not a football player and he became one of my top players. But, even though we barely finished with a winning record at 13-12, I vowed to never depend on football players again. From that day forward, they would simply be considered a bonus if they played. Reggie Garrett later played on two Super Bowl winning Pittsburgh Steeler teams. I never held any animosity toward him about not playing basketball, nor did I against Deryl McGallion, Coach McGallion's son. They both were great athletes and great kids. 1968-69 was just a bump in the road as far as I was concerned.

It was obvious to me that, if I wanted to build a winning basketball program that would be good every year, something would have to change where the junior high program was concerned. With the exception of Pat Day, who was a good coach in any sport, I was the only basketball coach in the school system. All the junior high coaches were hired to coach football and none of them had any interest in basketball. Had Coach McGallion not given me permission to do their scheduling, I doubt that they would have even played any games. But that was about to change. One of our high school teachers approached me one day and told me that she had a nephew that was graduating from a college in Oklahoma and that he was very interested in coaching football and basketball, but that his main interest was basketball. It just so happened that there was an opening in the junior high for a coach, and junior high coaching jobs at the time were hard to fill. Following my advice, she had her nephew, Richard "Dick" Strong, call me so that I could advise him as to how to apply. It would be almost impossible for him not to be hired because his teaching field was math, and math teachers were really hard to find. Sure enough, Coach McGallion approved his hiring as a coach but I'm sure Richard didn't mention his interest in basketball. When he arrived in Silsbee, I was surprised to see this very large "Baby Huey" looking guy who appeared to have never played a game of basketball in his life. But I took him under my wing and he adopted my system, including practice drills, one hundred percent. The junior high kids loved him. He coached them for the remaining six years of my tenure in Silsbee and retired there many years later. I'm sure that he lost a few games while I was around, but I don't remember any. Although he never coached the varsity team, no one deserves more credit than Richard "Big Dick" Strong for the rich basketball tradition in Silsbee that continues until this day, almost fifty years later.

I lost Pat Day as my junior varsity coach for the 1968-69 season. He was reassigned as the head baseball coach, and I inherited the baseball coach, Bo Tarver, to replace him. Bo was a fun guy to be around but was not serious about coaching or teaching. He was so high maintenance that I would have been much better off coaching both teams myself. Bo quit, or was let go, after two years and Ronnie Nash became my assistant and junior varsity coach. He held this position for the next four years until becoming an assistant principal. Ronnie and his wife Eileen were already friends of ours and they remain friends today. During my first couple of years in Silsbee, Ronnie was a math teacher but didn't coach. He did the filming for the football team and was already close to the coaching staff. He did a very good job for me during my best years in Silsbee and we had some great times together, both on and off the court. He later served for many years as a principal in Silsbee at the elementary, middle school, and high school levels.

The University Interscholastic League reclassifies schools, based on enrollment, every two years. But, because of integration, they ruled that a school must move into a higher classification after only one year if its enrollment increased as a result of the closing of the Black school in the district. Therefore, as a result of the closing of Waldo Matthews High School, Silsbee would have to play at least one year in Class 4A. This was a real challenge for us in 1969-70 because we were placed in a district with much larger schools such as Port Arthur Jefferson, Nederland, and Port Neches-Groves. The other schools in the district were Port Arthur Lincoln (a predominantly Black school), Orange Stark, and Vidor. Most of these schools were football powers but Jefferson, Lincoln, and Stark were also strong in basketball. Although we would have been a very good Class 3A football team that year, we had very little success against these larger schools, winning only against Stark and Vidor. Fortunately for me, basketball would do a lot better.

During the spring of 1969, I took a day off from school and went to Houston to visit with Don Coleman, the highly successful coach at Spring Branch Memorial High School. I was not satisfied with my high-low post offense and was looking for something that would better fit the players that I would have in the future. Don had spent some time with Coach Tex Winter at Kansas State University and was running his "Triangle" or "Triple Post" offense, although he had made some adjustments to fit his high school personnel. "Triangle" referred to the fact that there was almost always a triangle between a guard, forward, and strong side post man. "Triple Post" was a misnomer as far as I was concerned because the high post was actually a shooting guard who could attack the rim, and the weak side post was more of a forward who could rebound missed shots. With my own adjustments, I adopted the offense, calling it the "Corner" because there was always a player forming the triangle in the corner on the ball side. Many years later, Tex Winter became an assistant to Phil Jackson with the Chicago Bulls (and later the Los Angeles Lakers) where he installed the "Triangle" offense. I must admit that it didn't look much like the Silsbee Tigers of the early seventies, but I didn't have Michael Jordan or Kobe Bryant.

We had a very successful season in 1969-70, our only year in Class 4A. Our season record was 26-9 and we tied for the district championship with a 10-2 record. But we didn't make the playoffs because Thomas Jefferson of Port Arthur, while losing two games to other schools, won the tiebreaker by beating us both times. Our second game was in Silsbee and decided the playoff representative. I thought I had a great game plan against a school that was three times our size, but I was outcoached by my friend James Sharp. My starters that year were Grady Walters, Joe Price, David Matthews, Raliegh Garrett, and Mark Yawn. David later received a scholarship to play at Phillips University in Oklahoma. This team may have been the best one that I had in Silsbee even though we didn't reach the playoffs. Coach Sharp later replaced me at Kerrville Tivy when I left high school coaching in 1979 to become a college coach. A bit of trivia – A year after I left Kerrville, James Sharp entered high school basketball coaching history by winning a game against a San Antonio team that went ten overtimes. This is a national record that I believe still stands today.

Had we not spent that one year in Class 4A, it is very possible that we would have reached the state tournament in Class 3A in 1970. But a foundation for the future had been set. Joe Price and Mark Yawn were both juniors and the junior varsity team was loaded with prospects. We also had lots of prospects on the freshman team and in middle school. Because the UIL had raised the enrollment numbers to be in Class 4A, we returned to Class 3A where we belonged. This was good for all sports, not just basketball. The future looked good for the Silsbee Tigers and I was very pleased. I was also pleased that my wife, Pat, graduated from Lamar that year and was hired to be a physical education teacher and tennis coach at Silsbee High School for the coming school year. That meant two incomes and no tuition payments. We immediately started construction on a new swimming pool in our backyard and Pat could make extra money teaching swimming lessons. Since I had never seen her with a racquet in her hands, I didn't think that she had much of a future as a tennis coach.

I was expecting to have a good year in 1970-71 and I was not fazed when Mark Yawn decided not to play basketball when football season ended. I had vowed two years before to never again depend on football players until they showed up ready to play after football season. Fortunately, our other two-sport athletes, James Hunter and William Walters, showed up ready to play. Because there were too many 3A schools in our area, our district was divided into two zones and we were in the west zone with Livingston, Cleveland, Liberty, and Crosby. None of these schools had strong basketball traditions but they had recently integrated and had a lot of good athletes. Even though we were pretty good, we lost at Crosby by one point before beating them later at home by more than forty points. We then beat a very good Little Cypress team, coached by former Buna star Melvin Ellison, for the district championship. Joe Price, James Hunter, and David Brown all made the all-district team. William Walters and Marvin Kelly were our other starters and we also had a very deep bench.

Our bi-district opponent was Dulles High School of Sugarland, a suburb in Fort Bend County southwest of Houston. I don't remember much about that game except that we won by eight points and were matched against Aldine Carver for a spot in the state tournament. Carver was one of the many predominantly Black high schools in the Houston area that had long histories for success in basketball before they were allowed to compete in the University Interscholastic League. We played them in Pasadena at San Jacinto Junior College and the gym was packed. Carver had great athletes but we did too and we matched them point for point for the entire game. The lead must have changed hands twenty times. Late in the game, Carver got ahead by four or five points so we went to our full court press and got to within one point with maybe twenty seconds remaining. Joe Price hit a jump shot from the top of the key with less than ten seconds left to put us ahead by one. But, without calling timeout, a Carver player threw the ball the full length of the court. It hit the top of the backboard and accidentally bounced into the hands of another Carver player who made a layup as time expired. They had beaten us by one point on a fluke shot denying us a berth in the state tournament. One of our players, Marvin Kelly, thought we had won the game and was doing cartwheels out on the court. Coach Nash rushed out and gave him the bad news. We were all crushed at losing a chance to play in Austin and I was particularly disappointed for Joe Price, our only senior and one of the best kids I ever coached, who would never get that chance. I coached for more than thirty years and never had a more crushing defeat. We ended the season with a 27-7 record.

Joe Price was not recruited by Division I schools and, because he was on the district winning baseball team, was not able to tryout at NAIA schools or junior colleges. As a result, the school year was near its end and Joe had no place to play basketball the following year. At that time, there was a publication that listed all the college programs in the state with information concerning coaches' names, phone numbers, etc. Late that spring, after baseball season finally ended, I got on my home phone and started calling all the small colleges and junior colleges in alphabetical order. They all told me that they had no scholarships available until I got to Schreiner Institute, a two-year school in Kerrville. The coach there was Dr. Bill Campion. He knew of our success in basketball in Silsbee, said he had a scholarship available, and offered it to Joe sight unseen. Joe had no idea where Kerrville was but he accepted the offer and a pipeline between Silsbee and Schreiner began. Not only did Joe Price play there but so did David Brown (maybe the best player in both Silsbee and Schreiner history), Michael Dabney, Ricky Scott, and Larry Davis. This was also the beginning of a long friendship between Coach Campion and me. He later became a college basketball referee and officiated several of my games after I became a college coach. He has had a long career as a junior college president in both Texas and Florida.

Things didn't go well for Pat in her first and only year of teaching at Silsbee. The other girls' gym teacher had been at the school for many years and was used to what we called "the three R's" of Silsbee PE --- Roll out the ball, Relax, and Read the paper. Pat was hired because an increasing enrollment necessitated a second girls' gym teacher. She had just graduated with a degree in Physical Education and was "gung ho" about implementing everything she had learned in her classes at Lamar. But the students, who were used to choosing sides and leisurely playing volleyball every day, didn't take too well to Pat's approach. She got no help from the other teacher and the administration didn't think P.E. was important enough to get involved. She resigned at the end of the school year and took a job at Evadale, just seven miles away, as girls' basketball and track coach. Evadale, a small Class B school, was a tax wealthy school district because of the paper mill there, and she got a pretty good pay raise. In addition, Ronnie Nash's dad was the superintendent there and we knew Pat would get along just fine with the administration.

By the time the basketball season ended with such great disappointment in 1971, it was obvious that Silsbee had become a force in high school basketball in the Southeast Texas area and that football and basketball could both do well in the same school. But I still had some walls to climb. There is no doubt that we had done well because of the off season program that the school board had demanded a few years back. This was an advantage that we had over schools that still wanted to keep basketball "in its place". But there were still some things that Coach McGallion would not allow. For example, none of the three gyms in the school district could be open for informal basketball activities during the summer or outside the school day. Some of my players got around that by driving the ten miles to Kountze where they could play informal games at the abandoned Black school gym. I even provided the transportation on many occasions. But, even better, I got the city council to appoint me to the parks and recreation board. One of our recommendations to the council was that the city would purchase the abandoned Waldo Matthews campus and convert it to a community center. And, of course, the centerpiece of the park was a couple of nice basketball courts. After the construction of those courts, there was never any need for me to worry about not having "open gym". A few years later, we went even further in cementing the basketball tradition in Silsbee when we started a Little Dribblers program.

1971-72 was truly a banner year for Silsbee High School athletics. The football team had an excellent year, advancing all the way to the state quarterfinals before being defeated by Brenham 21-19. The baseball team, under Coach Pat Day, won district for the second year in a row. A lot was expected of the basketball team since we had done so well the year before and had four starters returning. My best two players were David Brown, a 6"5" inside player, and James Hunter, a 6'2" forward. David was probably the best basketball player in school history and James was no doubt the best pure athlete to ever put on a Silsbee Tiger uniform. Marvin Kelly, a great rebounder, and William Walters, an experienced point guard, were also back for their senior years. Taking Joe Price's place at off guard was a studious little sophomore named James Simmons. Eddy Fobbs, a 6'5" junior, was the sixth man but he played almost as many minutes as the starters. Knowing that we would be pretty strong, I scheduled tough opponents for non-district play. We opened with seven straight wins before being upset by West Orange in their tournament. Our only other loss was by one point to a very strong Houston Westchester team in the finals of the YMBL tournament in Beaumont. We were ready for district play and breezed through the first round without a loss.

Joe Price, David Brown, James Hunter

Since we had been successful in basketball for a few years, attendance at our home games was always good. We had standing room only crowds when we played some of the top Houston teams. In fact, we even paid them a guarantee to come to Silsbee and play us. That year we had an open date between the first and second rounds of district, and invited Houston Yates to play in Silsbee. I think Coach McGallion paid cash to the coach out of gate receipts which probably explains why we never had a problem scheduling the games. Yates was a Class 4A school with a great athletic tradition and they beat us by twelve points. After breezing through the second round of district play undefeated, we were off for a week before our district playoff game with West Orange. We scheduled two warm-up games, one against defending Class 2A state champion Kountze and the other against Wheatley High School of Houston. Wheatley, under Coach Jackie Carr, had already won several Class 4A state championships and they were the top-rated team in the state in any class at the time. Eddie Owens, a future All-American at UNLV, was a senior that year and could fill up a high school gym by himself. I'm not sure what Coach McGallion told me to offer Coach Carr to bring his team to Silsbee, but I do remember that he turned down the first offer. They eventually came, we had to turn away hundreds of fans, and they gave us a big-time butt kicking by a score of 98-69. But at least we beat our Hardin County rival Kountze 77-69.

Our district championship playoff game against West Orange at Lamar University's McDonald Gym was close, but we prevailed by a score of 54-49, and advanced to the bi-district game against Sugarland Dulles, the same team that we had beaten in bi-district the year before. We beat Dulles by thirteen points to advance to the regional finals against Wilmer-Hutchins, a school just south of Dallas. The game was played in Nacogdoches and the winner, just like the year before, would advance to the state tournament in Austin. Wilmer-Hutchins was a predominately Black school with a strong basketball tradition and some very good athletes. But we also had developed a pretty strong basketball tradition and had some great athletes as well. We jumped out to an early lead but couldn't seem to get ahead enough to put them away. The game stayed relatively close throughout but we eventually won by a score of 72-64. We had gained Silsbee's first trip to the state basketball tournament in Austin! I can't explain how happy I was. I had been there before as an assistant but this would be my first as a head coach. Had we not been on our way to Austin, I would have been very disappointed even though we had won more than thirty games and three of our four losses were to some of the best Class 4A teams in the state.

The four Class 3A teams at state that year were Silsbee, Cuero, Henderson, and Odessa Ector. Henderson was coached by an old friend of mine, Leroy Romines, a native of Carlisle, where I had coached a few years before. Cuero was known more for football but had a good 6'11" player that year. Ector was a predominately Black high school in a large West Texas school district that had not fully integrated. We were paired against Ector in the state semi-final game. We had not had a chance to scout them but I had talked to some coaches in the west Texas area that had played them. All I could find out was that they were an up-tempo team with good athletes at every position and that they had a very experienced coach in Al Ogelsby. Even though we were accustomed to large crowds in our average size high school gym, I think that my kids were overwhelmed by the large crowds that always packed Gregory Gymnasium for the state high school basketball tournament. James Hunter played very well but the others were a little tentative. But the fact was that Ector was just a better team, at least that night, and we lost by a score of 81-68. No team, with the exception of Wheatley, had scored more than eighty points against us that year and only two more had scored more than seventy against our sagging man-to-man defense. I was disappointed in our poor showing but was, nonetheless, proud of what we had accomplished. It was a great experience for our kids, the school, and the community. James Hunter was later named to the All State Tournament Team. Ector went on to win the state championship against Henderson.

Even after almost a half century of great Silsbee basketball teams, I repeat my belief that David Brown is probably the best basketball player in Silsbee Tiger history. He was the first player in Silsbee to score forty points in one game. David was not a great student and had to attend junior college, following Joe Price to Schreiner Institute in Kerrville, where he once scored forty-eight points in one game. He later played at Memphis State University (now Memphis Univ.) where he was an outstanding player. James Hunter, probably the best overall athlete in Silsbee history, played football at Grambling, and had a great career as a safety with the Detroit Lions in the NFL. Marvin Kelly walked on as a basketball player at Lamar University and was eventually awarded a scholarship. James Simmons, who was only a sophomore, played basketball at Rice University, received a law degree, and is now a successful attorney in the Houston area. Unfortunately, David was killed in a shooting a few years back in Lake Charles, Louisiana, and James Hunter died of a sudden heart attack in 2010 at age fifty-six. In the spring of 2017, after Silsbee had won its first state championship, I attended a reunion of the 1972 state tournament team. Almost all the living members of the team were there and we had a great time reliving the memories of that memorable season. We even allowed Joe Willie Price to join us even though he graduated in 1971. But, like Dick Strong, nobody has contributed more to the Silsbee High School basketball tradition than Joe Willie Price.

Growing up, I was very interested in anything having to do with social studies. Even as a kid, I read almost every word of the daily newspaper and saved the sports section for last. Had I not decided to make coaching my career, I would have majored in history or government in college and gone to law school. My dad instilled in me a love for politics which has endured for my entire life and, as a high school history and government teacher, I encouraged my students to be prepared each day to discuss current events, which we did at the beginning of each class. I always pounded the point to my students, many who thought that history was a waste of time, that understanding the past is an important component to being prepared for the future. Until maybe the late seventies Texas, with the exception of a few counties in the Hill Country, was solidly Democratic at the state and local levels. There was not even a Republican primary and elections were always settled in the Democratic primary in March. But I was a conservative and became a Republican before I was old enough to vote. As a result, I never voted in a Democratic primary or, even in a Republican one until I moved to Kerrville in 1975. My first vote was in the general election of 1960 when I cast my vote for Richard Nixon for President over John F. Kennedy. But, since I voted a straight Republican ticket, all of my national, state, and local candidates lost.

There were so few Republicans in Hardin County in 1972 that the Democrats recruited the few that they could find to work the Democratic primary election in Silsbee. Elections were so hotly contested among local Democrats that they couldn't trust their own to conduct a fair election. Pat and I, and a few others who admitted to being Republicans, worked at the polls that spring and were actually paid for our time. The presidential race that year was between Richard Nixon and George McGovern and the Texas State Teachers Association, an affiliate of the National Education Association, endorsed McGovern. In protest, I dropped my membership in TSTA and several of my colleagues followed suit. Most of them probably did so just because it gave them an excuse to save the twenty dollars a year on membership dues. As a result, Silsbee ISD became one of the few school districts in the state without 100 percent membership in TSTA. I feared that I may lose my job but my principal, Weeks Crawford, was my good friend and assured me that I had nothing to worry about. He may have saved the twenty bucks himself even though he was a lifelong Democrat. Nixon won Texas that year with sixty-six percent of the vote and even Hardin County went heavily for him. But it would take several decades for Democrats to lose control in the courthouses of most east Texas counties.

When the school year of 1972-73 rolled around, I faced some uncertainties both in my career and in my personal life as well. Things had not gone well for Pat in her new career as a coach and she complained all the time. She lost game after game and rejected all my efforts to help her. I began to realize that this was a marriage that probably should have never happened. I sometimes felt more like a father than a husband and, when she told me that she didn't care to have children, I knew that the end was in sight. Finally, we agreed to a divorce and I moved out to a trailer in Lumberton, which was then a tiny community between Silsbee and Beaumont. Many years later, probably in 2003 or 2004, I received a call from a man I didn't know to inform me that Pat had been murdered by her then husband, who also committed suicide. Although I had not seen or heard from her in many years, I was extremely saddened to hear this awful news.

We were due to drop off a bit in basketball after our "final four" year in 1971-72. James Simmons was our only returning starter although we thought we would have Eddy Fobbs, our sixth man, back also. However, we later discovered that Eddy had spent two years in the eighth grade and a UIL rule prohibited senior eligibility after five years from the time a student first enrolled in eighth grade. This rule was designed to prevent parents from holding their kids back to gain maturity for athletic purposes. Eddy was 6'6" as a senior but he was so tiny in middle school that he didn't even play basketball until high school. But, in spite of only one player returning, I felt that we could do well because of our successful feeder system. Michael Dabney, one of my best prospects ever, would be a sophomore, and Steve Albrecht, a 6'4" post man, had seen considerable playing time the year before. They were joined in the starting lineup by Charles Stanley, and 6'4" Mitch Dinkle. Both were tough athletic football players that had been in our basketball program for several years.

As it turns out, this group did not disappoint and it was one of my most rewarding seasons. After a tough non-district schedule, we marched through zone play undefeated, then beat Crosby for the district championship. Anahuac, a Class 2A school coached by my friend Russell Boone, was undefeated that year and was ranked number one in any class in Southeast Texas. We scheduled them in a warm-up game before the play-offs began. The game was played in Beaumont and was standing room only. They were probably the better team, but my kids played hard as always, and we prevailed 47-41. We then played Pine Tree, a suburb of Longview, in the bi-district

James Simmons and Michael Dabney, 1974

round in Nacogdoches. They were an all-White team and extremely well coached by Rex Ray. Our season ended that night by a score of 52-46. They went on to win the state championship in Austin and I always thought that it could have been us had Eddy Fobbs been eligible. In spite of not playing his senior season, Eddy was offered basketball scholarships but turned them down to help support his family. He has been a pastor at a small church in Silsbee for several years.

After the season ended in 1973, because of my personal situation, I felt it best that I leave town and obtain another job. Pat was dating another guy in town and I had fallen in love with a beautiful blonde divorcee, with four kids, from Houston named Joan (Jo) Asher. She had grown up in the small German community of Boerne in the Texas Hill Country and was a wonderful person. I had always wanted to coach in college so I took the first thing that was offered, a basketball coaching job at Brazosport Community college in Lake Jackson, on the Gulf Coast southwest of Houston. It was not really what I wanted in that there were no athletic scholarships or dormitories and all players had to be from Brazoria and adjoining counties. But, at least, it was a start and I would be leaving my personal problems behind in Silsbee. Just before the school year ended, Mr. Crawford, my principal, ordered a large cake and had a going away party for me at the high school. But things changed a few weeks later when I completed my driver education class that I taught that summer. When I returned the car the to the local dealership, a school board member that worked there told me that I needed to call Coach McGallion and discuss with him what they had done at the board meeting the night before. Coach McGallion informed me that they had offered a substantial pay raise and would relieve me of all football coaching duties if I would stay. This was too good an offer for me to turn down so, after receiving assurances from Coach McGallion that it was okay with him, I accepted and offered to continue to scout for football. When Mr. Crawford saw me afterward, he said that he wanted his cake back.

Jo and I were married on July 29, 1973, and we took a quick honeymoon to Las Vegas. While there, I got a call from my real estate agent that the house that Pat and I owned had been sold, thus giving me down payment funds for a house that we had already picked out right in the middle of Silsbee. Although we have lived in eight different houses since, Jo still says that this one was her favorite, and I agree. Her two youngest kids, Kelly and Darryl, moved with us and entered school in the sixth and eighth grades respectfully. It wasn't long before they were talking just like everyone else in deep Southeast Texas.

When school started in the fall, I wasn't sure how my fellow coaches, all good friends of mine, would react. I was already making a higher salary than they were, would be making even more now while coaching only one sport, and didn't have to work two-a-day football practices in the hot August sun. But it didn't take me long to find out. Several of them never spoke to me again and their wives treated Jo the same way. They even had a jar in the football coaches office in which a quarter had to be deposited every time one of them uttered my name. I understand that this still existed several years after I left. Only Ronnie Nash and Pat Day continued to speak to me although I'm sure they still had to pay the quarter. Someone jokingly told me years later that the new stadium was funded by the money that had accumulated in that jar over the years.

Jo was a real trooper. Although she had been a Houston housewife for several years, she was basically a small town girl and had no problem fitting in to her new surroundings. Because she was a bridge player, she developed more friends in town than I although I had been in town for several years. We were active members of the Silsbee Country Club and continued friendships with the same young couples that Pat and I had associated with. Kelly and Darryl both adjusted well to the country life. Kelly often spent weekends riding horses with friends who still lived in houses that didn't have indoor plumbing. Darryl was somewhat of a challenge but he loved the outdoors and we spent many weekends camping, hunting, and fishing at the area lakes such as Dam B and Sam Rayburn. Darryl was happiest when he was alone in my boat in the middle of the lake running his trot lines at midnight. We always knew that he was okay when we saw the flickering light of his Coleman lantern. You would think that he may have been born in a flat bottom boat on Village Creek in the middle of the Big Thicket. Leslie, Jo's oldest, was already enrolled in college in San Marcos, and Randy, her oldest son, was living with his father in Houston.

It was in 1973 that I heard about a basketball organization for kids called Little Dribblers. It was founded by the county judge in Levelland, west of Lubbock, and had spread to a few communities in Texas. I contacted them and they sent David Durham, an English professor at Sam Houston State University, to Silsbee to help us get it organized. I had no problem getting young adults in town who loved basketball to take charge and get the program off to a good start. Because I left in 1975, I didn't benefit from the many great players that developed in the program. But I am told by Silsbee old timers that Little Dribblers basketball is the main reason for the continued success of Silsbee High School basketball. Since 1972, when we made our first trip to the state tournament, Silsbee teams have been back there seven times. They lost in the final game at state in 2016 , but won it all in both 2017 and 2018. There appears to be no end in sight. Not to diminish their recent success, but it is true that Silsbee is now in Class 4A, which would be the equivalent of Class 2A when I was coaching there. Class 3A back then would be the same as Class 5A now and they may not have as much success today at that level.

When our off-season practices began in the fall of 1973, it was evident that we may be pretty good again. Although we had lost three starters to graduation, James Simmons and Michael Dabney were two of the top players in the area, Doug Almond had seen considerable playing time as a sophomore, and Ricky Scott was up from the junior varsity. In addition, Artie Shankle, one of the best athletes in high school, was now a sophomore and would probably make the starting lineup soon after football season ended. We won 24 games that year and lost only five but we had some setbacks. We lost to Little Cypress during the first round of zone play and ended up having to beat them in a sudden death playoff game for the zone championship. But our biggest setback was in the district championship game against Crosby. We had no problem with them in the first half and led by 17 points after the third quarter. The game was on a neutral court at Lamar University in Beaumont, and I had made a mistake by agreeing to allow both coaches to pick an official to call the game. We fell apart in the last quarter but still would have kept the lead had not the official picked by Crosby called us for three straight lane violations while the ball was still in the back court. I called time out and both I and the other official explained to him that lane violations apply only to when the ball is in the front court. He disagreed, we continued to fall apart, and eventually lost 69-68.

I felt really bad for James Simmons. He had been a starter for three years and was one of the best kids I had ever coached. James finished his high school career as an honor student and was voted by his fellow students as "Mr. SHS", which said a lot about how far race relations in Silsbee had progressed in just a few years. James Simmons is Black and was given this honor by the vote of a student body that was 85 percent White. He received a full basketball scholarship to Rice University and now is a successful lawyer in Houston. I had lost touch with him for many years but, when I attended a reunion in 2017 for previous Silsbee state tournament teams, I made sure to let him know that I have never been more proud of one of my former players than he.

Our loss to Crosby that year was when I first realized that I had been spoiled by my success. I realized that losses, even though they were few up to that point, were much more devastating than our many wins were satisfying. I've been told that when that starts happening it is time to change careers. I wasn't quite ready to do that just yet, but I did begin to explore other coaching opportunities. Being shunned by some of my fellow coaches who had been my close friends hurt me a lot. And, while my relationship with Coach McGallion remained professional, I was somewhat upset with him for allowing this juvenile behavior on the part of his assistants to continue. Jo had made so many close friends in town that she completely ignored the fact that she was also shunned by their wives.

Sadly, my last year at Silsbee was almost an exact replica of the year before. We lost seven games, all to Class 4A schools, in non-district play, then marched through our zone schedule undefeated. Michael Dabney had injured his knee the year before in a pick-up game and never fully recovered. But he still had a great senior year, along with fellow seniors Ricky Scott and Doug Almond. David Brown's younger brother Anthony was a junior on that team and had a great year as well. Artie Shankle played well also as did Larry Davis and Larry Taylor, who spilt time at point guard. Both Michael and

Anthony were named to the All-State team. But we lost again in the district championship game to Cleveland 74-72. We had beaten them handily twice in the preseason. This was my second devastating loss in two years that prevented another run at a state championship. I began to question my ability to win big games. In my nine years in Silsbee, we had been to the state tournament once but had lost in elimination games five times to teams that eventually made it to Austin. Two of those teams ended up winning the state championship. We may have won more games than any Class 3A team in the state during that nine year period, but we didn't have much to show for it. I was ready to try something else. We had won 209 games and lost 75 for a winning percentage of .736. A very large percentage of our losses were to larger Class 4A schools. Our record against schools in our own classification must have been more than 90 percent victories.

CHAPTER **12**

Four Happy Years as a "Kerr-Vert" (Kerrville Tivy)

SHORTLY AFTER MY ninth season in Silsbee ended in 1975, I heard that Tivy High School in Kerrville, a school with a great basketball tradition, had hired a new athletic director and that he was looking to replace the head basketball coach. They had won back-to-back state championships in basketball under Jim Reid in 1969 and 1970, but with a different coach, they had fallen on somewhat hard times in recent years. I immediately applied and was soon hired over more than one hundred applicants. They wanted me to start immediately so that I could have a couple of months of spring practice with the returning players. I left Jo and the kids in Silsbee so that they could complete the school year and moved in with Jo's mother thirty miles away in Boerne. We would have to sell our house and move to Kerrville during the summer. Only a few people would turn down a chance to move from humid Southeast Texas to the beautiful Texas Hill Country, but Jo was not overjoyed because she loved our house in Silsbee and had made lots of friends there. Plus, housing prices were much higher in Kerrville and we would probably have to find a place to rent. But I was ready for a change and looked forward to the future.

Although it has grown a lot in the past forty years, Kerrville was a town of about 15,000 people in 1975. Being nestled in the hills of the

Texas Hill Country, it is best known for the Guadalupe River, which runs right through the middle of town. It is also known for its nearby summer youth camps, music festivals, hunting ranches, James Avery Jewelry, and Schreiner University (Schreiner Institute at the time). Whereas Silsbee was a blue collar town, Kerrville had a vibrant professional and business community in addition to a large population of educated retired people from all over the country. There is no way and Jo and I would be able to join the country club. Another thing that would probably affect the basketball program was that the Black population was only three percent of the total compared with about fifteen percent in Silsbee.

My new boss Bob Boyd was all you could ask for, and then some, as an athletic director. He had been the head football coach at Garland High School, a suburb of Dallas, and had arrived in Kerrville just a few weeks before I got there. He brought his top assistant Randy Nunez with him. In the four years that I worked with Bob, I never once thought that he had any interest at all in trying to keep any sport "in its place" as many football coach/athletic directors in Texas are prone to do. One of the members of Tivy's two championship basketball teams, Stuart Caulkins, was already coaching at the middle school and Coach Boyd even took my advice and hired my former Silsbee player Joe Price to coach at the middle school as well. Neither Stuart nor Joe had played football in high school. There is no way I could complain about my new situation as far as to how basketball would be treated in the athletic program.

Although the talent level in basketball had fallen off since Tivy's championship seasons, they continued to win zone championships in their Class 3A district. But it was mainly due to the competition, which consisted of Fredericksburg, Uvalde, Carrizo Springs, Crystal City, and Southwest of San Antonio. Fredericksburg and Uvalde were strictly football schools and the others were not particularly strong in any sport. Also, Tivy had a larger enrollment than any of the others and many of its players concentrated on basketball. But, while they could win the district's west zone, they had always been beaten by a team in the east zone for the district championship. When I met with my players for the first off-season practice that spring, I could tell right away that I had my work cut out for me. Compared with what I had been used to in Silsbee, there simply was not much athletic talent.

That spring was a hectic one for me. Besides starting a new basketball program, I taught four history classes and commuted back and forth between Boerne and Kerrville every week day. On Fridays, I drove the 360 miles to Silsbee, then back to Kerrville on Sunday. I spent any spare time that I had looking for a house. Buying one in Kerrville was out of the question and there wasn't much of anything for rent. Besides, we would have to sell our house in Silsbee and there weren't many people looking to live there at the time. I couldn't wait for the school year to end. But eventually we sold our house in Silsbee and, just before the school year ended, I found a house to rent in a very nice neighborhood on Virginia Drive in Kerrville. The rent was $250 per month which was a bargain in Kerrville but would have been considered unthinkable at the time in Silsbee. When we finally drove out of our driveway in Silsbee for the last time, Jo broke down in tears. After all these years, she still says that this was her favorite house of all time. Many years later, while on a trip to New Orleans, we took a detour to Silsbee and found a grown up empty lot where our first house once stood. Needless to say, Jo cried again.

Other than scouting, I had not had any football coaching duties in Silsbee for the past two years. In Kerrville, I continued to scout for football and agreed to help coach the freshman team, but only during their athletic period during the school day. This was good because I would also be available to help with freshman basketball when football season ended. It also meant that I would teach three history classes instead of four. But I was also expected to coach football during two-a-day practices in August. It was during this time that I discovered what a challenge that we might face in trying to turn around a declining athletic program. There was very little talent on the football field and, even worse, the players gave very little effort. As a result, the team went 0-10 that year even though our district was one of the weakest in the state. Coach Boyd was a very good coach and I knew that he would not leave until he had completely turned things around. I just hoped that things would not be the same for my basketball team during my first season.

As it turns out, the basketball team in Kerrville wasn't all that bad that first year but it wasn't all that good either. I don't remember much about our non-district record but we, as expected, marched through west zone play undefeated only to lose in the district championship game to Samuel Clemens, a school in the Schertz-Cibolo school district near San Antonio. This was not an improvement at all from the past few years and I was not a happy camper. We simply did not have very good athletes and, like the football team, I thought that our effort was somewhat lacking. Although we had a winning record, it was not up to my standards. There were not many prospects for the next season either. All of our good prospects were freshmen so I thought that it may be a couple of years before we could turn things around. My old Silsbee Tiger team, under new coach Fred Williams, made it all the way to the state tournament that year. Fred was a great coach but he stayed in Silsbee for just one year. He later won a couple of state championships at Hebert High School in Beaumont.

During the fall of 1975, we learned that Jo was pregnant with her fifth, but my first, child. I couldn't have been happier and couldn't wait for his/her arrival in late April or early May. Adam Whitney Montgomery was born on the third day of May, 1976 at Peterson Memorial Hospital in downtown Kerrville. Adam is Jo's maiden name and Whitney was my father's middle name. Three of Jo's kids (Randy, Darryl, and Kelly) lived with us at the time and, along with their sister Leslie, who was in college, were just as happy as Jo and I. Kelly, the youngest, was already fifteen at the time and doted on her new little brother. Randy, who had been living in Houston with his father, moved in with us during the school year and graduated in the spring from Tivy High School. He was also a member of my first basketball team there. In the fall of 1976, Randy entered Texas A&M and became a proud member of the Corps of Cadets.

The spring of 1976 was hectic, to say the least for the Montgomery family. Not only did we have a precious new arrival in the family, but we were also informed by our land lord that he was taking an early retirement from his job in San Antonio and would be moving to the house he owned in Kerrville. We had only a month to month lease and we had to look for another place to live. We loved the house on Virginia Drive but, fortunately for us, we found another house, for the same price, that we liked even better on Jonas Drive, just a few blocks up the hill from the high school. We moved in just before Adam was born. Our next door neighbors on Virginia Drive had been Jim "The Snake" Nugent and his wife. Jim at the time represented the Hill Country in the Texas Legislature and was a Democrat. We became friends and I actually voted for him when he ran for re-election against a Republican. This almost came back to bite me when I ran for public office myself many years later in 2000. At a Republican primary candidate forum in Kerrville that year I was asked if I had ever voted for a Democrat. I told the truth and said that the only one that I had ever voted for was my former next door neighbor Jim Nugent. I was unaware that his Republican opponent from that long ago election was in the audience that night. But everything worked out in the end when I carried Kerr County by a large margin even though I was running against an incumbent in the Republican primary.

In the summer of 1976, I was hired as the program director for Camp Rio Vista, a boys' camp on the banks of the Guadalupe River between Ingram and Hunt. Although Adam was only a month old, Jo also worked in the office at the camp and it was an enjoyable, but not a very relaxing, experience for both of us. Jo had grown up in the Hill Country and I was new to the area. But I loved my new surroundings and was very happy with the decision we had made to move there. Most of our friends in Kerrville were the other coaches and their wives. Stuart and Debbie Caulkins, although much younger than we, were especially good friends. Jo continued to play bridge at least once a week and also took a part time job as a bookkeeper for a local businessman. One of her bridge partners was Sharon Woodul. She and her husband Frank became close friends and still are today.

Although my first team in Kerrville was made up mostly of seniors, I had two transfers that would be eligible the following year, and I thought that we had a good chance for improvement. Robert Hubble, the brother of Coach Boyd's secretary, was a 6'8" transfer from Medina, a small Class B school nearby. He had starred there in both football and basketball. Gary Grief, who is now the executive director of the Texas Lottery, was a 6'3" transfer from Odessa Permian. Although I didn't have great players returning or up from the junior varsity, I made a decision to keep the really good sophomore prospects together on the junior varsity. This turned out to be one of the worst decisions that I ever made in my entire coaching career. Two, and maybe three, could probably have started on the varsity team. One of them, Jon Chambers, became the best player I ever had at Tivy and even scored sixty points in one game.

In addition to my bad decision, the other coaches in our zone voted to divide the district schedule into two halves, with the winner of each half playing for the zone championship. This was an effort to end Tivy's domination in basketball, and it worked at least for one year. Crystal City was a predominately Hispanic school but their coach, Joe Betancourt, somehow managed to get a 6"5" Black kid to transfer in from New Braunfels and they were suddenly competitive. Uvalde hired a really good coach, Robert Capelo, and they also had some very good senior athletes that year. None was better than Vann McElroy who had a great nine year career in the NFL with the Raiders and Seahawks. None of this made any difference during the first half of zone play as we went undefeated. The second half was a different story, however, as we lost at Uvalde by two points. But Uvalde ended up losing to Crystal City, throwing the second half into a three-way tie. We felt that we should have been declared zone champions by winning one half outright and tying for the other half, while the others had merely tied with us for one half. But the district committee voted to allow Uvalde to play Crystal City for the right to play us for the entire zone championship. Plus, we would have to play on a neutral court in San Antonio.

If my decision to keep my sophomores on the junior varsity was a bad one, my coaching decisions in that playoff game were even worse. I was completely outcoached by Robert Capelo. Uvalde controlled the pace of the game completely. Although we weren't particularly an up-tempo team, they stayed close the entire game by their slow, patient pace. However we managed a small lead until the last shot of the game. With about a minute left, we had a one point lead, 38-37, they were in possession of the ball and held it for one shot. A kid named Tad Nuetze took the last shot from the wing and it, unfortunately for us, went in. We lost 39-38, I was terribly embarrassed, but had no one to blame but myself. I had made bad decisions all year long and they cost us.

Robert Hubble went on to be the leading scorer and most valuable player for the South team in the Texas High School Coaches All-Star game that summer. He later played both football and basketball at Rice University and had a short career in the NFL. Robert was the third of my former players to play basketball at Rice, following Jimmy Hubenak from Wharton and James Simmons from Silsbee. James and Robert even played together one season. These three young men all ended up with degrees from Rice, one of the most outstanding universities in the country.

It would have been have been difficult for me to have blamed others for my first two mediocre basketball seasons at Kerrville Tivy. I had good coaches below the varsity level and their teams did well. In addition to Coach Caulkins and Coach Price, Phil Demasco, who coached the junior varsity team, worked just as hard for me in basketball as he did for Coach Boyd in football. Our facilities for basketball, which included a 1200 seat gymnasium, were some of the best in the state at the time. The community loved basketball and I had the full support of my athletic director as well as my principal and superintendent. I guess I could have blamed things on a very small Black enrollment but I would have been ignoring the fact that the same was true of most of the other schools in the southwest quadrant of the state where we competed. Instead, I looked straight into a mirror and stared at the real culprit. I vowed to never let it happen again.

I had intended to return to Camp Rio Vista for the summer of 1977 but instead ended up running a fireworks stand during the Fourth of July season. Leslie had graduated from college in San Marcos and had married Tom Woods, who owned a small fireworks company with several locations in the area. He found an ideal spot just outside the city limits on the south side of Kerrville that just so happened to be owned by our former neighbor, State Representative Jim Nugent. Jim agreed to rent the location to Tom only if Jo and I agreed to run it. We ended up really enjoying it and continued to do so for the next two or three summers as well as during the Christmas holidays. Adam was just a toddler then but developed a love for fireworks that endures to this day. That same summer, our land lord notified us that he was taking an early retirement and would be moving to his house that we lived in on Jonas Drive. We loved this place and hated to pack up and move again. Tired of all of this, we decided to buy a place of our own and quickly found a modified A-frame house already under construction on West Lane near our first house on Virginia Drive. But the builder got bogged down, forcing us to have to live in a motel for a couple of months after the school year began. I still remember watching Reggie Jackson hit all those home runs in the 1977 World Series from our room in that motel on Sidney Baker Street across from Tivy High School. I've passed by this spot hundreds of times in the past twenty-eight years and always remember those days. My little boy Adam was not yet two years old at the time.

When the school year of 1977-78 began, I looked forward to having last year's sophomores on my varsity team. Malcolm March, a 6'3" Black kid with a big butt and a large Afro, was the only starter from the previous year who was returning. Along with Malcolm were five juniors (Guy Overby, Jon Chambers, Jessie Brown, Henry Michel, and Robert Wilbourn) who had been together since middle school. None of them were football players so we got off to an early start in the off season. Guy was a very good ball handling 5'10" point guard who could also score. Jon, the son of Schreiner College's athletic director, was a terrific athlete who was also a great tennis player. He was only about 6'1", but could attack the rim and shoot from the perimeter. Jesse was about 6'2" and was our second best scoring threat. Henry was a tough competitor and good athlete but was only 5'9" or 5'10". Robert was a 6'8" goofy acting character whose dad was a professor at Schreiner College. Other than being tall, he didn't look like an athlete but he could actually play when he really felt like it. All of these, with the exception of Guy Overby, were real characters and sometimes difficult to reign in. They had played together since seventh grade and had almost never lost a game. Looking back, I should have moved them up to the varsity as freshmen when I first arrived in Kerrville. Had I done that we may have eventually won two state championships.

We always played a brutal non-district schedule against mostly Class 4A schools in the San Antonio and Austin areas. I don't remember exactly what our non-district record was but I do remember that we reversed course from the year before and marched through both halves of zone play without a close game. Our district championship game was against New Braunfels and, for some reason that I also don't recall, was played on their home court. They were a very good team that year and beat us by three points. I still believe that, had we played in Kerrville, there would have been a different result.

I had no interest in leaving Kerrville but I had always wanted to coach in college if the situation was right for me. That spring, I learned that the basketball coaching job at St. Edward's University in Austin was open. Thinking not much about it, I called anyway and had them send me an application even though I had no idea what the job, other than coaching basketball, actually entailed. Lo and behold, the faculty athletic representative, who was also the head of the Education Department, called and essentially offered me the job over the phone without even meeting me. I agreed to at least travel to Austin and meet with him (his name was Dr. Glen Hinkle) but I

MY TEXAS LIFE IN THE (NOT SO) FAST LANE

was not impressed. The athletic director was a young baseball coach who, for some strange reason, I never met and my job title would be health and physical education instructor and men's basketball coach. St. Edward's was an NAIA school in the Big State Conference with schools such as St. Mary's, Southwestern, and Texas Lutheran. They had been awful in basketball for several years and, when I learned that the salary would be less than I was making at Tivy, I quickly declined and forgot about it.

Although we didn't make it to Austin, my fourth year at Tivy, 1978-79, was a very successful one. I had lost only one starter, Malcolm March, from the year before but had a capable replacement in Augusta "Gus" Benson, a 6'3" muscular junior, who had played on the junior varsity team the year before. We won twenty-eight games and lost only four, the best won-loss record in school history. Better even than that of either of the state championship teams of 1969 and 1970. Jon Chambers broke the school single game scoring record with sixty points in a non-district game against Holy Cross of

Tivy Antlers, 1979 district champs (Jon Chambers is standing next to me)

119

San Antonio, a record that had been held for many years by John Mahaffey, who went on to have a successful career on the PGA tour. We had no problem winning the zone title, and then got revenge by beating New Braunfels for the outright district championship. Our bi-district game was in Victoria against a very good Bay City team. They had been in our district many years before when I was at Wharton and were known mainly for their success in football. But that was before integration and they had become a power in both sports in recent years. Both teams played well that night and the lead changed hands several times. We led by five points in the fourth quarter but they came back late to tie, and the game went into overtime. We ran out of gas during that last three minutes and eventually lost 52-46. I was disappointed but was proud of my team. Bay City went on to win the state championship and I always felt that we could have been state champs had we won that night.

When that season ended, I had been a head coach for seventeen of my twenty years as a high school coach. We had made the playoffs eleven times and had reached the final four at the state tournament once. Nine of the eleven teams that eliminated us reached the final four and seven of them won the state championship. My only losing season was my first one at Calvert and we won at least twenty games in fifteen of those seventeen seasons. Today, high school teams in Texas reach the playoffs by finishing fourth in their district but during my high school coaching days, only the district champion made the playoffs. So, although there were many disappointments along the way, I am nonetheless proud of my achievements as a high school coach, and I am even more proud of the dozens of youngsters who gave their all for me.

A very small percentage of high school athletes in any sport go on to play in college. Only one of my players on my first two Tivy teams, Robert Hubble, played college ball. But, of the top seven kids who played in 1977-78 and 1978-79, five of them played basketball for at least one year in college. Two of them, Robert Wilbourn and Gus Benson, ended up playing for me for at St. Edward's University and I am proud to say that they both got their degrees. Jon Chambers, probably my best player ever at Tivy, turned down my offer of a scholarship at St. Edward's to play in junior college to keep his Division I hopes alive. Sadly, this never happened and he ended up finishing his career at Schreiner before it became a four year school.

As far as I was concerned, I had one of the best basketball coaching jobs in the state. Kerrville was in the middle of the beautiful Texas Hill Country and there were no efforts whatsoever on the part of the administration to "keep basketball it its place". Just as I had done in Silsbee, I had started a Little Dribblers program and was on the Parks and Recreation Board in the city which had resulted in basketball courts all over town. None of this had restricted Coach Boyd's efforts to rebuild a losing football program. In fact, football was doing much better than basketball. I had no intention of leaving unless I could advance up the ladder into college coaching. But I was reluctant to uproot my family. We had just moved into a new home, Darryl was out of school and had joined the Army, Kelly had one more year of high school, and Adam was approaching his third birthday. Life was good for the Montgomery family when an unexpected call from Austin came.

The call was from Dr. Glen Hinkle who had offered me the job at St. Edward's the year before. The coach who had taken the job, Rick Starzecki, had resigned after only one year and they were removing John Knorr as athletic director although he would remain as baseball coach. I was now being offered the dual job of athletic director and men's basketball coach and would also be an assistant professor (instead of instructor) of health and physical education, teaching no more than two classes per semester. Half my pay would be for teaching and one-fourth each for coaching and athletic director. Unlike the offer the previous year, my salary would exceed what I was making in Kerrville, but not by much. But, as an assistant professor, I would be automatically eligible for tenure after four years. Jo and I were happy in Kerrville and we didn't want to take Kelly away from her friends, but this may be the only chance I would ever get to coach in college.

We decided to go for it and I started the following week. I slept on a cot in the locker room during the week and drove back to Kerrville on weekends until the school year ended. We put our house in Kerrville on the market but had no success selling it so we rented it out for a several years. I found a nice house for rent in Barton Hills, a very nice neighborhood only three and a half miles from the St. Edward's campus on South Congress Avenue.

CHAPTER **13**

My Time on a Hill in South Austin (St. Edward's)

ST. EDWARD'S UNIVERSITY is a private liberal arts Roman Catholic university in the Holy Cross tradition and is located on a beautiful spot on Congress Avenue about three miles south of downtown Austin. Although it has over 5000 students today, there were only about 2300 when I arrived in 1979. It was founded in 1877 by Father Edward Sorin, who also founded the University of Notre Dame in Indiana. Probably half of the faculty and staff were either Holy Cross priests or brothers and lived on campus. Until the 1970's, a large percentage of the students were Anglo Catholics and were from all over the United States, but especially from the Midwestern states such as Indiana and Ohio. But in 1972, the College Assistance Migrant Program (CAMP) was added. CAMP was a federal program that gave migrant students federal grants to provide them with opportunities to attend college. As a result, there was a large Hispanic student population and the traditional Midwestern Catholic student population had declined.

I never doubted my decision to take the job at St. Ed's but I must admit that I was appalled of some of the things that I discovered that spring. I was shocked when I walked into the women's locker room in the 1930's era gymnasium and saw three open toilets that were not separated by stalls. Volleyball, at the time, was the only women's sport and the coach was Dr. Diane Daniels, who had been at the school forever. She had never complained about this as far as I know and I wondered if she had ever even noticed. My first reaction was to meet with my immediate boss, Brother Henry Altmiller, and inform him of this unthinkable problem. I'm not sure that Brother Henry had ever set foot in the gymnasium but he took action immediately after I offered to pay for the stalls myself. I didn't have to pay, Brother Henry authorized payment for the stalls, and he soon became one of my staunchest supporters.

Speaking of bosses, I had a lot of them at St. Ed's and they were all very liberal. Dr. Hinkle was my academic boss because he was dean of the Center for Teaching and Learning (fancy name for Education Department) which Health and Physical Education was a part of. Brother Henry was Academic Dean. His boss was the Executive Vice-President, Father Tom Wynberg, a bearded sandals and socks wearing individual that I couldn't imagine being a person of the cloth, much less the vice president of a University. Finally, the president of the university was Brother Stephen Walsh, who was the only one of the four that ever wore a coat and tie. Other than Brother Stephen and me, the only persons who looked professional at St. Ed's were the conservative professors in the business department. The others, except for Father Tom in his sandals, could have been mistaken for blue collar assembly line workers at a factory in Cleveland or Pittsburgh.

When I eventually waded through the maze of bosses and met with the president Brother Stephen, I realized that he wasn't particularly interested in athletics but that he was, nonetheless, willing to cooperate with me on my ideas as to how to improve the athletic department. I was surprised when he pulled out a list of suggestions that former Coach Starzecki had sent him for improving the basketball program. Most of the suggested changes were things that Brother Stephen was not even aware that were problems in the first place. For example, John Knorr had told me and the previous coach that a school rule required every scholarship athlete to pay at least $500 per semester out of his/her own pocket even after all scholarships and student aid had been considered. This meant that there was no such thing as a full athletic scholarship at St. Ed's even when combined with grants and loans. In the end, he told me to ignore all of John Knorr's supposed rules and to get with the athletic council, of which I was the chair, and draw up new rules for the athletic department for his approval. His only requirement was that we could not schedule games or matches against any schools that were not accredited by the Southern Association of Schools and Colleges. He also told me that the tennis program, under Bro. Emmett Strohmeyer, should not have to undergo any changes as a result of any new rules that the athletic council may approve. Bro. Emmett had been at St. Ed's almost all his adult life, was already in well into his eighties, and Bro. Stephen felt any changes might unduly upset him.

St. Edward's was a member of the National Association of Intercollegiate Athletics (NAIA) and competed in four men's sports (basketball, baseball, golf, and tennis) in the Big State Conference with St Mary's, Texas Lutheran, Huston-Tillotson, Southwestern, Mary Hardin-Baylor, and East Texas Baptist. The women's program competed in volleyball, basketball, and tennis but basketball was in its first year. Each school in the conference was limited to a total of sixteen men's scholarships each and could divide them up as they chose but were limited to ten scholarships in any one sport. We were currently awarding nine scholarships in basketball, four in baseball, two in tennis, and one in golf. I had no plans to recommend changes to this allocation. At that time, NCAA Division II was non-existent in Texas so all colleges that were not in Division I were members of the NAIA. In addition to the Big State, there were three other NAIA conferences. One of them, the Lone Star, was made up mainly of large regional state universities such as Southwest Texas, Sam Houston, Stephen F. Austin, etc. In order to advance in national NAIA competition, the Big State Conference champs had to get past the Lone Star Conference champ which was a very tall order, especially in basketball.

Our athletic facilities at the time were at least average for baseball and tennis and our golf team practiced at Lost Creek Country

Club. But the gymnasium was a whole different story. It was very old, needed lots of repairs, and was tiny with bleachers on only one side of the playing court. The locker rooms, restrooms, and coaches' offices were totally inadequate. Many colleges in the state refused to schedule us in basketball on a home-and-home basis, and any recruiting advantage that we may have had because of our location in Austin was completely negated by the terrible facilities. As far as athletic budgets, I'm sure that ours was near the bottom when compared with other NAIA schools. Every sport had only one paid coach. Besides myself as basketball coach, John Knorr coached baseball and taught health and physical education classes, Brother Emmett Strohmeyer coached tennis, and Jim Koch, an economics professor, was the golf coach. Dr. Diane Daniels reluctantly coached all three women's sports along with her teaching duties in health and physical education. I promised her that I would do my best to convince the administration to hire a basketball coach as soon as possible.

Although I was the men's basketball coach, I was determined to do everything that I could to have a healthy all-around athletic program. Before I made any decisions concerning other sports, I did so only after consulting with the other coaches and then getting approval from the athletic council which consisted of the other four coaches, the faculty athletic representative (Dr. Hinkle), two faculty members appointed by the president, and myself. Although I was concerned that Coach Knorr may be a problem because I had replaced him as athletic director, he and I got along just fine. Dr. Hinkle also was supportive of my efforts although I sometimes felt that he considered himself the true director of athletics. I had to be careful with him because, after all, he was my boss on the academic side of things which provided half my salary. I guess this is why he is the one that had offered me the job for the past two years in a row.

I didn't have any teaching responsibilities that first spring and summer so I had plenty of time to recruit for basketball as well as to establish myself as the new athletic director. With only nine scholarships available for basketball and a few scholarship players returning from an 8-19 team, I had to be extremely selective if I wanted to have a chance to turn things around. I had no experience on the college recruiting trail but I had lots of friends in the high school and junior college coaching ranks in Texas. Sometimes that can be a negative, however, because most high school coaches think that they have at least one player who can play at a small college, and junior college coaches think that their bench warmers can excel at that level. My phone rang off the wall that spring from coaching friends recommending their players for scholarships or tryouts. I had no assistant coach but Jimmy Fred Littleton had completed his eligibility the previous year and was a student assistant while completing his degree. His dad had been one of the most successful high school basketball coaches in Texas history and I considered him to be an unpaid full time assistant. He later had a long successful high school coaching career in San Antonio.

Don Loobeck, a 6'3" transfer from Alvin Jr. College, was the only decent holdover from the year before but he was a very solid all-around player. My first recruit was Larry Kruse, a 6'4" kid from Crockett High School in Austin, just south of the St. Ed's campus. We had played Crockett when I coached in Kerrville and I knew that he was a solid college prospect. My other top recruits were Johnny Campbell, a 6'0" guard from Blinn Jr. College, Greg Marshall from Stark High School in Orange, and Rick Hawkins, a slick 6'2" transfer from Schreiner Jr. College who was from The Bronx, NY. I had to use only a small amount of scholarship money on Rick because he was on the GI Bill and lived off campus with his wife and infant son. Don, Larry, and Johnny ended up being three of the best players that I ever coached. Greg was a great point guard but had academic problems and was there only two years. Our major weakness was a lack of height. However, we played hard and completely turned things around that first season, finishing with a 17-11 season record and third place in the Big State Conference, barely missing the playoffs since the top two teams in the conference advanced. At one point in the season, we won ten games in a row and didn't lose a game between December 3rd and January 26th. We even beat St. Mary's for the first time in many years and had an 8-4 conference record. To say the least, I was very pleased with what we accomplished that first year.

One of the highlights of that first season was a trip that we took during Christmas break to far west Texas for games against Sul Ross in Alpine and Abilene Christian in Abilene. Since we had games during the break, the basketball players were enrolled in a health class that I taught during a three week mini-semester. Our game with Sul Ross was scheduled for a Saturday night and we then were to play in Abilene on the following Monday. It was near the beginning of our ten game winning streak and I looked at the trip as a "bonding" experience for the team. Alpine is 400 miles from Austin but a longer route is south on IH-35 to San Antonio then west on old Highway 90 all the way to Alpine in the Big Bend National Park area. This route goes through Del Rio, a city on the Rio Grande River across from Via Acuna, Mexico. Jo and I had been to Via Acuna many times for weekend getaways when we lived in Kerrville so I was very familiar with all the activities there. But, with the exception of Alan Catalani and Mark Bird, who were both from San Antonio, none of the others had ever been across a national border before. I had arranged for the team to have dinner Friday night at La Macarena, a famous restaurant and night club that I had visited many times. We drove the team van (I was the driver) across the river, parked in a secure lot, and I allowed them to walk up and down the streets of a small city in a foreign country. Later, we walked to the restaurant and had a great time. I would later be embarrassed when we crossed back into the U.S. and the Border Patrol confiscated some tequila (Jo's margaritas are the best ever) I had bought. Only one liter per person is allowed and I had two. Mark Bird was twenty-one and knowledgeable about border crossings but the guy didn't buy his story that one of the bottles was his. He made me watch as he broke both bottles in a trash can. I still haven't lived that embarrassing moment down.

We spent the night in Del Rio then drove 200 miles to Alpine for our game on Saturday night. We beat Sul Ross pretty handily and drove more than 300 miles the next day to Abilene for our game with Abilene Christian on Monday. Abilene Christian was a member of the Lone Star Conference. It was very unusual for a Big State Conference team to win a game against a Lone Star Conference team. They had larger enrollments, better facilities, and more athletic scholarships. Given a choice between signing with school from that conference or ours, a prospect almost never picked the Big State school. But we played great that night and won going away 85-73. We did not lose again until late January, and I believe that trip brought us together as a team which allowed us to have a winning season, the first one at St. Edward's in several years.

Our location in Austin was not only a plus for recruiting, but also for rivalries and travel. Except for East Texas Baptist, 275 miles away in Marshall, all the conference schools were less than eighty miles from Austin. We were right in the geographic center of the conference. St. Ed's, St. Mary's, Texas Lutheran, and Southwestern had all been members of the Big State for many years, were close together, and had developed strong rivalries with each other over the years. The gyms were small but the crowds, mostly students, were substantial and usually raucous. I really enjoyed the atmosphere but I knew that we had to do something to improve the facilities and budget for athletics if we wanted to be competitive on a regular basis.

The financial situation for athletics was very difficult to solve in that there were very few sources for additional income to supplement our meager budget. Most colleges get income for athletics from gate receipts but most our fans were students and faculty and they were admitted free to athletic events. We had concessions at basketball and baseball games but the profits didn't even cover the costs for referees and umpires. There was a development office and I was enlisted by it to contact alumni for donations. But most of the alumni old enough to have accumulated wealth were old time traditional Catholics who no longer lived in the state and many of those who did were upset that their alma mater had changed drastically over the years and was so dependent on the federal government for its survival. In a nutshell, I would have to look elsewhere for funds in order to improve the athletic program. I soon found a partial solution but it had negatives as well as positives.

The term "giveaway game" refers to the practice of a small college agreeing to play a game on the home court or field of a larger division school in return for a monetary guarantee, thus allowing the larger school to pad its overall season won-loss record. The smaller school almost always loses the game but collects money for its underfunded athletic budget. Sometimes the payment for one game exceeds the entire yearly budget for that particular sport and, in the unlikely event that the smaller school wins, a lot of positive publicity for the smaller school's athletic program because the game is likely to be televised or at least broadcast by radio. "Giveaway" games are the primary reason for weak non-conference schedules in major college football and basketball. The major schools and their coaches are simply "buying" wins in order to have winning season records. We played one of those games my first year at St. Ed's when we traveled to play at UT-Arlington. I had added the game late when my old friend and then UT-A coach "Snake" Legrand called and offered a few shekels for us to come up and play a late season game. Over the next few years, I would schedule a lot of them at the expense of our won-loss record but to the benefit of our bottom line. My 17-11 season record that first year was the best that I would have. But there should have been an asterisk because we played only one "giveaway" game and the schedule had been arranged by my predecessor who was eager to reverse his 8-19 record from the year before. Also, we destroyed Southwest Assemblies of God twice and scored 129 and 125 points against them. They were not accredited by the Southern Association of Schools and would not be eligible to be on the schedule in the future.

Although I was director of athletics, my contract was on a nine month basis. Since the school year ended in early May and didn't start again until mid-September, I had a lot of time on my hands during the summer months. The university allowed me use the gym facilities for a one week basketball camp and one summer Jo and I returned to the campus of Schreiner College in Kerrville where we directed a three week camp, called Camp Murieta, for overweight girls. We also continued to operate the Kerrville fireworks stand for our son-in-law for a couple of years. Life was good for us in Austin. Barton Hills was a great neighborhood and had an outstanding elementary school for Adam. I had become an avid runner in 1976 when I worked at Camp Rio Vista, and I loved jogging on the trails along the Colorado River near our house. Kelly had moved with us to Austin for her senior year in high school, but, after about a month, she missed her friends and we allowed her to return to Kerrville to finish her senior year at Tivy.

Late in the school year of 1979-80, I was able to make good on my promise to Coach Daniels to hire a women's basketball coach so that she could concentrate on volleyball. After receiving the go ahead from the administration, I advertised the job and, even though the salary was low, I got lots of applicants. The outgoing coach at the University of Texas even applied. After interviewing several applicants, I settled on a young lady who was coaching at a small high school near Lubbock. Her name was Sharon McIlroy. She, like I the year before, had no recruiting experience so I even went on a couple of visits with her. Coach Daniels was happy and so was I. It took Sharon a while because our team had been so bad but she worked hard and ended up doing a respectable job.

I had also completed the task that Brother Stephen Walsh had demanded of me which was to draw up a new set of policies for the athletic department and present them to the athletic council for approval. Since he had said that any policies presented to him must forbid scheduling of non-accredited schools, I went even further by forbidding competition against schools whose teams were not active members of a nationally recognized athletic association for four year colleges such as the NCAA or NAIA. When I presented my proposals to the council there was hardly any discussion (I had already told Bro. Emmett that tennis was exempt) and every single item on the agenda was unanimously approved. I presented the policies to Brother Stephen, he approved them, and I fully expected that all coaches would comply.

Although we had four seniors on the squad in 1979-80, Don Loobeck was the only one that would be difficult to replace. Don was not only a talented player (he was our leading scorer) and tough competitor, but was also a great team leader. I was also losing my student assistant Jimmy Littleton, who had graduated and was starting a coaching career of his own. Since our primary weakness was lack of height, my recruiting efforts were aimed at signing taller players. That is tough to do for small colleges because most prospects that have both height and talent are scooped up by larger schools. So I looked mainly to junior colleges to fill our open spots for the coming year.

Junior college basketball in Texas has always been probably the strongest in the country. Most junior colleges in the other states, if they have basketball programs at all, don't have dormitories and also don't award athletic scholarships. A notable exception is Kansas but, except for a few scattered programs in the rest of the country, that's about it. As a result, the thirty or so Texas JUCO's that award basketball scholarships compete for players from high schools all over the United States. These players choose junior colleges either because their grades don't allow admittance to a four year school or because they haven't been recruited by a Division I school and want to keep their hopes alive to play at that level in the future. A very large number of these students end up at junior colleges in Texas. A great many of them never get a chance to play at the major college level and eventually end up at the Division II or NAIA level.

As a Texas high school coach for many years, I had developed friendships with many of the junior college coaches in the state and, when I became the coach at St. Edward's, I frequently got calls from them when they were looking for a place for some of their players to continue their careers. As a result, I was able to sign Marcus Jones from Navarro Jr. College (my alma mater), and Andre Glover from Tyler Jr. College. Marcus was a 6'5" forward who had played at Roosevelt High School in Dallas, one of the top programs in the state. Fortunately, he was a good student who had no problem gaining admittance to St. Ed's. Andre was a 6'7" inside player from Miami, Florida who had not seen a lot of playing time at a very strong Tyler JC program. Robert Wilbourn, who had played for me in high school in Kerrville, was now 6'9" and had played for one year at Schreiner but was eager to leave home to continue his college career. In addition, I had brought back Jerry Haines the year before after he had been dismissed by my predecessor. Jerry was a traditional St. Ed's Catholic Midwesterner from Cleveland, Ohio who, although somewhat hotheaded, was a pretty decent shooting guard. With these four additions, plus several players who contributed to our winning season the previous year, I felt that we would have an even better year in 1980-81.

As it turns out, my second team at St. Ed's was somewhat of a disappointment although I had no reason to expect better because our schedule was much tougher. In order to bring in funds, I scheduled away games with three NCAA Division 1 schools: Baylor, Hardin Simmons, and Houston Baptist. We were guaranteed money totaling several thousands of dollars from them. In addition, we played six games against Lone Star Conference schools and only two of them were at home. Most of the larger schools simply would not play us in our old and tiny gym. Because I had become friends with University of Texas coach Abe Lemons, we even moved some of our home games to the Frank Erwin Center and played a preliminary game prior to the Texas games. Only ten of our games that year were played in our gym, thus causing us to lose valuable home court advantage. But, unlike NCAA basketball with many at-large teams in the playoffs, the NAIA admitted only the top two teams in conference play. So I was willing to sacrifice a few non-conference losses in an effort to upgrade our program for extra funds and much needed exposure. We sought playoff appearances by finishing high in the conference standings.

One of the highlights of the '80-81 season was a five point loss to Baylor at the old Heart O' Texas Coliseum in Waco, a facility that was better suited for rodeos than for basketball games. In a game that was supposed to be an easy win for Baylor, we jumped out to an early lead and kept it until almost the very end. All our players, but especially Johnny Campbell, were exceptional that night. They had no answer for Johnny. I even felt sorry for Baylor coach Jim Haller near the end for he could not afford to lose to an NAIA school. But, with about three minutes left, he turned things over to his star Terry Teagle and, with some help from the Southwest Conference officiating crew, Baylor prevailed by a score of 76-71. I'm not much on moral victories but this was a notable exception. We pocketed the $8000 check, had a great post game meal at the famous Elite Café on the Circle, and didn't even have to spend the night in Waco. That itself was a pretty good reason to celebrate.

Going into conference play that year I felt that we had a genuine chance to make the NAIA playoffs, something that St. Ed's hadn't done since 1971. St. Mary's had not made the playoffs the year before but that was just a blip on the radar screen that was probably caused by a temporary loss of athletic scholarships two years earlier. They had developed somewhat of a basketball dynasty several years before under Coach Ed Messbarger who had success with older and more mature Army and Air Force veterans who had spent time in San Antonio, which is known as a military city. Unlike the NCAA, which has an age limit for athletes, the NAIA has no such rule. Coach Messbarger had left for Angelo State in 1978, and was replaced by his longtime assistant Buddy Meyer, who had been an All-American himself at St. Mary's. Buddy continued the great winning tradition and, except for that one year, St. Mary's continued to dominate in the Big State Conference. But even if we lost to them, we could still make the playoffs by finishing second in the conference.

We started conference play with a close win over Huston-Tillotson and lost our second game to East Texas Baptist by two points at home. But the one that eventually kept us out of a second place conference finish was a heartbreaking 70-69 loss to St. Mary's on our home court.

We also lost twice to Southwestern and they ended up with the second playoff spot. Seven conference wins against five losses was not quite good enough and I was very disappointed since we were 8-4 the previous year. Marcus Jones, Johnny Campbell, and Larry Kruse played great all year but Andre Glover and Greg Marshall were disappointing. Johnny was graduating in the spring and Greg and Andre would both be leaving because of poor grades. I had some serious recruiting to do if we were to improve. I had suffered through my first losing season since my first year of coaching but we still had our second winning conference record in a row, something that hadn't happened for the Hilltoppers in many years.

St. Edward's University Hilltoppers, 1981

Shortly after the season ended, I learned that the head basketball coaching job at Howard Payne University in Brownwood was open. I was not looking to leave Austin but Howard Payne was in the Lone Star Conference which was definitely a big step up from St. Edward's and the Big State. Although they were one of only two private schools in the conference (Abilene Christian was the other), they had good facilities, a full time assistant coach, twelve scholarships instead of nine, and paid quite a bit more. Also, they had competed quite well in basketball against larger state supported universities. We had played them four times already and were winless against them. Feeling that I had nothing to lose, I applied for the job and, along with two other applicants, I was granted an interview. The interview went well but, for many reasons, I wasn't very comfortable with the surroundings. Howard Payne is a Southern Baptist University. The president was a gregarious heavy set guy who reminded me of every Baptist minister from my childhood. Brownwood is about the same size as Kerrville but had the feeling of being a little on the dull side. So, on the drive back to Austin, I decided that I would call when I got home to tell them I was withdrawing from consideration. I'm glad I did because, three years later, Howard Payne dropped athletic scholarships and became an NCAA Division III school. Also, on that drive back to Austin, I learned on the radio that my friend Abe Lemons had been relieved of his duties as the coach of the Texas Longhorns.

My recruiting went very well that spring. I concentrated again on the JUCO ranks, bringing in Jimmy Wright from TSTI, Steve Martin from Cisco, Ellis Montet from Jacksonville College, and Bradye McClure from Ranger. Jimmy was 6'6" and had been a teammate with Marcus Jones at Dallas Roosevelt. In spite of the fact that everybody at St. Edward's bragged about the tough admissions requirements, he was admitted with a certification in sewing machine mechanics at TSTI, which was a two-year technical school in Waco. I called him "Singer" after the sewing machine company of that name. Steve was a raw 6'8" 250-pounder who I signed as a consolation prize in my unsuccessful efforts to sign his 6'10" brother Woody, out of Cooper High School in Abilene. In addition to these four, we also brought in Gus Benson, who had played for me at Kerrville, and Jerry Farias from Mission in the Rio Grande Valley. Because of our large Hispanic student population, Jerry was a perfect fit. He was only 5'9" but had broken all kinds of scoring and assists records in the Valley during his high school career and was a very good ball handler. In addition, he was one of the most coachable kids that I ever worked with. Bradye McClure's best friend at Ranger JC, Joe Bill, also came along as student trainer/manager. I gave Joe a free room in the gym and he used the restroom and showers in the men's locker room. Joe was, and still is, one of my favorite people ever. He later became a basketball coach himself and, as far as I know, is still coaching at Louise, a small school near Victoria.

A real plus for me that spring was the fact that Bro. Henry Altmiller was promoted to Executive Vice-President, which meant that I would have just one boss to answer to as Director of Athletics. I didn't know Bro. Henry that well and he didn't seem to know or care anything about athletics. But he was a straight shooter and seemed to take a liking to me because he saw me as being one as well. The only thing that we ever discussed during our infrequent meetings was finances. He thought that it was great that I was scheduling larger schools and was bringing in extra money that had not been factored into the budget. When I asked him to authorize a $3000 salary to hire an assistant, he immediately approved. When I advertised the job, I was shocked at the large number of applicants, many of whom had full time coaching jobs in the public schools. I eventually hired Ernie Nieto, a local Hispanic activist, who had played college basketball at Southwestern University. Bro. Henry and I continued to work together very well until he decided to retire from administration and return to the classroom. Things would fall apart for me after that, but more on that later.

My relationship with the baseball coach and former athletic director John Knorr had gone fairly well during my first two years at St. Ed's. But I was understandably a little uncomfortable around him. When I was offered the basketball coaching job three years earlier, he was the athletic director but I never met him. I think I was told that he was serving in the role on an interim basis and they had not decided who they were going to have as his replacement. The following year, when I was offered the job as both athletic director and men's basketball coach, I still didn't meet him until I was already on the job. I found him to be a very nice young guy but I wondered how he would react to having someone else come in, assume a role that he had held for the past two or three years, and suddenly become his boss. But he assured me that he was glad to be the baseball coach only and was relieved to not have the duties of athletic director. The only thing that he asked of me was to allow him to continue to do some fundraising for the baseball program without having to share the proceeds with the other sports. I was aware that he was talking about nickels and dimes and told him that I had no problem with that as long as he understood that the other sports could do the same. He seemed happy with my answer but that was before the basketball program started bringing in more than just nickels and dimes.

When the 1981-82 school year began, I was fairly confident that this would be a breakthrough year for the basketball program. But our non-conference schedule was even tougher than the year before. Instead of six games against Lone Star Conference schools, we had eight. We again scheduled three games against NCAA Division I schools but we replaced Baylor on the schedule with a game against Texas A&M in College Station (the Aggies paid more than Baylor for easy wins). I really didn't care about our non-conference record as long as we were increasing the bottom line and that we did well enough in conference play to enter the NAIA playoffs. That meant finishing either first or second in the Big State which I fully intended to do.

One day during the fall of 1981, a local Austin guy named Reynol Gray walked into my office unannounced and made a proposal to me to allow him to publish a basketball program. He would sell advertising to businesses in South Austin, publish the program, and spilt the proceeds with the university. He had a fund raising advertising business that had done most of its work in the Rio Grande Valley but he wanted to establish customers in the Austin area. I was skeptical, but intrigued, so I called references that he provided and they were all positive. But I told him that I would have to seek approval from my boss Bro. Henry Altmiller. Bro. Henry, always eager to bring in more funds, approved but warned me that, if anything went wrong, I would be held responsible. When I gave Reynol the okay, he then asked for a room at the university to establish a telephone bank. I quickly nipped that one in the bud without even asking for approval. But he went ahead without the phone bank and sold more ads that I ever thought possible. St. Ed's was Reynol's first client in the Austin area and he later went on to establish a fairly large advertising business that published calendars, schedules, programs, etc. for high schools all over the state. But this was before the internet boom that eventually brought down a lot of people who were involved in print advertising.

We started the 1981-82 year at 4-2 and both losses were to Lone Star Conference schools Howard Payne and Southwest Texas State (now Texas State). But I can't imagine what I was thinking when I arranged our non-conference schedule. Our next three games would be on the road against Houston Baptist on Nov. 29, Texas A&M on Dec. 1, and Texas A&I on Dec. 3. That was three road games in five days, and two of them were against Division I schools. Altogether we would be putting over 1200 miles on each of our 15 seat passenger vans. To make things worse, I had to be in Corsicana the day after our game in College Station to finalize a family land transaction with the Tarrant County Water District which was using its power of "eminent domain" to obtain property on which to build a dam to provide water for the city of Arlington.

Through a couple of complicated family inheritances, I had become part owner of Montgomery family property near Eureka in Navarro County. The tract of our land that the water district sought consisted of about 1050 acres of ranch land and its mineral rights. After a couple of years of back and forth with the water district, a judge ruled that $650 per acre was a fair price. Since I had lost all interest in cattle ranching after my dad died, I, along with my mother and sister, agreed to sell since we would keep our mineral rights. At that time there were thirteen shallow oil wells on the land that provided family members with varying amounts of royalty income each month. Supposedly, the wells would stay in production by the building of platforms above the water level. Long story short – I traveled to the Texas A&M game in my car so that I could sign away a portion of family property in Corsicana the next day. Coach Shelby Metcalf and the Aggies didn't show mercy on the Hilltoppers that night, beating us 104-57. I knew that we were in trouble when our trainer Joe Bill tapped me on the shoulder during the Aggie school song to inform me that Jimmy Wright was still practicing his free throws. Jimmy should have known better since his brother Rynn had been a star at A&M just one year before.

After the loss to the Aggies in College Station, I drove my used El Camino to my mom's house in Fairfield where I spent the night before traveling the thirty-five miles to Corsicana to collect a check at the office of our long time family attorney. By today's standards, the payment was not all that large but it was still more than I had made in my first fifteen years combined as a Texas high school coach and teacher. I returned the 156 miles to Austin that day in time to park my new found wealth in a short term Certificate of Deposit (the short term interest rate back then was 13%) at a Savings and Loan just up the street from the St. Ed's campus. I became an investor that day and have been a pretty successful one ever since. Plus, I have never paid a dime to a financial adviser. We would be traveling the next day 235 miles south to Kingsville for our third game in five days. Actually, we stopped for a much needed rest seventy-five miles north of Kingsville in Beeville. We lost that game to A&I, spent the night in Beeville, and returned to Austin the next day. I was worn out and I vowed to never again play that many tough games in such a short time on the road, no matter what the money guarantee might be. We beat Tarleton State one night later at home and got revenge two weeks later at home against Texas A&I. Big State schools almost never beat Lone Star schools so I was pretty happy going into the Christmas break. But I had never been so tired in my life.

In my four years at St. Ed's, we had a combined 15-1 record against Mary Hardin-Baylor and Huston-Tillotson, the two teams that usually finished at the bottom of the conference standings. But, unfortunately, this was the year that we lost to Huston-Tillotson by one point at their little gym just four or five miles away in East Austin. That loss ended up keeping us from finishing in second place outright behind St. Mary's. Instead, we tied with Southwestern and East Texas Baptist for second. We lost the coin flip and were forced into a two game playoff for a spot in the NAIA District IV playoffs. Fortunately, we won the flip for home court advantage and beat ETBU 69-64, then Southwestern 74-66 the very next night. We were then paired with Sam Houston who had finished first in their conference. If we could get by them in Huntsville, we would play the winner of Stephen F. Austin and St. Mary's for a spot in the NAIA national tournament in Kansas City. Getting past Sam Houston would be a very tall order. They had beaten us by eleven points earlier in the season, were one of the top rated NAIA teams in the country, and would have home court advantage.

But we had almost a week to prepare and we had won eight of our last ten games. I thought that we had a reasonable chance to win the game but, if the odds makers had posted a line on NAIA games, we would surely have been double-digit underdogs. But my kids didn't disappoint. We battled valiantly all the way and, with less than thirty seconds to go in the game and Sam Houston ahead by one point, Jimmy Wright stole a pass and dribbled all the way for what appeared was to be an unmolested layup. But a Bearcat player came from behind, and delivered a blow which knocked Jimmy to the floor out-of-bounds. I couldn't believe it when no foul was called. We had to foul, they made two free throws, and Sam Houston won 72-69. To say the least, I was livid!! I later learned that this was the first college basketball game for the official responsible for the no-call. But I was hesitant to complain because the guy who was in charge of assigning officials in both conferences was Ed Norris, a legendary former St. Ed's coach who was still working with me part time in the Phys. Ed. Department.

In spite of the loss, I was still proud of our team. We had started slow, played a killer schedule, and finished strong to make the NAIA playoffs for the first time in many years. We would be losing Marcus

Jones, who made the all-conference team, but most of the other players that saw most of the playing time would be back next year. That included Larry Kruse, Jimmy Wright, Gus Benson, Jerry Farias, Steve Martin, Bradye McClure, Ellis Montet, and Robert Wilbourn. Marcus finished his short two year career at St. Ed's as undoubtedly one of the top players in St. Ed's history. I can't believe that he has never been voted into the school's athletic hall of fame. But none of my former players have been voted in and it probably has something to do with who their coach was and with who is doing the voting. But I'll have more on that later. All that I can say is that Marcus Jones, Don Loobeck, Larry Kruse, Johnny Campbell, and Jimmy Wright have to be five of the best players in St. Edward's basketball history. It is a shame that none of them are in the school's hall of fame while many others, with much lesser accomplishments other than longevity, have received the honor.

Other than my assistant Ernie Nieto, I didn't tell anyone at St. Ed's about my family land deal and I didn't even give him any of the details. I guess Ernie may have explained to my players why I drove my own car to the Texas A&M game. Anyway, shortly after the basketball season ended, I started getting visits from the head of the development office (I don't remember his name). By the way, "development office" is a nice name for "begging office". This guy had a real tough job because donations from alumni to the university had dried up over the years because the few who had money to give were dissatisfied with the direction that the university had been heading. I had sometimes been enlisted to seek help from former athletes but there were not many living in the state and those who did were not very cooperative. But I had come to enjoy St. Edward's and, after a second or third visit from the poor guy, I wrote a $1000 check to the university. That doesn't sound like much but things were so bad that it may have been the largest check that they got that year. I soon got a nice letter of appreciation from the president, Bro. Stephen Walsh.

Also, that spring (or maybe the spring before), I got a visit from the new director of the CAMP (migrant) program who explained to me that the new administration in Washington under conservative president Ronald Reagan, was threatening to cut funding unless the program became more racially diversified. After almost ten years at St. Ed's, there had never been a single student in the program who was not Hispanic. This guy was from Florida and he wanted to enlist me to go there and recruit students in an area around Lake Okeechobee where there were a lot of Black migrant farm workers. He said that most of the high schools in the area were known for their strong athletic teams and that, since CAMP fully covered the freshman year, I wouldn't have to use scholarship money. When he offered to pay my expenses for a full week, I gladly accepted and soon both Jo and I were off to a working spring break vacation in Florida. Before leaving, I somehow came up with a list of all the basketball prospects from high schools in the migrant area (both boys and girls).

The two high schools that had most of the migrant students were Pahokee and Belle Glade, both on the shores of Lake Okeechobee. When we drove in to Pahokee, I felt at home when I saw a sign on the outskirts of town that said "Welcome to Pahokee, the boyhood home of Mel Tillis". Mel was always one of my favorite country western singers. Both Pahokee and Belle Glade could have been mistaken for poverty stricken towns in Haiti or any other of the destitute communities on the poor islands of the Caribbean. I met with the administrators and counselors at both schools, explained what the CAMP program at St. Ed's was all about, and when I left, I felt like the Pied Pieper with all these poor kids following behind in an effort to get out of all this poverty. I went up the road to several other schools in the area and my efforts eventually led to enough Black students being admitted into the program that the government was satisfied. Several of them were decent athletes who had stellar careers at St. Ed's. One of them, Ginger Brown from Pahokee, still holds several rebounding records for the St. Ed's women's basketball team. But Ginger is still not in the St. Edward's athletic hall of fame even though I have personally nominated her. I wonder why? Could it be that Dan Montgomery was responsible for her being admitted to the university? I wouldn't go so far to say that my efforts that spring saved the CAMP program from extinction but I will take some credit for satisfying the government's requirement that it become more diverse. And one last thing regarding my efforts to help CAMP – I even signed up the program's first Anglo student, Charlie Hoes, who was a 6'7" son of a cotton gin worker in Joshua, a small town south of Fort Worth. I have no idea how a worker at a local cotton gin qualified as a migrant but I do know that the federal government sometimes works in mysterious ways. Had my dad's gin not burned down before I was born in 1939, I may have qualified for CAMP myself.

Bro. Henry was not much of a sports fan and very seldom attended any athletic events. But one of the few basketball games that he did attend happened to be the one that a student hit a half court shot at halftime to win $100. Almost all colleges had done this for several years to boost attendance and so had we, although no one had ever made the shot. But Bro. Henry had never seen this before and thought that it was a great idea. But, concerned about how we covered the $100 payment to the lucky student, he called the next day to find out. I told him that I had kept a $100 bill of my own in my billfold just in case the shot went in. The next day I got a call from the business office to come pick up a check for $100. My boss, with whom I had nothing in common, and I were becoming big buds. I didn't know it at the time, but my friendship with Bro. Henry didn't sit too well with some of the other decision makers on campus.

When I became athletic director at St. Edward's in the spring of 1979, I let everybody know that I wanted to upgrade the program to a higher level. While I couldn't do much about the inferior facilities (although stalls separating the toilets in the women's locker room was a tiny start), I wanted to upgrade non-conference scheduling in all four team sports and to improve our chances to at least enter the NAIA District IV playoffs. St. Edward's had lagged behind in both of those areas for far too long. In order to boast of winning season records, prior coaches had scheduled inferior non-scholarship schools for non-conference games and had almost never finished near the top in conference play in any sport. Hardly anyone in the Austin area even knew that St. Edward's fielded athletic teams. Big State Conference scholarship limitations made it difficult for us to do well against schools in higher rated conferences but I felt that competing against them would get us more publicity and would also help recruiting. And, in the end, the only thing that really mattered was how we finished in conference play. But I got some push back, especially from John Knorr.

Although we had only four baseball scholarships, Coach Knorr believed in playing between fifty and sixty games a year and scheduled double headers as often as he could. Most knowledgeable baseball people know that pitching is the key to winning baseball games and that, with only four scholarships, it is impossible to have enough quality pitching to succeed while playing that many games in a period of three or four months. The schools that finished at the top of the conference standings every year (St. Mary's and Texas Lutheran) were the two that played only thirty or thirty-five games each year. But, in spite of not ever reaching the playoffs, John always boasted of a winning season although only he would know. I, as well as others at St. Ed's, suspected serious embellishment since he also falsely claimed that he played baseball at Notre Dame. He had no idea at the time that something called Google would come along and that the rosters of every baseball team in Notre Dame's history would be posted on the internet. But John also had some positives. He was a hard worker who took great care of the baseball field meaning that I didn't have to do much at all in that area. Also, he was a devout Roman Catholic and I always assumed that he did a good job in the classroom. And, except for his stubbornness about playing too many games, I always thought that he was a fairly competent coach.

The CAMP program at St. Ed's, through federal funding, was in charge of a summer program for migrant high school students at Ben Bolt-Palito, a tiny school district in South Texas near Alice. For some reason that I never understood, Dr. Hinkle had a summer job as some type of administrator for the program although he often bragged that

145

he spent only a couple of days each summer on site. But, after a new CAMP director was hired, Bro. Henry gave the summer job to him. This caused a nasty feud between Hinkle and Bro. Henry and I would later unwittingly get caught up in the middle of it. One was my boss on the academic side and the other was my boss on the administrative side, and each side was responsible for half my salary.

After almost three years on the job, Dr. Hinkle and I had hit it off very well. He loved sports, had strong opinions about college athletics, and often talked about his football playing days at some small college in Nebraska. He had been faculty athletics representative at St. Ed's for several years and was very proud of that. Although he was head of the Education Department where I taught a couple of classes each semester, he hardly ever discussed academic matters with me. He loved to play golf and was golfing buddies with Jim Koch, our golf coach, who was an Economics professor at St. Ed's. When I was hired, Glen told me that a requirement for using the golf course at Lost Creek Country Club was that we pay for two golf memberships there. And, wouldn't you just know it – Dr. Hinkle had somehow become the unpaid assistant golf coach which allowed him to play golf with Jim at Lost Creek at any time. I accepted this as fact and put the $3200 ($1600 for each membership) in my budget request to Bro. Henry every year. But when I met with him in the spring of 1982 to go over the proposed budget for the next year, he balked at approving more than one membership. He advised me to call the club and find out if we could still use the course with just one membership. He also opened the Big State Conference rule book and pointed out a rule that prohibited the faculty athletics rep from holding a coaching position. I went to my office and called the Lost Valley course director, who told me that they would be glad to have us with just one membership. I asked Bro. Henry to deliver the news to our soon to be fired assistant golf coach but he refused, saying that was my job as athletic director. I'm not sure that Dr. Hinkle ever spoke to me again. And, to make matters worse, he had tenure and I didn't. I was lucky, at least at the time, that he had no power to fire me. I was very disappointed that

Glen reacted in this way toward me because I was his friend and had enjoyed my relationship with him.

In spite of this petty controversy, I went about my business of preparing for the next season. Most of the members of the basketball team were returning so I had to bring in only two or three players. DeNell Davis , a 6'5" kid from Johnston High School, was the top player in Austin that year and I was able to convince him to stay at home and become a Hilltopper. DeNell was a very good kid and was probably a good enough player to sign at a mid-major Division I school. I also signed another former Dallas high school player, Barry Dowell, who was finishing up at Grayson Community College in Denison. Marcus Jones was graduating and would hard to replace, but I still looked forward to a banner year in 1982-83. My part time assistant Ernie Nieto was leaving to spend more time on his community activities so I would have to hire a replacement. Lots of high school coaches wanted to enter college coaching regardless of the pay so I had many applicants. But I was hesitant to hire someone who had no visible means of support, so I hired David McKey, whose wife Lori was a Certified Public Accountant and would have no problem finding a good paying job in Austin. David had coached for three years at Kountze, a small school in southeast Texas, but was presently employed at an oil refinery in Port Arthur. Although David and Lori were much younger, Jo and I became fast friends with them and we remain so today even though David was with me for only one season.

As a political conservative, I was opposed to tenure for teachers at any level. It was my view that, if a teacher or professor was not doing a good job in the classroom, the administration had every right to remove him or her and hire a more capable replacement. As a result, I never bothered to educate myself as to what the tenure policies at St. Edward's were. I had no idea that, if an assistant professor (whatever that meant) survived four years at the school, he or she had tenure and could not be fired except for the most egregious crimes such as murder in the first degree. I assumed that, if the department head never visited with me concerning my poor teaching performance, I must be doing a pretty good job and need not worry about tenure policies. But Dr. Hinkle was so upset with me over losing his golf privileges at the country club that he enlisted the help of John Knorr, who wanted to get his job of athletic director back, plus a few other tenured professors in the Education Department to vote against me receiving tenure before I completed four years of service. But I still was not too concerned because I couldn't imagine that a majority would vote against me and I knew that I had the support of Bro. Henry Altmiller, who had become a bitter enemy of Dr. Hinkle.

Life for us in Austin had been good for the past three years. Barton Hills was a great neighborhood with a great school, Barton Hills Elementary, just a few blocks from our house. Adam was completing kindergarten there and would be entering first grade in the fall. Two of Jo's kids, Leslie and Darryl, had jobs in Austin, Kelly was in nursing school at Schreiner in Kerrville, and Randy was married and living in College Station. We had good friends in the neighborhood, most of whom were parents of kids that were classmates of Adam. Jo had a part time job as a bookkeeper for a small company in South Austin and, although I had grand ambitions to climb up the college coaching ladder, I was pretty content to stay where I was, at least for the near future. Entering the 1982-83 school year, I felt that I had no reason to fret about my job security. But when Bro. Henry announced that he was resigning his administrative post and returning to the classroom in the fall, I began to worry a bit.

Bro. Stephen Walsh, our president, was out of the country a lot during my time at St. Edward's, supposedly because of the branch that St. Edward's had started in the Samoan Islands. When the school year started in 1982, he had been away for several months and nobody seemed to know when he would return. I guess that Bro. Henry had been the acting president in Austin since he was the executive vice-president at the time. When he stepped down that fall, we learned that Dr. Bob Mugerauer, the Academic Dean, would become the acting Executive Vice-President and that Sister Jean Burbo, the Dean of Students, would become Academic Dean. Even though he had been at St. Ed's since 1980, I had never met Dr. Mugerauer but I had seen him around campus a few times and I remember him as an unkempt, shaggy haired young guy who always wore sandals with no socks. The word around campus was that he was an extreme liberal, and he certainly looked the part. Sister Jean was a fixture on campus but I didn't know much about her. I had never seen either Dr. Mugerauer or Sister Jean at an athletic event.

In mid-November, just prior to our first basketball game, I received a call from Dr. Mugerauer's secretary who wanted to set up an appointment for me to meet with him in a couple of days. I assumed that this would be an opportunity to get to know my new boss in the administrative area for the first time. But, after we introduced ourselves, the first thing out of his mouth was to inform me that I had been denied tenure by a vote of my colleagues in the Center for Teaching and Learning (Education department), and that I would no longer have a job as an assistant professor at the university after the current academic year. That was shocking news for me but, when I asked how that would affect my position as men's basketball coach and athletics director, he seemed dumbfounded as though he didn't even know that I held those positions. In fact, I doubt that he even knew that St. Edward's fielded athletic teams. If I remember correctly, his answer was that he would have to get back with me on that. He never did so I assumed that I would have to wait for Bro. Stephen to return for an answer to that question. Meanwhile, Dr. Hinkle, John Knorr, and Diane Daniels all went out of their way to avoid any contact with me. That told me who in the department voted to deny me tenure. But I knew who they were anyway. Dr. Hinkle was mad about losing his golf club membership, John wanted his old job as athletics director back, and Diane was too lazy to get behind my efforts to upgrade the women's athletic program. In fact, Diane would have been perfectly happy with no women's program at all. The votes of these three to deny tenure for me had nothing whatsoever to do with my performance in the classroom.

Since a new basketball season was just beginning, I decided to, as best I could, put all of this out of my mind and concentrate on the season ahead. Other than my wife, I told nobody about it and, as far as I could tell, nobody on campus, other than those involved, knew anything about it. Bro. Stephen would eventually return from wherever it was that he had been and I would hopefully get some clarity from him. But I felt bad for my new assistant coach David McKey, who had quit a good paying job in an oil refinery to be my assistant for a measly $3000 per year. In addition, he was enrolled in classes at Southwest Texas State in San Marcos in an effort to obtain a Master's degree. So, on an early season trip to West Texas to play back-to-back games against McMurry in Abilene and Howard Payne in Brownwood, I delivered the news to him. I assured him that nothing was final and that I could possibly reverse things with a meeting with the president of the university.

As usual, our non-conference schedule was brutal, and we got off to a very slow start. But we had some good experienced players plus one or two good recruits and I felt that our conference chances were pretty decent. If we could get to the playoffs and do well there, I would probably have a good chance to move to a better coaching job anyway. One plus for us was that the Lone Star Conference had moved to NCAA Division II, meaning that we wouldn't have to compete against their champion in the NAIA district playoffs for a spot in the national tournament. In fact, for that one year, the second place team in our conference would play on the road against our first place team for the District IV championship. As it turns out, we finished again in a three way tie for second place with Southwestern and East Texas Baptist, which was an exact replica from the year before. But, because the Lone Star Conference had made a late decision to drop out of the NAIA, there was a long break between the regular season and the playoffs. As a result, I had scheduled season ending games on the road against two Division I teams, Hardin Simmons and Pan American. This meant that the playoff to decide which team would face St. Mary's for the District IV championship would be delayed for more than a week. We beat Hardin Simmons 67-64 in Abilene for the first win ever for a St. Ed's team against a Division I team. Three days later, we flew to the Rio Grande Valley to play Pan Am in Edinburg. Many of our players had never been in an airplane before. Jerry Farias was a legend in the Valley and his parents arranged for us to cross the border and have dinner at a nice restaurant in Reynosa. The following night, we lost to Pan-Am under its young coach Lon Kruger (now the head coach at the University of Oklahoma) but it was a great experience for our players and we looked forward to the upcoming playoffs. Pan Am gave us a hefty guarantee but they probably came out ahead because of the crowd that came out to see Jerry Farias play. It was very unusual at the time, and still is, for a Hispanic kid from the Rio Grande Valley to play on a college basketball team.

Unlike the year before when we had home court advantage against both Southwestern and East Texas Baptist, we lost both coin flips and had to play both on the road. Our game in Georgetown against Southwestern was a nail biter but we won by two points on a last second shot by Bradye McClure. Two nights later, we played 275 miles away in Marshall against East Texas Baptist. We always traveled by chartered bus to games that far away and, for this one, I chartered a second bus for our students. Because of my "lame duck" situation at St. Ed's, nobody seemed to want to be my boss, so I pretty much did as I pleased. I hadn't talked to anyone above my pay grade since November and both Glen Hinkle and John Knorr avoided me like the plague. But, for the first time, our students were excited about basketball and I was determined to take advantage of it. We beat ETBU that night 65-58, and were now just one game away from the NAIA national tournament. This would be decided just two nights later in San Antonio against St. Mary's and, while the team traveled on our two vans, I chartered a bus for the students.

Our game against St. Mary's that night was my biggest challenge ever in my four years at St. Ed's. It had been a trying year for me and we had not had a great year on the court. But, as usual, we had rallied near the end, and were now in a position to possibly do something that a Hilltopper team in any sport had never done – play in a national tournament. Just prior to tipoff, David McKey tapped me on the shoulder to alert me that three people (Glen Hinkle, John Knorr, and Sister Jean Burbo) were taking their seats in the stands behind us. I had never seen Sister Jean at an athletic event of any kind, and both Hinkle and Knorr had not, to my knowledge, been to a single basketball game all year. Plus, none of them had spoken to me since my meeting with Bob Mugerauer in mid-November. Now, here they were, supposedly supporting our effort to do something that no Hilltopper team had ever done. I told Coach McKey that they should be in the St. Mary's cheering section where they belonged.

We didn't play well that night in San Antonio and we lost by fourteen points. Larry Kruse was my first recruit and had been with me for four years. He was a great player at St. Ed's but didn't have a great night. Alan Catalani had also been with me for all four years and stuck with us in spite of not seeing much playing time. He was part of a prominent San Antonio family that was in the produce business, and could have attended any school in the country without an athletic scholarship. Had I been Alan, I would have probably transferred, but he didn't and I appreciated that. Larry married Liz Hernandez, a member of our women's team, and has had a successful coaching career at Harlingen in the Rio Grande Valley. He is in the top ten in several statistical categories of all-time St. Ed's basketball records but, even after I personally nominated him, he is still not in the St. Edward's Hall of Fame. But guess what? Both John Knorr and Glen Hinkle received that honor while both were members of the committee that did the choosing. Knorr had a mediocre coaching career at St. Ed's and Hinkle may be the only hall of fame member in the history of any school who was never anything more than a faculty athletic representative. And Diane Daniels is a member too. I was her boss for four years and I have never witnessed a lazier or more incompetent coach. Is it sour grapes on my part because I am not a hall of famer? Absolutely not. My overall record at St. Ed's was 59-62, which certainly doesn't qualify me for anything. It would be an absolute joke if I were even nominated.

After the season ended, I learned that Dr. Stephen Walsh was finally returning to the campus so I requested a meeting with him as soon as possible after his return to discuss my status at St. Ed's. When I arrived at his office, the first thing that he did was hand me a check for $1000, which was a refund for the donation that I had made to the university the year before. After assuring me that my job as athletics director and basketball coach was not in danger, he explained that he had to honor the decision of the Education Department to deny me tenure, and that my job as assistant professor would end at the end of the semester in May. Since this would mean that I would lose half my salary, there is no way that I could stay but I didn't tell anyone this. I resumed my job as if nothing had happened and eventually collected my full salary until the end of August.

Although I had not made my decision to leave public, word soon got out among members of the college coaching fraternity that I was out as coach at St. Ed's. Several coaches interested in replacing me called to inquire. One was Tom Pate, an assistant coach at Stephen F. Austin University in Nacogdoches. Tom, and his twin brother Ty, had played for me on the junior varsity team at Houston Jones High school in the mid -sixties. Their dad Harvey had been a long time top assistant to Guy Lewis at the University of Houston. I told Tom that I was not planning to return for just half my current salary but that I was holding off making the announcement as long as I was receiving a salary from St. Ed's. I also told him that, no matter what, he should never let it be known that I had ever been his coach. I also got him to promise me that he would try to keep my assistant David McKey. Tom never told anyone about his relationship with me and he was eventually hired as my replacement. But, as I predicted, John Knorr replaced me as athletics director and Tom had to work under him. Tom Pate did a credible job as coach for several years at St. Ed's before he was eventually fired as coach. But he stayed long enough to gain tenure as a professor and I believe that he still teaches at least part-time at St. Ed's. Tom also kept Coach McKey although he paid him only $1000. Coach McKey eventually became the winningest coach, in any sport, in St. Edward's athletic history as the women's basketball coach.

My relationship with the women's basketball coach Sharon McIlroy had been excellent and it continued that way throughout my ordeal. A policy at the time was that the athletics director had to sign off on all scholarships, both when awarded and also if and when they were revoked. One day during the spring of my final semester, Sharon asked me to sign off on the revoking of the scholarship of her very best player. I think that this was the only time that I was asked to do this for any coach during my time there. Sharon seemed a bit nervous and was vague as to the reason she wanted to take this action. The player in question was not only her top player, but she also made good grades and never had been in any trouble as far as I knew. I politely refused to sign and told her that I wanted to talk to the young lady myself before I would agree to do so. Sharon said that she would have her come by and visit with me. It never happened and, because I was occupied with determining my future, I forgot about it. But several months later, after I had left Austin, I received a call from an attorney who told me that the girl who had lost her scholarship had filed a lawsuit against St. Edward's, Sharon McIlroy, and me. She claimed that her scholarship had been revoked because she had broken off a relationship that she had with Coach McIlroy. I had no idea why I was part of the lawsuit because I was unaware of any sexual relationship between the two and had also not signed the scholarship revocation. But I was ordered to testify at a deposition in Abilene (I was living near there at the time). Lawyers for all parties were present at the deposition and I was presented with a copy of the scholarship revocation that I had supposedly signed. But it was obviously not my signature and I testified to that fact. I guess that everybody at the deposition believed that my signature had been forged because I was removed as a defendant in the suit and never heard another word about the case. I always thought that Sister Jean Burbo forged my signature on the form but I have no concrete evidence to prove that. Sharon stayed on as coach for one more year and was replaced as women's coach by my former assistant David McKey. To this day, I don't know what Sharon

McIlroy did and, if she did something wrong, I forgive her. All I know is that she did a great job in turning around the women's program at St. Ed's and that she was loyal to me until the very end.

In an effort to continue my college coaching career, I looked into every job that was available. But there weren't many and all of the few openings attracted scores of qualified applicants. I could have always returned to high school coaching but, after four years as a college coach, I was not ready to do that. I also was not particularly interested in coaching at the junior college level but, when I learned that my friend Tommy Collins was leaving Cisco Junior College, I called an old family friend from my childhood days, Carroll Scott, who was the vice president at Cisco at the time. Within a few days, Carroll had pulled some strings and I was offered the job there as men's basketball coach and physical education instructor. Although I would not be the director of athletics (which I was glad to know), I would still be making more money. In addition, Cisco offered twelve full scholarships for basketball, had a much larger recruiting budget, and the facilities were much nicer. Those were the upsides. But the overwhelming downside was that Cisco was a tiny burned out oilfield town that, as my wife put it after she visited, "had not one redeeming feature". But another upside was that my salary would start immediately and would not affect my continuing salary at St. Edward's, which didn't end until the end of August. I still was reluctant to leave Austin for such a nondescript location and considered changing professions, but Jo convinced me that I was too young to abandon my love of coaching basketball. I had done this for almost a quarter of a century and was still only forty-three years old.

CHAPTER **14**

The Wild and Wacky World of Juco Basketball (Cisco)

CISCO IS A small town off of IH-20, about 100 miles west of Fort Worth and forty miles east of Abilene. It is famous as the location of Conrad Hilton's first hotel as well as the Santa Claus Bank Robbery (a man dressed as Santa held up the bank in the 1920's). The junior college is located on a hill just north of downtown. By the time we arrived in the summer of 1983, it was obvious that the town, like most little oil boom and bust towns in West Texas, had seen better days. Most of the buildings on the main street, Conrad Hilton Boulevard, were either empty or would soon be. But Cisco Junior College seemed to be alive and well, mostly because of the large number of athletes, band members, and drill team members who lived on campus. If not for athletics, especially football, the college would have a hard time surviving. I doubt that more than ten students who were not involved in one of these three activities lived on campus while enrolled in classes at the school.

A real problem for us was finding a decent place to live. There were only a few nice homes in town but almost none were for sale or rent. However, we eventually found a nice place across the street from the Methodist Church and I offered $70,000 cash for it. We deposited $3000 in earnest money and planned to move in soon after closing. But Jo visited the town without me a few days later and found another

Cisco JC Wranglers, 1985 conference champs

house for rent for $400 a month. It was just as nice or nicer and was in a better location so we decided to back out of the other deal even though we lost our earnest money payment. I'm glad that we did because I'm sure that it would have been nearly impossible to sell if we ever left. We had no plans to live in Cisco for the rest of our lives but, as it turns out, we were pretty happy there. We became active in the Methodist Church and Jo quickly made several close friends, many of whom are still our friends today. Fortunately, Jo didn't have to work so she spent most of her time socializing with her circle of friends. Adam entered second grade that year. The schools were not as good as his elementary school in Austin but he adjusted quickly and did very well.

There is an old saying that "West Texans don't have much shine on them but they are some of the best people in the world". I found that to be true for the most part but many of our friends in Cisco had a little bit of "shine" on them as well. Probably our closest friends there were Jamie and Arlene Fry. Arlene was a part-time recruiter for the junior college and Jamie was a rancher who also owned liquor stores on two county lines (Cisco is in a dry county). Jamie had to stock his Putnam store with more tequila after we arrived because Jo makes the best margarita ever and, back then, she made them pretty often.

While we and many of our friends were Methodists, most people in Cisco were either Baptists or members of the Church of Christ. The Church of Christ (or "Campbellites" as members were often called) was very strong in West Texas, especially within a one hundred mile radius of Abilene where Abilene Christian University is located. An old worn out joke goes – "Where do Campbellites go when they die?" Answer – "Abilene". (Substitute "Baptists" for " Campbellites" and the answer is "Waco"). Anyway, we Methodists, as well as members of other "mainline" congregations, made up a very small minority of the population, and, since local school boards were controlled by members of the Baptist Church and/or Church of Christ, dancing was not allowed at school sponsored parties and proms. Anson, a small town north of Abilene, even had a city ordinance that prohibited dancing in the city limits. Thus the term -- "No dancin' in Anson". Some people say that even smiling is frowned upon in some towns in the area but I never believed that to be true.

CJC sponsored only three sports – football, men's basketball, and women's basketball. The basketball teams competed in the North Texas Junior College Conference against Ranger (only twenty miles away), Weatherford, Hill County (Hillsboro), McLennan County (Waco), TSTI (Waco), Southwest Christian (Terrell), Cooke County (Gainesville), and Grayson County (Denison). The football team was not in a conference at the time because six of the eight schools in the state that played football had kicked both Cisco and Ranger out of the conference because they refused to abide by the conference's strict thirty-three player squad limit. All schools were allowed thirty-three scholarships but Cisco and Ranger wanted to divide them up in a way that would allow more than one hundred players in an effort to fill up empty dormitories on campus. The other schools had enough full paying non-athletes to fill up their dormitories.

Except for our location at the far western edge of the conference, we had a decent situation relative to most of the other members of our basketball conference in that we awarded twelve full scholarships and the players could also keep half of any federal grants that they might receive. Only McLennan and Grayson had as good or better situation for basketball. Plus, since basketball requires far fewer players than football, there was no pressure on me to award partial scholarships in order to increase enrollment. But, in spite of these advantages, our location and small community with an almost all-white population made it a real challenge for me to recruit and keep players who could play winning junior college basketball. There were very few basketball prospects in west Texas high schools and, the few that were there were scooped up by the many junior colleges in the state located to the west of us. Almost all Texas high school basketball prospects that are destined for junior colleges reside in the inner cities and in some suburbs and small towns in the eastern third of the state. At least twenty junior colleges in Texas are closer to the prospects than Cisco and are in larger towns with larger Black populations. As a result, I had to do the best I could in Texas but I would also have to recruit players from states that had no junior colleges that awarded basketball scholarships. That would be the Deep South states. I decided that I would concentrate on the large metropolitan areas of Texas plus east Texas, Florida, Louisiana, and Arkansas. I already had contacts in Florida and the other two states made sense because both bordered on Texas and neither had junior colleges that awarded athletic scholarships.

The other guys in the CJC athletics department were great. Ace Prescott, the athletics director, was an older former football coach who did everything possible to make life easier for the coaches. Bob Keyes was the head football coach (he had only two assistants) and was great to work with. He and his wife lived in and supervised the dorm where the basketball players lived and the players all loved them. Ronnie Hearne was the women's coach and was one of the best coaches with whom I ever worked. He had an advantage in that almost all his players were from small towns in west or north Texas where girls' basketball was second only to football in the high schools. Both Bob and Ronnie were devout Christians and were both members of the Church of Christ. I knew that I would never have a problem in working with any of these three guys.

My predecessor Tommy Collins was a good coach but he didn't leave me with very good players. He had signed only one player for the coming year and, because I took the job late, most of the decent prospects had already signed with other schools. But, fortunately, my efforts to boost the CAMP program at St. Edward's paid off for me in a big way at Cisco. Anthony Bryant, a 6'5" rail thin kid from Pahokee, Florida, had been one of the first CAMP students at St. Ed's to make the basketball team. He had played sparingly during his freshman year but CAMP covered only the freshman year and my successor Tom Pate was not able to offer him a full scholarship. But I took a chance on him and he transferred with me to Cisco. But, more importantly, his friend Melven Jones was also from Pahokee, and was one of the best high school players in the state of Florida. Melven was a Division I prospect but his grades would not allow him to receive a Division I scholarship. So he came with Anthony to Cisco and, mainly because of him, we made the NJCAA playoffs both years that he was there. Melven was heavily recruited by Division I schools and he eventually chose the University of Florida over Miami University. Anthony signed with Valdosta State, a Division II school on the south border of Georgia.

In spite of the fact that Melven Jones was gone, we won the Northern Texas Junior College championship in my third year at Cisco with a 13-3 conference record, a full three games ahead of the second place finisher McLennan. The contacts that I had built in Florida were paying off and I had also succeeded in signing several good players from Louisiana. McLennan had been the dominant power in the conference for several years, largely because of their location in Waco, the largest city in the conference. They also had great facilities plus Waco had a large Black population and was located in an area near the large metropolitan areas where most of the best high school players in Texas came from. Also, Baylor oftentimes directed players their way who didn't have the grades to be admitted to an NCAA school. The best example is Vinnie Johnson, an NBA star, who played at McLennan before being admitted to Baylor. But, in spite

MY TEXAS LIFE IN THE (NOT SO) FAST LANE

Melven Jones from Pahokee, Fl, my best player ever at Cisco

of winning our conference, we lost in the first game at the regional tournament to New Mexico Junior College even though they were the fourth place finisher in the Western Conference. In my six full years at Cisco, we played in four regional tournaments and lost every game to a Western Conference team. This was probably the strongest junior college conference in the nation and produced many NBA players. It was very unusual for a team in our conference to win against a team from the West.

During my six and a half years at Cisco there were three different presidents. The first one, Norman Wallace, left after my first year and was replaced by Dr. John McCullough, a rough edged East Texan. Dr. McCullough was fired after four years at the helm and was replaced by Dr. Roger Schustereit. I always said that it would be easier to screw up a steel ball or a one car funeral procession than to screw up a junior college, but some of them tried anyway. Dr. Wallace was there for several years and did pretty much nothing to upset the status quo but Dr. McCullough thought, for some reason, that he needed to change things a bit. For many years the college, with only 600 students, was overloaded with non-teaching administrators who didn't appear to have anything to do. But they were suddenly put back in the classroom and one vice-president was brought in to replace all of them. Dr. McCullough also introduced a new salary schedule based on years of experience and hours towards a doctorate that, lucky for me, increased my salary quite a bit. All of the displaced administrators loathed the guy but I had no opinion one way or another. Then, after we won the conference championship, Dr. McCullough called me in and said he was tripling my coaching stipend. I was surprised that he even knew that we had won the championship but I was happy to accept anyway. I told nobody about the salary increase and I don't think that Ace Prescott, the athletics director, even knew. Looking back, I was one of the few people on campus that wasn't cutting the president's throat and he appreciated me for it. But after Dr. McCullough left, things weren't so rosy for me.

Like most of my colleagues in the JUCO coaching world, I was always looking to move up the coaching ladder. Most of the players at Cisco were from towns from far away. Unlike Austin, where the students had lots to keep them occupied in their spare time, there was no campus life and absolutely nothing to occupy their time in town. I spent most of my time trying to convince players to stay or dealing with mostly minor discipline problems that they were involved in on campus. Sometimes the problems weren't so minor and I had to send players home. In addition, only two of our opponents (Ranger and Weatherford) were located in easy driving distance, which meant long hours on the 20-passenger school van (which I drove) usually on school nights. Very few people in town had any interest in our athletic teams and about our only fans were the football players, who lived in a dorm next to the gym and had nothing better to do. Probably the worst part for me was the fact that many players had graduated high school with reading levels of sixth grade or below, requiring them to take development courses which didn't transfer to four year schools. Needless to say, I was always looking for another job but one at another junior college was not an option.

About the only advantage that we had over many of our opponents was that our players could keep half of the grant money that they would have received had they not been on an athletic scholarship. This allowed them to have some spending money and to be able to pay for trips home on occasion. Had this not been the case, I would have had to recruit players within a hundred mile radius of Cisco, and this would be totally disastrous. Not so bad for schools located near big metropolitan areas in the eastern part of the state, but not good for a place with our location. But after Dr. Roger Schustereit became president in 1988, changes occurred. He had a meeting with the three head coaches to get our input before making a final decision about ending the policy of allowing athletes to keep part of their grant money. The football coach at the time, Rick Frazier, didn't care one way or another since football was already being used to bring in over a hundred players with only thirty-three scholarships. Ronnie Hearne, the women's coach, was opposed to the change but it didn't affect him as much since most his players were Anglo kids from the area who didn't usually qualify for grants. But I respectfully outlined my reasons to oppose the change with no argument back and forth at all. He called us back in a few days later to announce that he was making the change, but that students already enrolled would be "grandfathered" under the old scholarship rules. I reluctantly accepted the change and never discussed it with him again. His goal for men's basketball was twenty-four students on twelve scholarships. This was way too many for a basketball roster but he didn't care as long as all twenty-four stayed through the twelfth class day since enrollment on that day determined the amount of funding provided by the state. For years, the busiest day at the service station/Greyhound bus station in Cisco was the thirteenth class day when football players learned that they had not made the traveling squad. Unfortunately, because of President Schusteriet's mandate, twelve basketball players would be joining them soon and most of them would be east bound. I soon stepped up my efforts to find another coaching job.

From a financial standpoint, our years in Cisco were good. Although my salary was not high, it was more than I had made at St. Edward's and my investments were doing well. In addition, we learned that the EPA was not going to allow the wells that would be under water on our former property to continue production so we were forced to sell our mineral rights and all future oil and gas production to the water district. The financial settlement was not what I wanted but my mother, sister, and I signed away our mineral rights for less than what we expected. But it was a fairly large payment to us anyway. The other two sides of the Montgomery family refused to sign and, as far as I know, have still not collected a dime of mineral royalties on the property. Jo and I always put most of any money that we luckily received into a conservative portfolio of stock and bond mutual funds and saved for the future. But we weren't entirely frugal, causing people in Cisco to wonder about us. Jo drove around town in a used, but nice, red Cadillac and we traveled extensively during the month that I was off in the summer. While we were in Cisco, we took two trips to Europe and one to Russia. And I've lost count of the number of cruises and Las Vegas trips. We also loved the Texas Hill Country, especially Fredericksburg. We even rented a small cottage just off the main square and visited there often. Fredericksburg wasn't the "theme park" that it is today but it was already becoming very popular with tourists and retired people from all over the country.

During the spring of 1986 I became almost laughingly involved in local politics. Our friend Jamie Fry wanted to run for county commissioner as a Republican. But Eastland County was staunchly Democratic at the time and the Cisco precinct had not had a Republican primary election since Reconstruction days. If you wanted to vote in a Republican primary, you had to go to the county courthouse in Eastland. And even then, there would be no candidates on the ballot below the state level. With no place to hold a primary election, we got the county Republican chairman Jim Keffer to allow Jo and me to hold the election at our house. With no elected precinct chairman, I was in charge of the election and Jo was named as my assistant. Jamie had no primary opponent and there were no other names on the Republican ballot for county positions. So it was just Jamie Fry for County Commissioner plus a few statewide candidates for various offices. No more than fifteen or twenty people voted that day and I got six write-in votes for precinct chair and Jo received five (she still receives a hard time from me about that). After the polls closed, as precinct chair, I had to go to our living room to conduct a precinct "convention" for four or five staunch followers of the televangelist Pat Robertson who was pushing for some kind of religious right resolution to be voted on at the county and state conventions. While I was conducting business of great importance in the living room, Jo, Jamie, and Jamie's wife Arlene were gulping down Jo's margaritas in the kitchen. After that day, other than for voting, I stayed completely out of politics until the year 2000. Jamie lost to the Democratic incumbent in November and he never entered politics again.

For the entire time that I was in Cisco, I looked for better coaching opportunities. But all the available jobs that were better than mine had scores of qualified applicants and I had never even been granted an interview. But that changed in the spring of 1989 when I became one of three finalists for the head coaching job at Western New Mexico University, a four year NAIA school in Silver City, New Mexico. Jo and I went there for my interview and absolutely loved the place. It was a small town located in the forested mountains of the western part of the state just east of the Arizona border. We had a great weekend there and I thought that I had a great interview. But, after returning home, I didn't hear from them until finally I got a letter saying that they were reopening the search. I was almost fifty at the time and had coached for thirty years. I pretty much gave up on moving up the coaching ladder at that point and my attitude wasn't all that great after that.

In spite of my bad attitude and the negative change in the scholarship situation, my basketball team performed surprisingly well during the first semester of the 1989-90 school year. The returning players from the year before were pretty good and we even beat Midland, one of the top JUCO programs in the country, in a tournament in Levelland just prior to the Christmas break. But I didn't like my team. There are always discipline problems on any college team but I had never experienced these kinds of problems before. The main problem was stealing. These guys stole from each other but they also stole equipment from the locker room such as shoes, towels, uniforms, basketballs, etc. We even lost the VCR player that we used to record games. It got so bad that, while players were in the locker room dressing for practice, my manager and I went to the dorm, entered the rooms (I had a master key), and hauled out tons of stolen goods. When I got back to the gym, I unloaded on them and we did nothing but "run lines" for the entire practice. I'm sure that a few were not guilty and some of them complained to the administration that I had invaded their privacy. But none of them quit. They all returned from Christmas break when practice began a few days before the second semester began in January. Among those that returned was Lewis Hicks, a super point guard who had not been eligible during the first semester.

Lewis was a definite Division I prospect out of South Garland High School in the Dallas area but his grades were not high enough for him to attend an NCAA school. I recruited him, as did many other JUCO coaches, but he chose to attend Paris Jr. College, a pretty good program, northeast of Dallas. I don't know what happened with him at Paris (I probably should have checked), but his high school coach called to tell me that he was no longer there, and asked if I would still be interested. Even though he would have to sit out a semester, he was such a great player that I took a chance and brought him to Cisco. After sitting out that first semester, he played during the conference season and didn't disappoint. He was a quiet kid and didn't outwardly cause any problems but, like so many other kids from a similar background, he had real problems in the classroom. Crazy me, I brought him back the following year even though he would not be eligible to play again during the fall semester. But surprisingly, he became eligible (or so I thought) and we would have him for the conference race in the spring of 1990. Things were looking pretty good for the Cisco College Wranglers, until they weren't.

During my last two years in Cisco, there was no athletic director. Ace Prescott had retired and there was really no need to replace him since there were only three athletic teams. Each head coach was responsible for his own program and, if there was an athletic director for a few things, I guess it would have been the college president. About the only thing that I can recall that needed a signature above that of the head coach was the eligibility certification list for each sport that had to be sent to the offices of the NJCAA. One of the assistant football coaches, Chuck Lawrence, was responsible for collecting the list from each coach. A couple of days before the certification list came due for the second semester, Coach Lawrence opened the door to my office to remind me about the eligibility list, and he also asked if Lewis Hicks had passed enough courses to be eligible. I replied in the affirmative but I thought it was a little strange that he would be asking specifically about Lewis. About an hour later, I got a call from Dr. Schustereit's secretary who requested that I meet with Dr. Schustereit the following morning. Sure enough, after checking the NJCAA rule book, I discovered that Lewis, because of an obscure rule regarding transfers from other junior colleges, would not be eligible after all. I was almost sure that the meeting scheduled for the following day would be about this matter. But I was wrong in a big way.

When I walked in to the president's office the next day, he got quickly to the point. My contract was not being renewed when it expired eighteen months in the future. I had no idea that I was on a two year contract and I had no plans to stay on for one more year anyway. The reason that he gave was "philosophical differences" which is a catchall phrase for "I really don't have a reason that I can explain, but I've decided to do it anyway". When pressed for specifics, he said something about the way I dealt with players even though he, or anyone else, had never talked to me about his concerns in this regard. I had no interest in staying for three semesters as a lame duck employee so I proposed a solution. I would resign immediately if I could be paid through my current contract year which would end in August. He agreed to poll board members and get back with me. A few hours later, I was no longer employed by CJC but would receive my monthly check (and insurance benefits) for the next eight months. But, before leaving the president's office, I told him about the ineligibility of Lewis Hicks. I'm sure that he had never heard that name before. I felt bad for my friend Coach Hearne, who would be tasked with coaching both the men's and women's team for the rest of the year. He was a very good coach and ended up finishing second in conference play. But I didn't bother to tell him about Lewis and they ended up having to forfeit all the games in which he played. I have no idea who certified Lewis as being eligible since Roger Schusteriet knew that he wasn't.

CHAPTER **15**

Living in a "Theme Park" and Life After Coaching (Fredericksburg)

I HAD NO idea what the future might hold for me. I was fifty years old and, after being turned down for the job at Western New Mexico the year before, I had little desire to look for another college job. Another JUCO job was completely out of the question and I had no interest in returning to the high school ranks. But I didn't have to make a quick decision because I would be paid for the next eight months for doing nothing. We had lost our lease on our first house in Cisco several months before because the owner wanted to move back in, and we were presently leasing a smaller house from one of our best friends. The lease on it wouldn't expire until the end of May. We still had the cottage in Fredericksburg and I had (stupidly) invested in a charter bus business in San Antonio which caused me nothing but problems, both financially and in my marriage. Long story short – I spent most of my time that spring shuttling between San Antonio, Fredericksburg, and Cisco. Adam was in eighth grade and Jo was substitute teaching almost every day in Cisco. But her last day was the one in which she had Dr. Schustereit's daughter in her fifth grade class. She got no more calls to substitute after that.

One night that spring, at a cocktail party that Jo and I attended in Cisco, a mid-level administrator at CJC told me that Roger Schustereit had frequently complained that the men's basketball coach (me) was the highest paid employee on campus below the administrative level. I had never thought about it since I was making only $32,000, but it may have been true given the fact that I was on an eleven month contract, had twenty-eight years of teaching experience plus twelve hours above a master's degree, and had been given a healthy coaching stipend increase by the previous president for winning a conference championship. Maybe this was the "philosophical difference" that Roger was talking about when he met with me in January.

After leaving Cisco, I didn't keep close tabs on the basketball team there. The following year, Doug Galyean, the coach at Ranger High School, became the coach. But he had to recruit players under Roger Schustereit's scholarship rules which took away any advantages that Cisco had over some of the other schools. He stayed for two or three years but resigned in the middle of the season, causing Ronnie Hearne to have to take over both teams again. After that, they went through a few more coaches before deciding to drop men's basketball altogether several years ago. They are probably the only college in the country today that has a football team but not a men's basketball team.

My coaching career had ended after thirty and one-half seasons, twenty-seven and a half of them as a head coach. My only losing seasons were my first one at Calvert in 1959-60, and my last three seasons at St. Edward's when I sacrificed wins for money to help finance our program. I don't know what my overall won-loss record as a coach was because I don't have any records from my last six plus years at Cisco. But I'm sure that my win total for all those years is close to six hundred.

Although we were in pretty good shape financially, I must admit that I felt some pressure after losing my job. But, during my thirty-plus year coaching career, I had faced numerous "pressure" situations. So has every coach who was in the profession for as long as I had been. But, putting all things into proper perspective, I'll quote a former NBA player whose name I can't recall. When asked if he felt pressure when he stepped to the free throw line with the game on the line, he replied, "No man, real pressure is six kids and two biscuits".

When we left Kerrville for Austin in 1979, I felt that we would probably return to the Hill Country sooner or later. We had the small rental cottage in Fredericksburg but it was too small for the three of us and all of our belongings. But we eventually stored our furniture in town and moved in. After a short stay, we found a larger place to rent in a neat historic building downtown on West Main Street which we loved in spite of all the tourists who sometimes mistook our place for an antique store. But Adam, who was entering high school at the time, got a dog and our landlord wasn't too happy with that. Soon after, we found a nice house with a swimming pool just three blocks off of Main Street and have been there ever since. At the time, I thought that we paid too much for it but, because of Fredericksburg's popularity with retirees, it is now worth at least five times the amount that we paid in 1991. The saddest part about our move back to the Hill Country was that Jo's mother, who lived in Boerne, unexpectedly passed away just prior to our move to Fredericksburg.

Jo soon found employment as a bookkeeper at the Admiral Nimitz Museum Foundation and, soon afterwards, I was hired as a yellow page ad salesman for United Directory Services (UDS), a small company that published several area-wide telephone directories in the Austin, San Antonio, and Hill Country areas. I had some experience in sales during the summers of my coaching career, and I quickly became the company's top salesman. In fact, I made more money my first seven months on the job than I had made in a year as a teacher/coach. I continued to do well all throughout the nineties until unbridled competition in the yellow page industry and the sudden growth of the internet brought an end to my new career. Eventually, UDS was bought out by a larger company which made things even worse, and my phone directory sales career ended in August, 2001. Although there were "characters" of all kinds in that business, I made lots of friends and I especially enjoyed the relationships that I developed with small business owners in the area.

Adam adjusted well in Fredericksburg and graduated from Fredericksburg High School (home of the Battlin' Billies) in 1994. He, along with a few of his friends, enrolled as a freshman at Texas A&M in the fall. Several years before, my mother and I each put $10,000 in a tax exempt college fund, and when he graduated in 1998, there was nine cents left in it. The nine cents is still in the fund at Fidelity Investments although I have tried several times, without success, to close the account. Adam was a great art student in high school, but he always had a dream to do something in the movie industry. A&M didn't have a film degree of any kind so he got a degree in economics. Soon after his graduation in 1998, he headed out to California, rented an apartment in the middle of Hollywood, and got a job in the mail room of a talent agency. He later got a job at Imagine Television, Ron Howard's company, and eventually was hired at Sundance Film Festivals, owned by Robert Redford. He has been the senior manager for programming for the Sundance Film Festival since 2005. I'm extremely proud of Adam and what he has accomplished and I love telling all my friends in Texas that "My boy is pretty big out there in Hollywood".

Somewhere along the way, Adam met and fell in love with a beautiful girl named Elizabeth Daly, who had grown up in Illinois and Florida. They eventually married and, in 2008, had a beautiful girl named Abigail or simply "Abbey". I don't know what we would do without the three of them and we don't get to see them nearly enough. Elizabeth worked at Sundance for a while and also was an executive for a non-profit organization that benefits the homeless population in Los Angeles. She is now is doing well in the real estate business there.

MY TEXAS LIFE IN THE (NOT SO) FAST LANE

Our Hollywood triplets – Adam, Elizabeth, and Abbey

CHAPTER **16**

Becoming "That Other Guy"

DURING MY LONG career in education and coaching, I guess I considered myself somewhat of an authority on both. When I left the profession I continued to be interested in sports but more so as a fan and observer rather than in coaching techniques and strategies. But education was different. I had taught at almost every level including six public high schools, a four year university, and a junior college. As a result, I became somewhat opinionated about the state of education in the country, especially in Texas. Public schools are burdened with compulsory attendance laws (which I wouldn't change) that require them to educate just about everybody who doesn't attend a private school or is home schooled. It is almost impossible to provide enough quality teachers (at low salaries) to educate so many children, especially when many of them have little interest in becoming educated. The task is multiplied by many other things such as changing demographics, which means the schools have to deal with the fact that so many students are far behind in English when they enroll.

But where I really became aware of our failures in public education was at the junior college level where open enrollment is the norm. A large percentage of the students at that level are simply not prepared for college work even though they have graduated from high school. Most of the athletes at Cisco had below sixth grade reading and math levels and had to take developmental courses before they could even enroll in regular college classes. The teachers of these courses were great and most of the students advanced to college courses fairly rapidly, which I thought was proof that this could have been done at the high school level had anybody bothered to care. So, after I left the profession, I became interested in solutions and read a lot about education. I became a follower of Dr. Thomas Sowell and William Bennett who were both conservatives with common sense ideas about how to improve public education. But I was just an interested observer and had no plans to re-enter the profession or to do anything regarding education. That changed in 2000, more than a decade after I had changed professions. In fact, it changed in a very big way.

I could have always run for a seat on the local school board if I'd wanted to be active in education reform. But my son had gone through high school in Fredericksburg and I felt that the local schools were in pretty good hands. My only complaint had to do with the athletic program where, at the time, football was emphasized at the expense of the other sports. But I had become more interested in the academic side of things and an unwritten requirement for local elected office at the time was a German surname and long term residency in Gillespie County. Besides, I didn't really want to become active in politics anyway. My mind changed in 1998 after I read an article written by Paul Burka in TEXAS MONTHLY magazine about the Texas State Board of Education (SBOE) which painted most board members as a bunch of bumbling idiots who fought among themselves as well as against almost all of Governor George W. Bush's efforts to reform public education. I learned that the leader of the group fighting Gov. Bush was a fellow Republican, Dr. Bob Offutt, who was my representative on the SBOE. Dr. Offutt was a dentist with offices in San Antonio and New Braunfels and, although I had never met him, I had handled his yellow page advertising (through his office staff) for several years in our New Braunfels area phone book. Before reading the TEXAS MONTHLY story, all I knew about him was that he had been on the board for two terms and his name was on the Republican primary ballot, always unopposed. Because of political gerrymandering, the district was heavily Republican so he never had a problem winning the general election.

I knew enough about politics and elections to know that in "down ballot" races in primary elections, some voters (myself included), will skip those races if they know nothing about the candidates. But research shows that about eighty percent of uninformed voters will cast their vote for a familiar name on the ballot and, if there is not a familiar name, they will almost always pick the candidate with the most common name such as Smith or Jones. State judge and State Board of Education races are the best examples of "down ballot" races in Texas because they are either state wide or in very large districts, making it difficult for candidates with little name recognition to be successful. Every SBOE district in Texas is twice as large as a state senate district and ten times larger than a state representative district. Each district has a population of about 1.5 million and virtually nobody has any idea who his or her representative on the SBOE is. Even some people who are political activists and regular voters in primary elections are included in this group of clueless people. I doubt that even five percent of regular Republican voters in any district have any idea about who represents them on the SBOE.

With all of this in mind, I made a tentative decision to become a candidate in the Republican Primary for State Board of Education, District 5, which covered twenty-five counties stretching from McLennan County (Waco) on the north to Wilson County (Floresville) southeast of San Antonio. But I waited until the last day to announce just in case someone with a better candidate name than mine decided to announce. That didn't happen, so I drove to Republican Party headquarters in Austin, paid the filing fee, and officially became a candidate for public office for the first time in my life. In the box that asked if I planned to spend more than $500 in my campaign, I checked "No". I would soon have to make a revision in order to legally accept the flood of checks that began to arrive within a couple of weeks. Upon learning about what I had done, Jo's response was

"You've done what?" But she quickly jumped in to the campaign and supported me all the way. Although she was not my official campaign treasurer (Lukenbach founder Hondo Crouch's son-in-law, John Graham, was), she handled most of the day-to-day finances of the campaign.

The year 2000 was a presidential election year and Governor George W. Bush was seeking the Republican nomination in the primaries. His major competition came from Sen. John McCain and Steve Forbes. The important New Hampshire primary was fast approaching as the year began and lots of Texas Republicans were in New Hampshire volunteering to help Gov. Bush. One day in early January, something strange, but beneficial to me, occurred when Bob Offutt and former SBOE member Donna Ballard appeared on stage in New Hampshire with Steve Forbes. I was watching TV at the time and was shocked to see this spectacle play out before my eyes. Bob was the leader of a six-member group of far-right Republicans on the board who had fought most of Bush's education reform efforts and Donna was a wacky former member of the same group. The Bush people in Austin referred to members of this group as "wing-nuts". Bush's signature slogan of campaign was "No Child Left Behind", and Bob and Donna had traveled all the way to New Hampshire to call him the weakest education governor in Texas history. I couldn't believe the gift that had been handed to me and I quickly began efforts to take advantage of it.

This was only a couple of days after I had announced my candidacy and I'm sure that no one in the Bush camp had any idea that Dr. Offutt had a primary opponent. My first call was to Senator David Sibley. I had coached David on the junior varsity basketball team at Jones High School in the mid-sixties and I hadn't talked to him since 1991 when our 1965 state championship team was honored at the state basketball tournament in Austin. He was furious at Dr. Offutt but had no idea that he had a primary opponent. He thanked me for the call and said "I'll see what I can do". A few days later, I received a call from someone in the Bush campaign who wanted to arrange a meeting for me with the campaign manager Karl Rove. The meeting was to take place in Austin the day after the New Hampshire primary. The person who called asked me not to say anything to anybody about the scheduled meeting, and the only person that I told was my wife Jo.

In the meantime, I hit the campaign trail, which was a long one considering the size of the district. I already had received a few small campaign contributions, which covered my gasoline expenses for trips to campaign forums in most of the counties. I had never campaigned before but I had made a few speeches at meetings and coaching clinics during my career and could handle myself pretty well in front of small groups. I also knew enough about campaigns to pick out three or four issues, be well informed on those, and keep the message simple. I also was not afraid to tell the truth about how I stood on issues when answering questions rather than try to figure how the questioner wanted me to answer. But the big issue was Bob's trip to New Hampshire. I actually felt sorry for him when he was sometimes booed when introduced. It was pretty brutal and he usually didn't even show up unless the meeting was in the San Antonio area where he lived.

A few days before my scheduled meeting with Mr. Rove, I received a call from Jack Christie, a Bush supporter and former chairman of the SBOE. Although I had told no one other than Jo about the meeting, he somehow knew about it and advised me that, since the Bush team was big on appearances, I should wear a suit or blazer with a conservative tie, and make sure that my shoes were freshly shined. I hadn't paid for a shoe shine in years but I took his advice and paid eight bucks for one. When I arrived at Bush campaign headquarters in downtown Austin that day, I was surprised when the other three people at the meeting (Karl Rove, Ted Delisi, and Adam Goldman) were all wearing polo shirts, blue jeans, and sneakers. This was the day after Bush's big loss to John McCain in New Hampshire and Karl was not in a good mood. Most of his anger, however, was directed at Bob Offutt even though Bob's candidate Steve Forbes had finished a distant third behind Bush and John McCain. Karl had a blue blazer hanging on the door and put it on when he was called for an interview on CNN during my meeting with him. Otherwise, I felt way over dressed.

My meeting with Karl consisted mainly of him giving me a list of all the county Republican chairmen in the district with their phone numbers. He didn't tell me that he had already contacted most of them which explained why I had already received phone calls from many of them. He also didn't tell me that he had contacted several Bush donors on my behalf which explains why I began to receive contributions from people that I didn't know. Ted Delisi, who was at the meeting and had purchased Karl's direct mail business, would be my primary contact person along with Adam Goldman, a young guy who worked with both Karl and Ted in some capacity that I never understood. Ted's mother, Diane Delisi, was a state representative from the Temple area and had already called me to offer her support. But these guys, all directly involved with the Bush presidential campaign, had bigger fish to fry. I was somewhat embarrassed, and a little bit overwhelmed that they had been distracted by my candidacy in a lowly SBOE race. After that meeting, the only time that I remember ever talking with Karl was when I ran into him and Senator John Cornyn at a shopping mall in Austin. Ted and I talked frequently by phone during that campaign and he did some work for me on my re-election efforts in later years. As for Adam Goldman, he accompanied me to a few campaign events that year but I eventually lost track of him. I understand that he went to Washington and was an aide to President Bush.

One of my biggest supporters turned out to be Sen. Bill Ratliff, who later succeeded Rick Perry as Lt. Governor. Sen. Ratliff was more of a statesman than a politician and had often clashed with Bob Offutt's faction on the Board. Since Karl's team was busy with the presidential campaign, Sen. Ratliff suggested that I hire a friend of his, Bill Tryon, to be my campaign manager. I followed his advice and Bill did a great job for me. Ted Delisi produced some direct mail pieces for me and I assume he and Karl were at least partially responsible for a mailer that was very critical of Dr. Offutt and paid for by a political action committee (PAC) in Virginia that I had never heard of. The primary election was held in March and I won by a margin of 60% to 40%. I won every county in the district except for one and had spent more than $90,000, the most ever in an SBOE race. Sometimes I wish that I had stuck to my original plan to not spend more than $500 just to make a point that name commonality has more to do with winning "down ballot" primary races than anything else. I think that I would have won anyway, but not by twenty percentage points. The day after my win in the primary, a reporter in Austin asked Gov. Bush to comment on the results. I don't remember his exact quote but he referred to me as "that other guy". My son Adam has never let me live that one down and still sometimes calls me "that other guy".

I still had to win the general election in November but that would be a mere formality since the district was heavily Republican and the Democrats didn't even offer up a candidate. Facing only token opposition from a Green Party candidate, I prepared to take office in January. Sometimes I wonder why I even bothered to do this since it was not a salaried position and, unlike so many others who used the SBOE to launch candidacies for higher office, I had no plans, at my age, to do so. I had never even attended a State Board of Education meeting but I did so before I took office in January. To say the least, I was shocked at what I saw. I also learned that, even though SBOE terms were for four years, I would have to run again in two years because of redistricting after the 2000 census. That was not something that I looked forward to.

CHAPTER **17**

My Introduction to the Wild and Wacky World of the Texas State Board of Education

BEFORE CYNTHIA THORNTON and I were elected in 2000, the board was comprised of nine Republicans and six Democrats. Six of the nine Republicans were ultra-conservatives, or "wing-nuts" as Karl Rove called them, and the other three were considered moderates and generally supported Gov. Bush's education initiatives. The governor appoints a chair from the sitting members and Chase Untermeyer from Houston was the current chair. Since Cynthia had won an open seat that was held by a Democrat, the Republican majority would soon be 10-5 and the number of "moderates" would increase to five. I didn't consider myself to be a moderate but, compared with five of the others, I guess that I may have been. All of the far right members with school age children, except for one, either homeschooled them or sent them to private schools. They had a right to do this and still be on the board but it seemed a little odd since the board has nothing to do with non-public education. Four members of this group were extremely religious and very good people. One was an Evangelical preacher from a tiny west Texas town who almost never expressed a view on any subject except for textbook content. Another was an elderly genuine Christian lady from the Panhandle who seemed to have little knowledge about workings of the SBOE. She usually came to the board meetings in Austin on a Greyhound bus. Bob Offutt and David Bradley, an opinionated and abrasive guy from Beaumont without a college degree, were the leaders of this group, and they traded their votes on social issues in return for votes on Permanent School Fund issues, which the others knew nothing about. When I took my seat on the board, it was obvious that Mr. Bradley would pretty much control the votes of this five member group. But in order to have his way on financial issues, he would have to get three more votes from somewhere. But, until I took my seat on the board in January, he would need only two. And, as I would observe from attending the meetings, he and Dr. Offutt would do almost anything to get those two extra votes before I joined the board in January.

The only constitutional power granted to the SBOE is management of the Permanent School Fund (PSF) which, at the time, was a little over $20 billion. The other powers of the board were "statutory", meaning that they were granted by the state legislature. The most important of those powers were writing school curriculum standards, setting graduation requirements, approving textbooks submitted by publishers, and granting (or taking away) charters to groups and individuals who wished to establish charter schools. But the legislature could also take away powers from the board or could even pass legislation on its own, which 'trumped" the powers of the board. So, with the exception of the PSF, the SBOE's power depends on how much power the legislature decides to exercise on its own or how much it grants directly to the Texas Education Agency or to local school boards. The powers to write curriculum standards and to approve textbooks that conform to them were very important ones and also ones that caused a lot of controversy. The biggest controversy between some far right board members and Gov. Bush occurred because those members refused to vote for new English Language Arts standards that Bush wanted. Even though nine of the fifteen members were on his side, he wanted unanimous approval, and he made changes to appease the other six with no success. He finally gave up and urged the chairman to call for the vote, and the new standards were approved by a vote of 9-6. That controversy may have been the reason that I was elected in 2000, although I think that I would have won anyway because Montgomery is a more common name than Offutt.

Because of controversies such as this, the legislature had gradually chipped away at the Board's power. For example, the Commissioner of Education, at one time appointed by the SBOE, was now appointed by the governor. And, although management of the PSF was a constitutional power that couldn't be taken away by legislators, the board could no longer hire and fire the executive director of the fund. That power was now in the hands of the Commissioner of Education, who answered directly to the governor. I doubt seriously that any other public investment fund in the nation has an executive director that is not hired by its governing board. In addition, when I arrived at the SBOE in 2001, the board had almost absolute power over charter schools. But most of the charter schools approved before that time performed so poorly that the legislature took most of the powers of the board away and gave them to the Commissioner of Education.

Some board members didn't seem to know what the board's powers were and had taken their seats thinking that anything that had to do with public education in Texas could be affected by them. Many times, a member would introduce an issue or policy change only to be informed by Texas Education Agency (TEA) counsel that the board could only pass a resolution on that particular issue or policy. After about a year of voting on meaningless resolutions, I introduced a resolution to prohibit SBOE resolutions. Needless to say, it didn't pass but I think that it got more than one vote.

My predecessor Bob Offutt had been elected in 1992 when Democrats had a majority on the SBOE. To his credit, he worked hard to change that by recruiting Republicans in several districts until they held a 9-6 majority. Since several Republican members owed their seats to Dr. Offutt, he became the undisputed leader of the far right faction, most of who had been on the board for only a short period of time. So when he lost in the March 2000 primary, he would attend only three or four meetings before I was sworn in on January 1. I attended most of those meetings as an observer and saw that he was not about to go out quietly. He was chairman of the five member finance committee which handles PSF matters and David Bradley was the vice-chairman. A major responsibility of this committee is to recommend financial managers for the $20 billion fund which, at the time, was the second largest public endowment fund in the nation. Managers could make millions by managing just a small portion of the fund and board members were not about to allow the executive director and his team to have much of a say as to which managers were hired. They were determined to do it all on their own regardless of their knowledge, or lack thereof, about financial matters.

Every year, some management contracts expire and Requests for Proposals (RFP) are required from money management firms who seek lucrative contracts to manage parts of the PSF. So after all the RFP's had been received, Chairman Offutt called for a meeting of the committee to consider them on a day in August, 2000. But before the meeting convened in the afternoon, three members (Offutt, Bradley, and Democrat Joe Bernal) were observed eating lunch at an Austin deli along with Brian Borowski, Joe Alderete, and Russell Stein. Borowski was an unofficial "informal" advisor to Offutt and Bradley. Alderete was a close friend of Bernal who had lost his seat on the San Antonio city council after being indicted for felony theft, and Stein represented First Union Securities as the Board's performance consultant who, in his job, had nothing to do with recommending money managers to the Board. Yet Stein, who lived and worked in Houston, was having lunch in Austin with three members of a five member committee. The Texas Education Agency employees who reported the lunch meeting said that the six were at adjoining tables passing papers around between them. If the three board members were discussing state business of any kind, it would be a violation of the Open Meetings Law which prohibits a quorum of state officials having a meeting without posting it in advance. The three board members were indicted for a misdemeanor violation of the law but the charges were later dropped when they agreed to attend an ethics training class and to not violate a law more serious than a traffic violation.

In addition to the required orientation for new board members conducted by the Texas Education Agency, I attended an orientation for state board members in Washington sponsored by the National Association of State Boards of Education (NASBE). I had been told ahead of time by other board members to expect almost nothing but liberalism at the meeting. They were right but, since the leaders of the association thought that I was close to the Bush people in Washington (I wasn't), I was asked to serve on the government relations committee which met twice yearly, once at the annual NASBE convention in various cities and once in Alexandria, Virginia. I gladly accepted and attended two meetings before Governor Perry curtailed out-of-state travel after 9/11. It was at the convention in San Diego that Jo attended with me that we met our future daughter-in-law, Elizabeth. That alone made my short term on the committee worthwhile.

When Cynthia Thornton and I were sworn in early January, 2001, the chairman of the SBOE, Chase Untermeyer, came from Houston to attend the ceremony. He was appointed chair by Gov. Bush and had served only one term. I, and probably most other members, assumed that he would continue in that role under the new governor Rick Perry. Chase was very over qualified for the State Board of Education. A Harvard grad, he had already compiled a successful resume by serving in both the Reagan and George H.W. Bush administrations and had returned to Houston where he was involved in several business and civic endeavors. Unlike some board members, he had a calm demeanor and was a good leader respected by all factions on the board. Except for being over qualified, I felt that he was the perfect person to be chair of the SBOE. But for some reason that I never understood, Gov. Perry decided not to appoint him for another term as Board chair. However, he didn't immediately appoint a successor so the board was not allowed to meet until he did.

My swearing in ceremony in Jan., 2001

Most board members felt that Geraldine "Tincy" Miller, a Republican from Dallas, who was the daughter-in-law of real estate mogul Henry S. Miller, would be the next chair. Tincy had been a board member forever. I think she may have been elected back when doctors in her wealthy Highland Park neighborhood all drove Buicks with holes in the fender. But, after all those years of service, she had never served as chair. Most of us thought that this would be the year, especially since her family members were big donors to Republican candidates. And there was no question that she expected and wanted the appointment. But, surprisingly, that didn't happen. One day in January, I attended a luncheon at a downtown Austin hotel honoring some teachers. As I was walking into the banquet room, Dr. Hugh Hays, a deputy Education Commissioner, intercepted me to ask if I had talked with Robert Scott, an education adviser to the governor. According to Dr. Hays, the governor was finally about to announce his choice for board chair, and it was between Grace Shore and me. When I told him that I had no interest in the appointment, he gave me Scott's phone number and I rushed to the pay phones in the hotel lobby (I didn't have a cell phone) to let him know. Fortunately for me, I ran into Ms. Shore on the way and she told me that the governor's office had just called to tell her that she had been appointed as the new chair. Tincy Miller and Grace Shore were both members of the so called "moderate" Republican faction of the Board but that was about to change in a big way before I had attended my first board meeting. As for me, I was relieved, but shocked that I was even under consideration because I had never talked with anyone in the new governor's office.

CHAPTER **18**

Charter Schools and the "Textbook Wars"

GRACE SHORE WAS a former math teacher from Longview in east Texas. She and her husband had, over several years, built a successful oil field supply company and they were just about the finest people that you could ever meet. Grace was active in the Republican Party in Longview and Governor Bush had appointed her to the Board when Donna Ballard moved out of the district. She ran for a full term in 1998, but didn't have an opponent in the Republican primary. Her district, like mine, was heavily Republican so she had never had to campaign to win in November. I thought she was the best choice to chair the Board, but many of my Republican colleagues disagreed, especially Tincy Miller. Tincy spewed her wrath at both Grace and Rick Perry and it was obvious that she would do almost anything to make sure that Grace Shore lost her seat on the Board in 2002. Tincy had never been considered a "wing-nut" before but she suddenly aligned herself with the far right faction, meaning that there were now just four "common sense" or "pragmatic" conservatives (Grace Shore, Chase Untermeyer, Cynthia Thornton, and myself).

Ms. Shore's first order of business was to end all the problems and controversies surrounding management of the Permanent School Fund. David Bradley and Joe Bernal were removed from the Finance committee and assigned to other committees. She also notified First Union about Russell Stein's indictment and they immediately replaced him in his role as performance consultant for the PSF. As usual for new members, I was assigned to the Planning committee whose main order of business had to do with charter schools. Mr. Bradley wasn't too happy about his new assignment to this committee but he quickly began wheeling and dealing with charter school holders and hopefuls just as he had done with PSF consultants and money managers before.

At my very first meeting in February, I again wondered why I had bothered to do this. There was no salary associated with the job but, at least for a while, we got free health insurance from the state. But my main concern was the boring meetings. Most people have no idea what the real powers of the SBOE are. This includes the general public, the education community, and even some board members. Public testimony is allowed at both general and committee meetings and most of the testimony is from people, with strong opinions about public education, who are recommending action on things that are, unbeknownst to them, not within the Board's power. Many times, they had been invited to speak by board members who were confused themselves about the Board's powers. I agreed with the chair that we should show respect and stay in our seats during their ramblings as much as possible. But, I must admit, I sometimes had a hard time staying awake. I think I may have even looked forward to more controversy, which there was sure to be plenty of, just to bring an end to the boredom.

Jim Nelson, a Bush appointee who was an attorney and former Odessa ISD board member, was the Education Commissioner when I first joined the Board. He was a very nice guy who worked hard to implement the governor's education agenda. But many board members, who were not Bush fans and still upset that their power to appoint the commissioner had been taken away, were not cooperative. I was already aware of this disconnect but became even more so after a lunch meeting that I had with Commissioner Nelson, Chairman Untermeyer, and Margaret LaMontagne a few months before I was sworn in and before Bush was elected President. Margaret was Bush's education advisor and would later be named his Secretary of Education when he was President under her new name of Margaret Spellings. She is now the president of the University of North Carolina. At that meeting, I found out that Commissioner Nelson, like the future President Bush, was no fan of the far right faction of the SBOE. I liked Jim and did what I could do to make his relationship with the Board workable. But Democrats opposed him because he was appointed by a Republican governor and "wing-nut" Republicans opposed him because they thought that he was appointed by a RINO (Republican in name only) governor.

One of the biggest education controversies in Texas in 2001 involved charter schools, which are nontraditional public schools that are not subject to some of the same regulations that apply to traditional ones. The state legislature had authorized the establishment of charters in 1995 and a few schools began operating in the fall of 1996. The State Board of Education was given broad oversight authority over these schools including granting of the charters, taking them away, and approving changes that some charter holders requested after they had begun operating. In 1998, the board had approved almost every charter application, causing real problems since so many of the charter holders were not qualified to operate a school. I, like most everyone else, didn't know much about this new movement but I had always been in favor of more choices for parents in deciding what is best for their children. That included private school vouchers as well as charter schools. I was on the Planning committee that held charter school hearings and recommended action to the full board. Rather than attempting to just "wing it" regarding charters, I turned for guidance to Patsy O'Neill, the executive director of the Resource Center for Charter Schools, located in San Antonio. I found this group to be one that played no favorites and was truly dedicated to the betterment of education in Texas through school choice. But many charter schools that had been approved in 1998 continued to under-perform and were under poor and sometimes corrupt leadership. The superintendent of the largest charter school network at the time didn't even have a college degree but several board members, for whatever reason, insisted on approving this network to expand. Long story short – the legislature finally lost confidence the board's ability to clean up the situation and transferred most of the oversight authority to the Commissioner of Education. The board, however, kept its power to authorize charters until that, too, changed in 2013.

Prior to 1995, the SBOE had wide powers where textbooks were concerned. But some board members had demanded that publishers make so many content changes based on their ideologies or religious beliefs that the state legislature barred the board from editing content. So, during my time on the board, a textbook could not be rejected unless it was found to have factual errors, did not meet curriculum standards, or failed to meet physical manufacturing standards. But that didn't stop some board members from trying to influence content. They, with the urging and help from outside individuals and groups, attempted to do this by using a broad definition of the term "factual error" as well as changing curriculum standards to fit their beliefs. Some even said that content, such as creationism, left out of a book was a factual error because it was an "error of omission". David Bradley had once even ripped off the cover of a book that he didn't like because of its content, and then said that he couldn't vote to approve it because it didn't meet manufacturing standards. But the most egregious example of SBOE overreach concerning textbooks was when members demanded that a picture of a woman carrying a briefcase be replaced with a picture of a woman putting a cake in an oven.

Beginning in the early 1960's, before the term "culture wars" had become popular, a homely and somewhat eccentric couple from Longview named Mel and Norma Gabler were the chief "textbook police" in Texas. They were famous for compiling lists of what they thought were factual errors in textbooks. In a way, the Gablers offered a great service since they actually found lots of factual errors such as wrong dates and misspelled words that publishers needed to change. But they also caused controversies because many of their so-called "errors" were actually opinions, based mainly on their political and religious beliefs. For many years, they attended every SBOE meeting and gave their lists of alleged errors to board members, reporters, and anyone else who wished to have a copy. But by 2001, they were up in age and had turned most of their work over to Neal Frey, a guy that I never met nor talked to. As far as I know, neither Mr. Gabler nor Mr. Frey ever attended a board meeting during my tenure, but Ms. Gabler continued to attend, usually staying at the same hotel as board members. I frequently gave her a ride to and from meetings and she never once mentioned textbooks to me. However, she told me more than once that I was her favorite board member because I handled matters with respect and common sense that, in her opinion, was not true of some members. Mel Gabler passed away in 2004, and Norma left this earth in 2007, shortly after I left the SBOE. I never met Mel but I loved Norma even though I think that she may have been misguided and misinformed in some ways where textbook content is concerned.

My first experience with the "textbook wars" occurred in 2001, when environmental science books were up for adoption. All of the books, except for an advanced placement book offered by a small publisher, were unanimously approved. The lone exception was a book that was already used at the college level and the publisher was not willing, for financial reasons, to make changes for use in public schools. After all these years, I don't remember the exact details but I do remember testimony about a few minor errors in the book that would have been easy for a larger publisher to change. I voted with the nine other Republicans on the board to reject the book but it was not because I had enough scientific knowledge to know one way or the other about the subject matter. I had simply listened to testimony from what appeared to be experts and made my decision. The small publisher eventually sued the SBOE as a whole as well as the individual members, including myself, who had voted against them. The suit eventually died in the courts and I don't remember ever being sued again as an SBOE member.

Several outside interest groups such as Texas Eagle Forum, Citizens for a Sound Economy, Texas Public Policy Foundation (TPPF), and Texas Freedom Network (TFN) were active in attempting to influence the textbook selection process. Most were conservative groups but TFN was a liberal leaning one. But, with the exception of TPPF, they didn't conduct actual reviews or make up lists of "factual errors" as the Gablers had done. I considered TPPF to be a mainstream conservative organization because several of their active members had supported my candidacy in 2000 against Bob Offutt and they had done so at the urging of Karl Rove and other center-right Republicans. But, when TPPF botched a social studies textbook review process that resulted in some of the most liberal history books ever approved, the organization got out of the textbook review business. I'll have more on that later.

CHAPTER **19**

Redistricting, Re-Election, and (God forbid!) Terri Leo

SBOE MEMBERS ARE elected to serve four year terms. But, after the census is completed every ten years, districts are redrawn by the legislature and all members have to run for re-election even if they have been in office for only two years. I may have known this when I ran for the first time in 2000, but I hadn't given it much thought until it was called to my attention at my first board meeting. As a result, all state elected officials who represented districts began scrambling around to find a redistricting plan that would be favorable to them at election time. But the legislature adjourned in May without adopting redistricting plans and Gov. Perry refused to call a special session. This meant that the responsibility for redistricting was in the hands of the federal courts. At the time, I knew little about the process so I didn't really get involved at all until Tincy Miller and her husband Vance hired some guy to draw up an SBOE map that took almost all of the Hill Country counties away from my present district. Two alternate plans that the legislature left on the table were more acceptable to me. I don't think that Tincy and Vance were out to get me but, in their efforts to remove Grace Shore from office, their plan would rearrange the other districts in a way that, probably unintentionally, affected me more than any of the other members. Most board members, unaware of Tincy's intentions, were okay with her plan and a majority of them, including Ms. Shore, signed on to it. The board's five Democrats, all minorities, loved it because it packed even more minorities in their already safe districts and four Republican members were indifferent because they had no plans to run for re-election. As a result, I was almost alone in my efforts to have one of the other two plans adopted. It became pretty much a battle between Tincy and me.

Ms. Miller was difficult. One day she was your friend and the next day she was your enemy. She may have been on the board for twenty years but her experience level was one year repeated nineteen times. At my very first meeting, she repeated her often stated belief that the state legislature was intent on "raiding" the Permanent School Fund for money that would be spent on things other than textbooks, which she believed was in violation of the state constitution. I respectfully challenged her on that and the board's attorney, David Anderson, explained that the corpus of the PSF couldn't be spent for anything, but that income from it was to be distributed to the Available School Fund (ASF). He further explained that the money in the ASF must go to textbooks, but that any money left over was to be distributed on a per capita basis to school districts. That should have settled the issue but Ms. Miller continued to incorrectly state that the constitution limited income from the PSF to textbook purchases even though she had been voting for years on a per capita expenditure for non-textbook items. I guess that she never bothered to read the clause in the constitution that dealt with the PSF. But it was true that the legislature often put pressure on the board to increase income from the PSF to cover costs for programs that it created without funding them such as health insurance for teachers.

SBOE redistricting was assigned to a federal court in the northern district of Texas, located in Dallas. John Cornyn was the state Attorney General at the time and his office represented the state. Although I had no redistricting plan of my own to submit to the court, they took up my fight to oppose the Miller plan on the grounds of extreme political gerrymandering, packing of minorities in just a few districts, and the dilution of voting strength of rural voters. Tincy's plan would give urban voters an incredible amount of influence in almost every district even though most school districts were located in rural areas. As a small town guy, I was concerned about the reduced power for voters in rural districts as population in Texas shifted to urban areas. I was called to testify in front of a federal judge in Dallas on September 12, 2001, one day after the horrible attacks now known as 9/11. I was hoping that the hearing would be postponed but it wasn't, so I traveled alone to Dallas on the afternoon after the attacks so that I could be in court the next morning. Security at the federal courthouse was so tight that the court proceedings had to be delayed. My heart really wasn't into it but I answered all questions from the attorneys on both sides as well as some from the judge, who seemed to side with the state's argument. But his decision would not be announced until November. He eventually sided with the Millers probably because most of the other board members supported it, at least where their districts were concerned. I was disappointed but accepted it and I still don't believe that the Millers were out to have me defeated. Tincy could be tacky at times but Vance was really just a "good old boy" who had no axe to grind but would also stand by his wife. I actually enjoyed his company at the few social events that we both attended during my time on the board.

With some of my Republican colleagues still reeling over losing their leader Bob Offutt in 2000, I was sure to get a primary opponent in 2002. I was correct but I lucked out because the person recruited to run against me had an almost unheard of surname, "Deats". Jim Deats was a friend of Offutt's who had unsuccessfully run for public office several times before, twice for Congress and once for the State Senate. He had served as a school board member in Boerne but was removed from office when it was discovered that he lived outside the school district. So in spite of some baggage, he had some familiarity in the district because his name had been on the ballot several times before. Not expecting much of a problem, and also because I hated asking for money, I decided to depend on the few donations that friends and strong supporters were willing to give. The large donations that I had received two years before had dried up because Karl Rove and his team were frying bigger fish in Washington. But my opponent didn't receive much money either. However, he worked extremely hard and was all over the district campaigning. But he had no message where education was concerned and relied on the belief that he could convince voters that he was a better and more conservative Republican than I. I could hardly wait for the election in March to arrive because I was worn out trying to keep up with him. Governor Perry endorsed me about two weeks prior to the election and I eventually prevailed by a sixteen point margin.

While elections are officially decided in the general election in November, legislative and SBOE districts are so politically gerrymandered that Texas elections are almost always settled in the March primaries. As a result of the 2002 primaries, there would be six new members. But only one incumbent, Chairwoman Grace Shore, lost her seat. With financial help from Vance and Tincy Miller, Grace was defeated by Linda Bauer from Houston's northern suburbs. Grace had never had a primary opponent before and didn't seem to understand that incumbency isn't much of a positive factor in down ballot races in large districts. Walk into a room of one hundred primary voters and ask if they know who their state representative is and maybe fifty will raise their hands. Ask the same question about their SBOE member and you may have two hands go up in the air. Ms. Bauer was recruited by the far right after Tincy's redistricting plan shifted voters to the southern part of the district where Ms. Bauer lived. Ms. Shore didn't realize that it might negatively impact her so she signed off on the plan. She didn't spend much money or time campaigning and seemed to be more worried about my race than ensuring her re-election. It wasn't even close. Grace was defeated by almost thirty percentage points. But there was a gross miscalculation on the part of those who recruited Linda Bauer. Before her very first meeting in 2003, Ms. Bauer realized that she couldn't be a part of the wacky "wing nut" faction and became a reliable vote with the more mainstream Republican faction on the board.

Against my better judgment, I got involved in some of the other primary SBOE races in 2002. Some of my Republican colleagues were active in opposing me so I guess you could say that I used the "self-defense" argument to justify my actions. My biggest victory was the election of Patricia "Pat" Hardy, a former social studies teacher, who won an open seat in the Fort Worth area. Pat was very active in the state social studies teacher organization and I met her at a convention in Galveston where I had been invited to sit on a panel. She reluctantly agreed to run for an open seat that was held by a member of the far right faction, Dr. Richard Neill. I liked Dr. Neill personally and would not have gotten involved had he run for reelection. He handpicked his successor but Pat won in a landslide against his candidate who had a Muslim sounding name. I'm proud to say that Pat Hardy has been a very productive and reasonable conservative member of the board for the past sixteen years. Bob Craig, an attorney and Lubbock ISD school board member, won an open seat in west Texas. Bob, who was probably over qualified for the SBOE, was a great board member and became my best friend on the board for the next four years. But I had nothing to do with recruiting him to run in 2002. I think that Mike Moses, a former Commissioner of Education and Lubbock ISD superintendent, was largely responsible for that.

The 2002 election cycle also saw the term of Chase Untermeyer come to an end. For some reason, the new governor Rick Perry had decided to replace Chase as the chair of the board. Some people in the know say that the governor's advisers felt that Chase had not done enough to reign in the board's far right faction. That may have been true but I was still disappointed that my friend decided not to run for reelection in 2002. But he went on to bigger and better things when President George W. Bush appointed him as ambassador to Qatar a few years after he left the SBOE. Chase sat next to me for two years during my tenure on the SBOE and, in those two short years, I learned a lot from him about how it is more important for a public servant to be a statesman rather than a pure politician. Sadly to say, his successor was nothing more than a pure political junkie. Her name was Terri Leo, and she may have been the most repulsive person that I have ever known.

Terri Leo was an attractive forty-something year old former teacher from Spring, a northern Houston suburb. I had never heard of her before but I soon learned that she was an extreme political activist who had tried unsuccessfully to unseat SBOE chair Jack Christie, a Bush supporter, a few years before and that she had been recruited by Bob Offutt. When she learned that Chase Untermeyer was not running for reelection in 2002, she jumped into the race and won the primary against a guy named Doug Cannon. So, although I didn't know who she was, she already had it in for me because of her support for Offutt. She didn't seem to have much of an opinion about improving education for Texas kids but was quick to point out that she had attended every state Republican convention since 1984. Unlike Chase, who was more of a statesman than a politician, Terri was just the opposite. And she would be sitting in a chair next to me for the next four years. My immediate thought when I learned of her win was "Have a nice day Dan". Over the next four years I would learn that Terri was not satisfied unless there was a controversy going on that attracted the news media to board meetings. She loved attention from the media. One of my colleagues commented that "The most dangerous place to be in the SBOE meeting room is between Terri Leo and a television camera." And one last thing about Ms. Leo – she claimed to be a graduate of Texas A&M even though she actually graduated from East Texas State University in Commerce several years before it became part of the Texas A&M University system.

CHAPTER **20**

Liberal History Books and the Permanent School Fund

TEA COMMISSIONER JIM Nelson resigned in early 2002. I liked Jim and supported him every way that I could but it was no secret that he wasn't comfortable with many of the SBOE members. I don't know that this played much of a role in his decision to resign but I assume that it did. He was succeeded by Dr. Felipe Alanis who had worked at TEA before and had been an assistant chancellor of the UT system as well as superintendent of schools in Odessa. Dr. Alanis was a nice, even tempered guy who went out of his way to get along with everybody, which was impossible to do considering all the political factions on the board. For some reason, Gov. Perry removed him after only a little more than year on the job and replaced him on an interim basis with Robert Scott who had been an education advisor to both Bush and Perry. Robert lived in New Braunfels, which was in my district. When I ran for a position on the board, he was working for Gov. Bush and had called me to offer his support but asked that I not reveal to anyone that he had done so. Both Robert and I have been out of the public arena now for several years so I am revealing his support for me for the first time.

Because of redistricting, the district that I represented had become a little more Democratic, but not enough so that I had much to worry about in the 2002 general election. But I had a credible opponent in Donna Howard, who had lost to Cynthia Thornton in 2000 but was now running against me because redistricting placed her in my district. Donna was very liberal but was intelligent and well versed on education issues. In addition, she was a very nice lady. I won with fifty-nine percent of the vote and Donna later won a seat in the Texas House of Representatives and is still there today. I believe that she may be the only Anglo Democrat in the 150-member Texas House. She represents a district in Travis County (Austin) which is the only county in Texas with an Anglo majority population that is reliably Democratic. Where the State Board of Education is concerned, every Republican member since 2000 has been Anglo and every Democratic member has been either Hispanic or African American. This racial/ethnic divide on the board raised its ugly head when social studies textbooks were up for adoption in 2002.

The most active group involved in the social studies textbook adoption process was the Texas Public Policy Foundation (TPPF}, a conservative leaning think tank whose board chair was Dr. Wendy Gramm, wife of former Senator Phil Gramm. At the time, TPPF was not considered to be a far right organization and I had received support from some of its most active members. But the woman who had the title of "Director of Education Research" for the foundation was Chris Patterson who, for some reason, had avoided me "like the plague" from the day that I first arrived. In fact, the only board members that I ever saw her talking with were members of the board's far right faction although, as far as I knew, all Republican members respected the work of TPPF. Vance Miller was even a TPPF board member and no one considered him to be too far to the right. But Chris screwed up in a big way when she paid $100,000 to sixteen textbook reviewers, some who turned out to be big time liberals. One of them even said that one of the textbooks didn't give Roosevelt's New Deal enough credit for ending the Great Depression and that Reagan was given too much credit for the economic boom in the 1980's. Textbook publishers, always eager to please everybody in order to get their books approved, offered to make changes regardless of who was demanding them. When my Republican colleagues relented to liberal changes rather than embarrass TPPF, the Democrats on the board doubled down by demanding that even more liberal changes be made. The end result was that the most liberal social studies textbooks in Texas history were approved and I was the only board member who voted against their approval. This was in spite of the fact that many of my colleagues accused me of being "in the pocket" of at least one publisher because of my close personal friendship with Reese Washington, a former high school football coach and semi-retired Prentice Hall employee. But the record from those days will show that my lonely "no" vote was aimed mainly at liberal changes that his company was agreeing to make after the timeline for making changes had expired. And my friendship with Reese Washington after all these years is just as strong today as it has ever been.

I was so upset at the outcome of the social studies textbook review process that I wrote an op-ed piece and sent it to all the major newspapers in the state. In it, I explained that I was concerned that a supposedly conservative organization (TPPF) had commissioned a textbook review that had resulted in the adoption of some of the most liberal social studies textbooks in state history and that these books would be adopted for use in public schools throughout most of the country. This prompted a quick response from TPPF president Jeff Judson who seemed to be unaware of what I was talking about. It was obvious to me that SBOE issues were on the backburner at TPPF and that an organization dedicated mostly to economic and the size of government issues had no desire to be involved in textbook content discussions even though they had just spent $100,000 of donor money on a flawed review of social studies books. When Jeff contacted me I agreed to a lunch meeting in San Antonio with him, Chris Patterson, and John Kerr, a TPPF board member who had supported me in my 2000 campaign. I don't remember much about the meeting but I do know that I never saw Ms. Patterson again at an SBOE meeting and that TPPF has never again been involved in textbook reviews.

Jeff Judson resigned his position as president of TPPF a few weeks after the meeting. Vance Miller later told me that Jeff got "crossways" with TPPF chair Wendy Gramm and that the $100,000 textbook review process played a part in his resignation. I always thought it was strange that, after almost two years as an SBOE member, my first conversation with Ms. Patterson occurred at that lunch meeting even though she attended every board meeting and was also a resident of the district that I represented. Shortly after the meeting, the word "Education" was stricken from her title and she became simply the TPPF's "Director of Research".

As 2003 began, everything was put on hold where the SBOE was concerned. Board Chair Grace Shore was gone and Governor Perry was taking his time in naming a replacement. Because of all the past controversy surrounding the board, he probably wanted to keep board members out of town for as long as possible. Tincy Miller, as usual, wanted the job but I'm sure that some of the governor's advisers were opposed. Because I was the lone board member who had received Perry's endorsement in the 2002 primary, I was frequently mentioned as a possibility. But I had no interest in herding cats, which is what I would have had to do considering the three distinct factions that existed. I knew people close to the governor but I didn't know him that well, and I was never interviewed by his appointments adviser. In late March, the governor announced the appointment of Ms. Miller so the scheduled January and March meetings never happened. As a result, the first meeting of 2003 did not occur until April.

Things didn't go well for the new chair at her first meeting. Since she had aligned herself for the first time with the far right faction during the past two years, her choices for vice-chair and secretary were defeated, which made little difference except for the fact that the three board officers decided memberships on the board's three committees and Tincy was outnumbered 2 to 1. As a result, Bob Craig and I, along with Linda Bauer, were assigned to the Finance committee while David Bradley was buried again on the Planning committee. Bob and I were determined to finish cleaning things up where the

Permanent School Fund was concerned and it didn't take us long to do so. Tincy eventually joined us in our efforts and became a reliable vote on the common sense Republican side of the board. As I said before, she could be your friend one day and your enemy the next. But she generally remained on my side for the next four years and was a reasonably good board chair in spite of her lack of knowledge about some of the most basic issues that came before the board.

I was happy to be assigned to the Finance committee which had authority over PSF issues. The value of the Permanent School Fund at the time was about $20 billion and it was a little scary that a fund of this size was managed by a group of fifteen mostly obscure people, many of whom didn't know the difference between a stock and a bond. It was even scarier that a former high school and small college basketball coach (me) had more investment experience than most the other fourteen decision makers simply because he had received a relatively small inheritance several years before and had turned it into a decent sized investment portfolio without having ever used the services of an active money manager or adviser. But not all was bad since there was a staff of investment professionals, headed by an executive director (that the board had lost power to hire and fire), that operated within the Texas Education Agency. I had no plans to "rubber stamp" everything that they recommended but, at the same time, I also had no plans to micromanage the fund as some members had tried to do in the past.

The executive director of the PSF when I arrived was Paul Ballard and some board members, Republican and Democrat, almost never agreed with anything he did or with any advice that he offered. In addition, there was strong suspicion of collusion involving board members, money managers, and consultants. Grace Shore had done her best to clean things up and had made some progress but she never had enough votes to completely solve the problems because two Democrats usually voted with David Bradley and his Pied Piper like followers on PSF issues. But, against the wishes of new board chair Miller, Bob Craig and I were named chair and vice-chair of the five member finance committee and real progress was made in a relatively short time frame. But this was after an exasperated Paul Ballard had given up and handed the reins over to Holland Timmins.

Texas State Board of Education, 2003 (I'm standing on the far right)

Any income produced from the PSF was required to be deposited into the Available School Fund (ASF) and used first to purchase textbooks for all the students of public schools. Any money left over was distributed to the schools on a per capita basis. No money could be spent from the corpus of the PSF so that it could be left to grow to provide textbooks for future generations. This was not a problem in the early years of the fund since it included only fixed income investments, such as bonds, that produced interest. But, in order to provide growth for future generations, the board had been allowed to invest in stocks for the past several years and board members had voted to hire outside active money managers for most of the fund's assets. Since money from the fund's corpus could not be spent to pay the managers, almost $125 million from the ASF had been spent in the past seven years alone on management fees. State legislators, most of who were elected on the promise of not raising taxes, were always looking for money from other sources to pay for public education. As a result, they were always demanding more income from the PSF. Many board members frequently accused the legislature of "raiding the fund" at the expense of the children's textbooks. Even I became frustrated with legislators over their desire for more money that they couldn't find from looking under seat cushions. But their demands eventually led to a solution that would also end most of the controversy surrounding the fund. I am proud to say that I played a big role in finding that solution. It is called "indexing" and it was almost unheard of at the time for large pension and endowment funds.

For several years, there had been a large body of evidence that active money managers had a difficult time outperforming their benchmarks such as, for example, the S&P 500 Index for large cap growth stocks. This was not because managers were necessarily incompetent but, instead, it was due to the fact that their fees had to be subtracted from any value that they added. In addition, research showed that even those that did well one year were just as likely to underperform the next. Therefore it made sense to me to purchase indexed mutual funds and simply match the benchmarks. I had switched to indexing for my own investment portfolio a few years back, put everything on "automatic pilot", and had been pleased with the results. I realize that there is a big difference between a relatively small personal investment account and a $20 billion fund but, like coaching a middle school basketball team compared with coaching an NBA team, the fundamentals are basically the same. PSF managers, for the most part, had not done poorly and the fund had grown but most of them had not added value compared to the indexes after millions of dollars were subtracted for fees. Holland Timmins showed me research that his staff had done that showed that, had indexing been in effect for the last several years, the fund would have benefited by over $750 million after subtracting management fees.

When I suggested switching most of the PSF assets from active to passive management, I got pushback from some board members, financial management company lobbyists, and from the consultant who had recommended the managers who had cost us all that money in the first place. The mere mention of index funds put such a frown on the consultant's face that you would think that he was suffering from hemorrhoids. Some board members who were friends of money managers opined that the constitution did not allow the board to invest in mutual funds, which index funds are. I argued that, if that was true, we were already violating the law since internal staff had always kept cash parked in a money market fund, which was a mutual fund itself. I asked Ms. Miller to request an opinion from the Attorney General, and his office soon answered that the board could invest in mutual funds. We really didn't have much choice since the legislature demanded more money, and satisfying their demands didn't leave anything for management fees. In addition, most index funds cost less than ten basis points to manage while we had been paying thirty basis points for active management. Eventually, enough board members agreed and most of the fund's assets were moved to a passive portfolio consisting of index funds from various asset groups, both domestic and international. While I was proud of my role in this effort, I must admit that I soon became a bit bored as a member of the committee because, with indexing, there were few decisions to make. But my boredom was short lived because biology textbooks were up for adoption that year and there promised to be a circus atmosphere at board meetings in the very near future and Terri Leo would most certainly be the circus director.

CHAPTER **21**

"Strengths and Weaknesses" (The Biology Textbook Debate)

PROBABLY THE MOST important statutory power that remained in the board's hands in 2003 was approving curriculum content for K-12 public education and the adoption of textbooks that conformed to the curriculum. Textbook content is very important in that most teachers use the books as a way to satisfy the curriculum requirements. When I taught in public schools in the sixties and seventies, I don't recall ever seeing a curriculum document for my courses. I would bet that it is still true that a great majority of public school teachers consider the textbook to be the written curriculum for their classes and use it almost exclusively to develop their lesson plans. In fact, today textbook publishers furnish teachers with a teacher edition textbook which almost always contains suggested lesson plans. The Texas textbook adoption process is also very important in that many smaller states are forced to accept the books adopted by the larger states because publishers can't afford to publish books that differ in content for each state.

Where science was concerned, one of the curriculum requirements that the board had passed was that both "strengths and weaknesses" of scientific theories be taught. This supposedly applied to all scientific theories but nobody seemed to care except for the theory of evolution. I felt that this was a reasonable requirement but I really didn't feel qualified to determine what those strengths and weaknesses were without hearing from actual scientists. Of course, I had enough common sense to know that this issue was really about the old evolution vs. creation debate and which one should be taught in public schools. As a Christian, I personally believe that all things are created by God but, as a lifelong Methodist, I don't believe that the science of evolution is in conflict with my beliefs. "It takes just as great a God to create man from an amoeba as from a mold of clay" is a statement from my first college biology teacher, Dr. Roy Reese, and it comes back in my mind every time I think about this issue. I'm not sure where that statement ranks on a list of the most important ones ever spoken (probably not very high), but it nonetheless made an impression on me.

In spite of my personal feelings on the issue, I grew up in a very "Bible belt" part of the state and many of my Baptist and Assembly of God friends and relatives were strict Biblical literalists who believed that the earth is only a few thousand years old and that there were two dinosaurs on board an ark with two human beings, one named Noah, during a huge flood. I attended more than my share of tent revivals, camp meetings, foot washings, and muddy pond baptisms during my childhood days and, as a result, I know religious fundamentalism when I see it. I never personally witnessed a church "snake handling" but there is an old and tired saying that, "In east Texas even the Presbyterians handle snakes". I also believe in the inerrancy of Bible teachings but in a philosophical rather than strictly in a literal way. But, putting aside my personal religious beliefs, my upbringing caused me to sympathize with religious fundamentalists who had taught their kids at home and in church one thing about life's origins only to have them attend a taxpayer supported school and learn something different. And I would never dismiss their concerns with the statement that "they always have the option to send their kids to private schools". After all, they pay school taxes just like the rest of us. I don't consider myself to be a religious fundamentalist but I sympathize with them just the same.

It really made little difference what anyone's religious beliefs were concerning evolution in that the U.S. Supreme Court had already ruled that the teaching of creationism in public schools violates the establishment clause of the constitution. The four religious fundamentalists on the board understood that so they developed a strategy to attack evolution by demanding that the "weaknesses" of evolution be included in the textbooks along with the "strengths" even though they didn't think the theory had strengths. In my opinion, that was fair enough but I had examined the books and had talked to scientists. I concluded that the books all covered the questions of evolutionary theory such as gaps in the fossil record and the sudden explosion of life forms during the Cambrian explosion which occurred hundreds of millions of years ago and had lasted tens of millions of years. The books also covered the historical "frauds" in the theory such as the Piltdown Man, Haeckel's drawings, and the "peppered moth" photographs. In fact, Dr. David Hillis, an evolutionist biology professor at the University of Texas and a one of my constituents, alerted me to the fact that one of the smaller publishers still had an illustration similar to the fraudulent Haeckel drawings in a textbook up for adoption. I quickly contacted a representative of the company and he assured me that the drawings would be removed. So, in my view, the "weaknesses" of evolution theory had already been satisfied by all publishers with biology books up for adoption, and a majority of board members agreed. But evolution opponents had another option. It was known as Intelligent Design, a vague supposedly non-religious theory supported by a strange group of scientists at the Discovery Institute that was headquartered in Seattle. One of their leading spokesmen was Jonathan Wells, a follower of the Rev. Sun Myung Moon and author of the book, "Icons of Evolution", which was a list of ten falsehoods and "weaknesses" of evolution that he said were in public school biology textbooks. The four staunch creationists on the board said that they didn't want intelligent design to be taught in classrooms but they sided with the ID scientists anyway because they represented a common enemy against the teaching of evolution. I guess you could compare this unlikely alliance with the U.S.-Russia alliance against Germany in World War II.

Two hearings were held and the second one in September attracted 138 people who wanted to give their opinion. David Bradley, the leader of the anti-evolution faction, didn't even bother to attend. There was a board rule that only Texas residents could speak at textbook hearings. But several out of state residents, including several representing the Discovery Institute, signed up to testify anyway and a vote taken to waive the rule failed. I had no problem with hearing their testimonies but I felt that it would be unfair to others who didn't come to Austin from out of state because they were honoring the rule. However, we did vote to allow them to testify after all others had finished as long as a quorum wasn't present. Needless to say, I didn't stay to listen and they finally finished at 1:15 the following morning. Terri Leo enjoyed every minute of the spectacle and, because of concerns for my safety, I made sure not to invade the space between her and the television cameras.

A vote on the biology books was scheduled for the board's November meeting. Books could be placed on one of three lists: conforming, non-conforming, and rejected. School districts could choose books from either the conforming or non-conforming lists, but it was unusual for a district to choose from the latter. Things were reasonably quiet for me between the hearings and the November meeting until about two weeks prior to the meeting when I began to hear from a few stake holders. My first call of any significance was from Peter O'Donnell, a wealthy investor and philanthropist from Dallas, who had donated money to my political campaigns. He was considered by some to be the father of the Texas Republican Party, having helped build it from zero in the 1960's to the dominant party in the state. His foundation had donated tens of millions of dollars to science and medical research and he was concerned that negative publicity from the biology textbook controversy might hinder those efforts in Texas. He informed me that he and others had met with Governor

Perry recently and he assured them that he favored adoption of the biology books but that, for political reasons, he didn't want to speak out. I knew that Tincy Miller lived in Mr. O'Donnell's Highland Park neighborhood so I asked him if he had spoken to her. His reply was something to the effect that talking to her would be a waste of time. I assured him that approval of the books was a certainty but that I could not guarantee that the debate wouldn't produce negative publicity. Rick Perry could have done that but he didn't have the courage to do so. For that reason, I lost a lot of respect for the governor.

A few days before the vote, I got a call from Robert Scott, whose title was now Chief Deputy Commissioner of Education, but he was really the interim Commissioner of Education because Governor Perry had yet to name a successor to Felipe Alanis. Robert wanted my assurance that I was on board with approving all of the biology books with one vote because he was making that recommendation at the governor's request. When I asked why didn't the governor just come out and make his wishes public, Robert's reply was something to the effect that the governor was a religious man himself and didn't want to go against the board's hard core creationists because he didn't want to alienate the religious right. In other words, I was being asked to take the heat and I was willing to do so simply because I had done my homework and I knew that all the biology books up for adoption satisfied the board's requirement that they comply with the Texas Essential Knowledge and Skills (TEKS), the official name for the state curriculum. My religious beliefs had nothing to do with it. Neither did politics. As far as I was concerned, my only obligation was to my oath as an elected official to uphold the law. Postscript: I lost even more respect for Rick Perry when he ran for President in 2012 and, during a televised candidate debate, he had a "vapor lock" and couldn't remember one of the three cabinet departments that he wanted to eliminate. All he could say was "Oops". It was the Department of Energy and he is now the head of this very department and, as far as I know, he has not mentioned eliminating it. Again, I promise, I'm not making this up!! And I'm not making this one up either – As a student at Texas A&M, Rick Perry made a D in a course called "Meats"!! As the old Yankee manager Casey Stengel loved to say, "You can look it up".

Most issues under consideration at the SBOE were assigned to one of three committees and textbook selection would normally be assigned to the Instruction committee. But, because the issue of textbooks was so controversial, it had for several years been considered by the Committee of the Whole, made up of all fifteen board members. Like the three other committees, the Committee of the Whole met on the Thursday prior to the regular board meeting on Friday. So, whatever the board decided in committee on Thursday was usually adopted on Friday unless new information was made available to board members overnight. But the issue of textbook adoption was different. It was not unusual for the vote on Friday to be reversed from the one the day before. The interim commissioner, at Governor Perry's request, was recommending that all fourteen biology books be placed on the conforming list and, on Thursday, a motion was made to accept his recommendation. But David Bradley, without stating a reason why, moved that only two books be placed on the conforming list and that the other twelve be placed on the non-conforming list. The original recommendation from the commissioner passed with an 11-4 vote and David then withdrew his motion, only to make a different motion the next day to place only two books on the conforming list but one of them was on his nonconforming list the previous day and another was on his conforming list. This, of course, made no sense because no changes were made by publishers overnight. When asked to explain his reasoning, he went mute and all the books were later approved by the same 11-4 vote.

Two of the board members on the hard right were extremely good people and I believe they were sincere Christian fundamentalists. Gail Lowe, from Lampasas, was a somewhat matronly and quiet lady who never uttered an unkind word to anybody and there was no doubt that she was sincere in her strict religious beliefs. Don McLeroy, a mustachioed dentist from Bryan, was somewhat "goofy" but was also

213

a good guy who was an admitted "young earth" creationist. I have no idea how he had time for root canals because he seemed to spend most of his time trying to disprove the science of evolution and advancing creationism as an actual science. I've spent enough time already talking about Terri Leo but I never thought that she had a sincere ideology about anything other than calling attention to herself. As for David Bradley – he was hard to explain. He never graduated college and many of my colleagues thought that he was ignorant but, in my view, nothing could have been further from the truth. I would never question someone's sincerity where religious beliefs are concerned but it always appeared to me that David, the leader of the far right faction, went along with the fundamentalists in order to get their support on PSF and charter school issues. He already had two Democrats on board with him on PSF issues so he needed a few more Republican votes to get anything passed. Everybody thought that he and I were fierce opponents and we may have been. Chase Untermeyer, who sat at a desk between us for two years, once drew a cartoon of David launching a rocket from Beaumont to Fredericksburg. But our frequent disagreements didn't stop us from having a beer or margarita together on occasion at the Texas Chili Parlor across the street from the hotel where board members usually stayed in Austin. I guess that you could say that my relationship with Mr. Bradley was "somewhat complicated" except where the beers and margaritas were concerned.

CHAPTER **22**

My Final Years Dealing with Democrats and "Wing Nuts"

IN SEPTEMBER OF 2003, the voters approved a constitutional amendment to allow the SBOE to adopt a total return spending plan for the PSF. This meant that money could be spent from the fund's total value, which included capital gains and reinvested dividends and interest. While money to pay active managers still depended on a legislative appropriation, this would allow the board to invest more in stocks that had a greater potential for growing the fund over the long term, which would give us a better chance to guarantee intergenerational equity (student population growth plus inflation) for the future. I favored this move but I realized that the downside might be that there could be a move to more risky investments such as private equities and hedge funds which would mean higher management costs. However, I had an open mind because "diversification" is my second rule in investing and I was at least willing to listen to the pros and cons of alternative investments. And, I digress, but my first investment rule is "Buy low, sell high" and number eight is "Never invest in anything that eats, needs fixing, or floats on water".

Sometime in early 2004, Governor Perry named Shirley Neeley, the superintendent of schools of the Galena Park Independent School District near Houston, as the new Commissioner of Education. Dr.

Neeley had been named the top superintendent in the state the year before because Galena Park, in spite of being one of the state's most diversified districts, had recorded very high scores on the Texas Assessment of Knowledge and Skills (TAKS). Shirley was a very gregarious and upbeat lady with an extremely positive outlook about the future of education in the state. I thought that she was an excellent choice and she was immediately approved by the state senate. Dr. Neeley stayed in office for the rest of my time on the board and I enjoyed working with her in spite of her somewhat annoying "cheerleader" approach to almost everything.

There were several important issues on the board's agenda in 2004. For the PSF, the main decisions to make were whether or not to index international investments and setting an annual payout rate for the fund which had just changed from income to total return. As for indexing internationals, I felt that it was a no-brainer. We had already indexed large cap, mid cap, and small cap domestic stocks which saved the fund millions of dollars in management fees. But two board members, both Democrats, were very close to at least one of the two companies that were still managing our international portfolio and I wasn't sure if we could convince a majority of the members to do what I thought was prudent. One of the companies was so desperate that they offered to lower their fees almost to the point that they would be paying us. That offer sounded too good to be true and it was. The real problem was that they had underperformed their benchmark which was the equivalent of an international index. So, after costing the fund millions of dollars in gains, they were offering to lower their fees so that they continue to do so. Go figure!!! I expected David Bradley and his three supporters to side with the two Democrats as they usually did, but they surprised me and voted to fire the international managers and go with indexing. As for the payout rate, the board eventually, after a lot of haggling, decided on a four percent per year payout rate which was less than the legislature wanted but was one that I thought was reasonable.

Another issue on the board's plate that year had to do with teacher certification. The board had lost most of its authority over this issue a few years before to a new board called the State Board for Educator Certification (SBEC), but the SBOE maintained authority to reject its actions. One of the actions of SBEC that year was a proposal to grant two year temporary certificates to teachers in grades 8-12 to teach in subject matter areas of their majors without taking the necessary education courses for a permanent teaching certificate. Because of my personal experience as a public high school teacher who had labored through mostly useless college education courses and had also been a faculty member in a college education department, I strongly favored this proposal. I always felt that I was at least a decent social studies teacher but I admit that I could have been much better had I taken more upper-level history and government courses in college instead of wasting my time in courses that supposedly taught me how to teach instead of what to teach. During my career in the public schools, I witnessed teachers struggle to teach subjects for which they had very little knowledge. I acknowledge that pedagogy (how to teach) is important, especially for elementary teachers, but it is not nearly as important as subject matter knowledge. So, needless to say, I supported SBEC's proposal even though all of the board's Democrats voted against it. I still can't explain why a matter such as this has anything to do with politics.

Another of the board's powers that had not been taken away by the legislature was the ability to determine graduation requirements. On the surface, this seemed to be a very important power except for the fact that only the legislature could appropriate money, so anything that the board passed that had a fiscal note could go into effect only after the legislature appropriated the funds. So in 2004, when some board members wanted to increase the science graduation requirements from three to four credits, there was lots of pushback from legislators, some board members, local school districts, and teachers who taught electives or directed extra-curricular activities. Taking away electives didn't sit well with athletic coaches, band directors, fine arts teachers, etc. who didn't want to lose students from their respective programs even though some of these programs should not have occurred during the school day in the first place. The result was that school districts frequently sought waivers from the TEA to allow middle school courses to count toward graduation from high school. But most board members, who had not darkened the halls of a public school building since their high school days, were unaware of all of this and were prone to favor tougher graduation requirements in order to please those constituents who were for more rigorous requirements.

Increasing the science requirement was particularly difficult because qualified science teachers were already in short supply and, in addition, many schools lacked enough science labs that would be needed. The vote to add the fourth year of science for the recommended program, after much haggling, eventually passed with an 8-7 vote and, because of teacher shortage and financial concerns, I voted against it. The vote was not only bi-partisan, but Republicans from both factions voted on both sides which was unusual on controversial issues. However, implementation for the 2007-08 school year was contingent on funding, and, after all these years, I'm not sure whether or not it was ever implemented. But, even if it was funded by the legislature, it was still partially an unfunded mandate because capital outlays, such as science labs, are required to be paid for by local property taxes. As a conservative, I would never vote for an unfunded mandate.

In another issue, health books were among those up for adoption in 2004. Because some issues such as marriage, sex education, birth control, etc. were required to be taught in the health curriculum, there was sure to be some controversy and Terri Leo, always seeking the limelight, was geared up for a fight. Hearings were held in July and September and lots of people testified for and against the books, based mainly on their respective beliefs. But beliefs, according to the law, didn't count unless they were also facts backed up by empirical evidence. I had many friends who were employees of the textbook publishers and I was sometimes accused of "being in the pockets of the publishers" in spite of the fact that I had been the lone SBOE member to vote against a history book published by one of my best friend's employer, Prentice Hall, in 2002. By 2004, publishers were more aware of the board's politics and did everything that they could to avoid controversy. At the time, there was a state law prohibiting gay marriage and Terri Leo demanded that Holt Rinehart and Winston, a company whose sales director was a friend of mine, demanded that their health book define marriage as being between and man and a woman. Since this definition was state law, I agreed with Terri that this was not an unreasonable demand as long as the change was initiated by the publisher and not the board. My friend's company complied without action from the board, and that pretty much solved the problem. As a result, all of the health books were approved. Now that the Supreme Court has ruled against state laws that outlawed gay marriages, I would assume that textbook publishers are now free to define marriage differently without interference from SBOE members.

2004 was an election year but I had a four-year term and was not up for re-election. But Linda Bauer was and she, who was elected as a far right candidate, was now a target of the far right faction headed by David Bradley and Terri Leo. Linda was never comfortable as a board member but was slow to announce her plans about running for re-election. In the end, she decided to run but she didn't put up much of a fight and Barbara Cargill, who was recruited by Terri Leo, ran against her in the Republican primary in a heavily Republican district and won. I didn't know anything about Ms. Cargill but, when I had a chance to meet her, I was pleasantly surprised because, other than being attractive, she didn't seem to have anything in common with Terri. She was a former science teacher who now ran her own science camp in the Woodlands, north of Houston, and, like I, was a member of the United Methodist Church, not exactly a bastion of religious fundamentalism. I was so impressed that I even gave her a small contribution to help her retire her campaign debts. Little did I know that she would turn against me two years later when I was up for re-election even though we got along very well during her first two years as a member of the SBOE.

When the year 2005 began, legislative leaders expressed their displeasure with the board over its decision to ignore their request to set the payout rate from the PSF at 4.5%. Their search for money without increasing taxes was not successful and they demanded that we reconsider so that they could meet our request for purchasing textbooks. In November, I had reluctantly voted for the 4.5% rate but had been forced to settle on a rate of 4.0% when not enough of my colleagues would go along. That had been okay with me because I believed that a higher rate would endanger the board's goal to provide intergenerational equity for the future. But the legislature persisted in its demands and Commissioner Neeley urged Ms. Miller to call a special meeting in early January to reconsider. Ms. Miller complied and, after much haggling, the board unanimously approved a 4.5% payout rate. Had we not done so, I think that it was very possible that the legislature would have attempted to disband the SBOE with a proposed constitutional amendment. Looking back, that may have been a good thing.

Our first regular meeting in 2005 was scheduled for February, and, because of a family commitment, I was unable to attend the Committee of the Whole meeting on Thursday. But, to the surprise of my colleagues, I had requested to move from the Finance committee to the committee on Instruction. I felt that I had accomplished my mission where the PSF was concerned by helping to rid the board of the politics and corruption caused by active managers and that I had little more to accomplish by being a member of this committee. Besides, I was on an education board and it seemed to me that, of the three committees, Instruction was the one most closely associated with education. So, although I was not present when the committee assignments were announced, Ms. Miller honored my request and I became a member of the committee on Instruction. Some members thought that I had been punished by the board's officers for being too assertive on PSF issues but nothing could have been further from the truth.

MY TEXAS LIFE IN THE (NOT SO) FAST LANE

There wasn't much controversy on the Instruction committee largely because the development of curriculum standards and textbook adoptions were so important that they were assigned to the Committee of the Whole. During the early part of my time on the committee, I received a call from a lady who was a constituent of mine to tell me about a problem that her daughter faced at her high school. The dad was a doctor at one of the state's top hospitals and the family had moved to Texas after the daughter had already entered high school. She was now a senior, a member of the school debate team, an honor student, and was scheduled to graduate the following spring. But, unfortunately, she was informed that she couldn't graduate until she had completed a required course called Communications Applications (basically a ninth grade level speech class). The state that she came from had no such requirement and, besides, most of the students in her new Texas high school had completed the course requirement in middle school. I informed the mother that I would look into it and that it shouldn't be a problem because most board members would surely agree that debate team membership would most certainly substitute for the course. After all, the physical education requirement could be satisfied by athletics, marching band, ROTC, cheerleading, and who knows what all else. When I was in high school, even vocational agriculture and home economics substituted for Phys. Ed.

But there were no approved substitutes for this course so I met with TEA staff in an attempt to find some to introduce to the board. They suggested Public Speaking, Speech Communications, and Debate. I brought the matter up at the Instruction committee and both Terri Leo and Mary Helen Berlanga agreed that substitutions should be offered as long as the courses were not less rigorous than Communications Applications. But I ran into a roadblock in Ms. Miller who, as chair, made the decision as to whether to bring matters up before the full board. Thinking that former commissioner Mike Moses and I were friends, she informed me that he had been opposed to substitutions for this course. But Commissioner Neeley was also my friend and she was in favor of my efforts. When it became evident that Ms. Miller wouldn't budge, the commissioner cornered me at a board meeting and said "Coach, don't worry about it, I'll take care of it". I don't know what Commissioner Neeley did, but a few weeks later I got a call from the girl's mother thanking me for solving the problem for her daughter. However, there still were no substitutions for the course for other students. But I am proud to say that I got the ball rolling and now the speech requirement can be satisfied with Communications Applications, Speech Communications, Public Speaking, Debate, and Oral Interpretation.

I was no longer a member of the Finance committee so I didn't keep up with PSF issues as closely as I had in the past. During my first four years on the board, our investment advisor was Callan Associates, based in San Francisco. Their representative was Carl Deane and his job was to offer investment counseling services such as asset allocation and recommending firms to manage the assets. Mr. Deane was highly respected by all board members and most of us considered him, rather than his firm, to be our adviser. They charged us only $75,000 per year for their services and I often wondered how they could break even at this rate after paying Mr. Deane's expenses to travel back and forth from San Francisco to Austin several times a year. After all, the PSF was a $20 billion fund and $75,000 amounted to a grain of sand on a large beach in comparison. But, in 2005, I found out when an article appeared in "Forbes" Magazine that was critical of Callan for some of their practices in recommending managers for large pension and endowment funds. They had an investment conference every year called Callan College and charged fees to management firms to attend. It just so happened that all thirteen firms that had been recommended to manage PSF assets were paying members of Callan College. As far as I know, however, they were never found to have done anything illegal. But, for me, this didn't exactly pass the "smell test".

Like most board members, I liked Carl Deane and hated to lose his services. But as a prudent fiduciary, as I was sworn to be, I thought it would be prudent to issue an RFP rather than to automatically renew Callan's contract when it expired that year. My decision was made easier when Mr. Deane announced his retirement. As a whole, the firms recommended by Callan had added value to the fund but they had still underperformed their benchmarks by a collective $750 million over the years when you considered the $125 million that they had been paid. But in spite of all of this, some members, especially David Bradley, didn't want to hire another firm. However, knowing that Callan could respond to the new RFP, the board's decision to issue the RFP was unanimous. After the internal staff narrowed the field of respondents to four firms, the finance committee met to interview them. Since all board members could attend the meeting, it became almost a Committee of the Whole.

Before this meeting, I was almost sure that Callan would be rehired because David Bradley had two Democrats on his side and four Republicans followed faithfully along with him on PSF matters in return for his vote on "culture war" matters such as textbooks. That was seven votes, eight made a majority, and you never knew how Ms. Miller would vote on anything. But a crazy thing happened at the meeting when Callan was interviewed and one of their male representatives was sporting an earring. At a break, I asked Gail Lowe (probably the most fundamentalist of all the members) if she noticed the earring. Her answer was "yes" so I knew that Callan's days as our adviser were about to end. But I still questioned them about the poor performance of the managers that they had recommended over the years and the guy with the earring replied that their job was to recommend managers not to manage the money for them. That answer sealed the deal and a new consultant was soon hired.

There were thirty-seven endowment funds in the nation with over $1 billion in assets and, unlike the PSF, almost all of them had investments in alternative asset classes such as real estate, private equity, hedge funds, etc. However most of them were managed by professionals and I wasn't sure that this was something that the PSF should do because of the lack of investment knowledge on the part of board members, including myself. We each had an investment adviser but they didn't receive compensation even for their travel expenses. As a result, only a few of us consulted with our advisers. My adviser John Bell lived in Austin so he was probably the most active one. At any rate, after consulting with John, I was somewhat reluctant to vote to approve new asset classes for the fund although internal PSF staff tried to convince me based on the fact we needed more diversification with less risk in order to provide intergenerational equity for a growing student population that was becoming more difficult to educate each year.

Toward the end of 2005, the board had a meeting in which Holland Timmins, executive director of the PSF, made the case for alternative investments. I suspected that internal staff had some personal interest in this in that they needed something more than indexing in order to pad their resumes for higher paying positions at other endowment or pension funds. Mr. Timmins, who I respected a lot, pointed out that the PSF had been underperforming its peers and, in his opinion, it was because the PSF was investing in only stocks and bonds. He was correct about that even though our fund was doing quite well without alternative investments. But, after listening to his presentation, Ms. Miller adjourned the meeting after passionately pointing out that the PSF was still the top performing endowment fund in the nation. The number of eyes that rolled was astounding because the board's chair was essentially calling the executive director of the fund a liar. I had a hard time remaining silent after her ridiculous comment. But I did and so did everyone else in the room.

Although the issue of bilingual education was never an action item while I was an SBOE member, there was lots of discussion about this controversial issue. As a conservative, I had always followed the Republican mantra in favoring immersion over bilingual education as the best way to educate non English speaking students. But I later learned that I was wrong because I really didn't understand the issue. At the time, my stepson was married to an educated Hispanic lady who was in no way a hard core liberal. She explained to me that, although immersion was fine in teaching people to speak and understand conversations in another language, it was not good in learning to read and write another language, which is necessary in staying on grade level in courses such as math, science and social studies. In other words, conversing in a second language is one thing but reading and writing a second language is a completely different thing. So it began to make sense to me that students should be taught in their native language in subject specific courses while they were also learning English in their language classes. This is what is truly meant by bilingual education even though most people don't understand that.

CHAPTER **23**

The Election of 2006 (and After)

MY SECOND TERM was expiring in 2006, and I was sure to get an opponent (or opponents) in the March 2006 Republican Primary. Although they voted with me a majority of the time, my far right colleagues had never forgiven me for defeating their almost cult-like leader Bob Offutt in 2000. And I must admit that I had helped recruit candidates to oppose some of them on occasion. They had made a mistake in 2002 when they recruited a bad candidate with an unusual name to run against me and they were not likely to repeat their mistake. It is common knowledge in politics that a far right candidate has a better chance of winning in a Republican primary against an incumbent if the incumbent can be forced into a runoff. That's because runoffs attract the more activist voters and voter turnout is usually very low. It is said that runoffs attract only those voters who drive around town all year long looking for "vote here" signs. So when I drew two opponents in 2006, I suspected that my colleagues recruited both of them.

Mark Loewe was a relatively young guy from Austin who sometimes testified before the SBOE, usually about what he thought were failings of the Texas Education Agency. In his most recent testimony, he had made wild accusations that there were mistakes on the TAKS exam and that TEA knew about the mistakes but had failed to correct them. Some members, especially Don McLeroy, always seemed to agree with any citizen who criticized the Agency, and I noticed that Don huddled up with Mr. Loewe for a fairly long period of time after his testimony ended. I had no idea what this guy's party affiliation was but I wasn't totally surprised when he announced as a primary opponent of mine. Not long after his announcement, one of the newspapers in Austin reported that he was active in a local atheist organization. I strongly suspected that Don McLeroy, a religious fundamentalist, had unwittingly recruited an atheist who was also a conspiracy theorist to run against me.

Ken Mercer, from San Antonio, was a local political activist who had served one two year term in the state legislature after defeating a Democrat in a predominantly Democratic district in 2002. Ken was a right-winger who had won in the primary against an establishment Hispanic business woman who was hand-picked to run by the local Republican Party leaders. As a result, he was not a favorite of party insiders in Bexar County and they probably felt there was little reason to offer much help to him in the general election against the Democrat Raul Prado. But Ken had the election handed to him on a silver platter when, a few weeks before the election, Prado was indicted on corruption charges and would eventually serve a prison term. As a result, Ken served for two years as a backbench member of the legislature. When he ran for re-election in 2004, he was defeated by a Democrat even though George W. Bush carried the district by a comfortable margin.

I didn't know Mr. Mercer that well but I had crossed paths with him a few times at political events in Bexar County and also at the state capital during his short legislative term. I found him to be a very amiable guy but I didn't know much else about him. I had no idea that he had any plans to run against me in 2006 until I saw him at a 2005 board meeting and heard rumors that Terri Leo was introducing him to several other board members. I soon got a call from the Bexar County Republican chairman that Ken was planning to run for my seat. And, by the time he announced, he had gathered a long list of endorsements and some of them were state legislators who later told me that they had no idea that he was running against a Republican incumbent when he asked for their endorsement. I knew that this was going to be a tough race because Ken had a very good candidate name and he also had some name recognition in the district because of his one term in the legislature. I also knew that I would likely face a runoff and I knew that far-right candidates had an advantage in runoffs.

As for money, just as in 2002, I didn't actively seek contributions. I had a few people with money and an interest in education that had contributed in the past so I had enough to compete and I didn't think that either of my opponents would raise much money either. The district was so large that, in order for money to do much good, there would have to be lots of it. Campaign signs were out of the question but one thing that I didn't think about was that Ken had kept his signs from his legislative days and all he had to do was cover the word "legislature" with "State Board of Education" and have the altered signs placed at the voting sites. Campaigning consisted mostly of candidate forums at Republican club meetings throughout the district and I knew that I could hold my own at those. But probably less than five percent of eventual primary voters attended them. Mark Loewe didn't appear at any of them and Ken attended most of the first ones but didn't do well. He was a large man with kind of a stuttering speech pattern and he didn't seem to know much about public education. Like most of the far-right board members, he sent his two young daughters to a private Christian school. As the campaign went on, he stopped coming to the forums almost altogether. He didn't have to because he got a $35,000 contribution from James Leininger. That was enough money for mailers and robo calls depicting me as a flaming liberal who would do all kinds of bad things detrimental to our school children. One of the calls was from his two young daughters, one of whom was only nine years old. That was disgusting and I lost all respect for the man. Merle Haggard recorded a song titled "The Roots of my Raising Run Deep" which partially describes my feeling about this incident. The roots of my east Texas "raising" would never allow me to stoop so low. I would much rather lose an election than to arrange for my nine year old child to become involved in an outright lie just so that her father could return to the political arena.

Dr. James Leininger is a wealthy physician, businessman, and philanthropist from San Antonio. He founded Kinetic Concepts, a medical technology corporation, as well as several other successful businesses such as Promised Land Foods, Sunday House Foods, and Plantation Seafood Co. Politically, he is best known for founding the Texas Public Policy Foundation (TPPF) and for his almost laser focused support for school vouchers. He had financially supported several conservative politicians including George W. Bush and Rick Perry, and, although the State Board of Education has nothing to do with school vouchers, in the 1990's, he almost single handedly financed the campaigns of several conservative SBOE candidates including Dr. Bob Offutt. But when Dr. Offutt campaigned against Bush in the 2000 Presidential primary, he suspended funding for SBOE candidates. I met Dr. Leininger on one occasion at a political event at the home of former actress Susan Howard outside of Boerne and found him to be a very nice, but somewhat shy, man who had very little to say to anybody. I'm not sure about this, but I may have been the only SBOE member to ever meet Dr. Leininger personally and our conversation that day was too short for me to get around to letting him know that I am a strong supporter of vouchers, even the private school ones. I didn't talk about vouchers much at campaign events because, in my role as an SBOE member, I knew that I would never have a chance to vote on the issue. So, if he thought that the $35,000 that he gave to Ken Mercer would help to achieve vouchers in Texas, he was sadly mistaken. The same would have been true had I been on the receiving end of his money. To me, throwing around that kind of money to accomplish nothing is foolish and is something that I would never do. David Bradley was probably one of my colleagues who convinced Dr. Leininger to donate to my opponent and David was an opponent of vouchers because he thought that they would negatively impact homeschooling. Go Figure!!! Like Merle Haggard sang, I believe that the roots of Dr. Leininger's "raising ran deep" but I also believe that he had a tendency to listen to the wrong people, which is why he made zero progress in convincing policy makers to approve vouchers in Texas. Had he been better informed, he would have discovered that, unlike Mr. Bradley, I was a strong supporter of private school vouchers but only the legislature has the power to approve them.

When early voting started that year, there were old Ken Mercer legislative signs at every polling site that had been altered to reflect his new run for the SBOE. Ken had enlisted the help of young homeschoolers from all over the district to place the signs even though the SBOE had no power whatsoever over home schools. And, besides, no one could have been more supportive of the right of parents to homeschool their kids than I. But I am not a demagogue and I would have never campaigned to support or oppose something over which I had no control. But my opponent, Ken Mercer, evidently had no problem with doing so as long as it would help him become an elected official again, regardless of the position. He, unlike I, was a pure political junkie who wanted to be elected to something.

On the day of the election, I knew that I would not fare well but I still felt that I would at least make the runoffs. I was right but barely. Ken got 49.8% of the vote and I was saved for another month only because Mark Loewe, an atheist, received almost 7500 votes after doing no campaigning at all. He would have probably doubled that total had he simply removed the first "e" from his last name. You would think that an atheist running in a Republican primary would receive almost no votes but this was the State Board of Education, and almost nobody has any idea who the candidates are much less what they stand for. But robo calls, mailers, polling place signs, and familiar candidate names are all very powerful and can overcome lack of knowledge on the part of voters, especially in down ballot races. I considered dropping out of the race altogether to save counties the expense of conducting a runoff but, when I discovered that there were other runoffs in every county in the district, I decided to stay the course mainly because I didn't want to give in to a candidate who would stoop so low as to have his children send out a false negative message about me that they were too young to understand. Even though I stayed the course, I lost in the runoff by a large margin to a lesser qualified candidate and suddenly became a lame duck member of the State Board of Education.

Looking back, I may have done a few things differently, but not many. I probably wouldn't have become involved so much in the races involving my colleagues. But that wouldn't have kept them from being involved against me. I had been defeated very decisively even though I had almost never received any negative feedback from any of my constituents. My only Republican enemy in the district that I was aware of was Adam McManus, a talk show host on a Christian radio station in San Antonio, whose ratings were so low that his listeners couldn't fill up a tent at an east Texas camp meeting revival. Candidates that he endorsed in Republican primaries almost never won and his views were so controversial that he was fired twice by his own radio station. When I first ran against Bob Offutt in 2000, my advisers told me not to agree to go on any show that was obviously supporting my opponent. I didn't have to worry about McManus in 2002 because he had been fired and was no longer on the air. But, in 2006, he was back at the station and I agreed, against my better judgment, to appear on his show although I knew that he was supporting Ken Mercer. But, to prove that none of that mattered, in 2010 he supported a qualified fundamentalist Christian candidate Joanie Muenzler against a strange homeless guy named Tony Cunningham in the Republican primary in a very Democratic district. Cunningham was undoubtedly the most unqualified candidate ever and I have no idea where he got the money to pay the fee to get on the ballot. But he won by a margin of sixteen percentage points which is more evidence that common names have more to do than anything in down ballot primary races and it also proved that an endorsement from an overly opinionated and uninformed person like Adam McManus is completely useless. McManus was not a preacher. But he was a religious zealot and he brought back memories of my father who didn't care for preachers who involved themselves in politics, especially those who told church members how to vote. He once said that "preachers should save souls, marry people, preach funerals, and keep the grass mowed around the church". My dad had little use for those who mixed religion with politics. His son couldn't agree more.

I would not be the only lame duck member of the SBOE for the rest of the year. Cynthia Thornton, a Republican, and Joe Bernal, a Democrat, didn't run for re-election. Cynthia had been elected with me in 2000 and Joe, a former state senator from San Antonio, had been elected in 1996. Cynthia's husband convinced her not to seek re-election because of an encounter that she had with David Bradley in which she accused him of physically threatening her. I don't know the details of the encounter but I do know that, because of Mr. Thornton's concerns, security at board meetings were increased after Ms. Thornton's accusations. I also know that Mr. Bradley was a very abrasive individual with a hot temper who could sometimes let his emotions overcome him. As for Joe Bernal, he was getting up there in age and simply felt that it was time for full retirement. Joe and I didn't agree on many things but we were still friends and our friendship didn't start with our membership on the SBOE. Joe was also a basketball referee at one time and had officiated some of my games when I coached at Tivy High School in Kerrville. Tincy Miller also was a lame duck chairwoman because she had served as chair for four years which was all that was allowed under the state constitution.

During my six years on the board, the far-right faction's power was limited because they never had more than five members at any one time. But, beginning in 2007, they would have seven. Ken Mercer was very much on the far right and Ms. Thornton's replacement was Cynthia Dunbar, who was reported to be so far to the right that she made all the others seem like left wing liberals. Dr. Bernal's replacement was a young Democrat named Rick Agosto, a principal in one of the money management firms that we had fired. Joe had hand picked him to run and he won in an uncontested primary and had only token Republican opposition in the general election. Joe and another

Democrat, Rene Nunez, almost always voted with David Bradley on PSF matters and sometimes on other issues, so it appeared that the far-right group might be back in power because Joe Bernal and Rick Agosto were very close. I'm sure that shady money managers were anticipating a bonanza from the results of the 2006 elections.

I dutifully served out my eight lame duck months as a member of the SBOE with no problems. I don't remember any important items that came before the board during that time, at least none that caused any controversy. I guess that my far right colleagues stayed quiet while waiting for January when they would have a better chance of advancing their far right agenda. When I left, like all outgoing members before me, I got a resolution recognizing my service as a member of the board. And Cynthia Thornton, Joe Bernal, and I also got a replica of the chair that we sat in with the State of Texas seal inscribed on the back rest.

Soon after I left the board, Governor Perry fired Commissioner Neeley and replaced her with Robert Scott, who was the current deputy Commissioner and had served as interim Commissioner before Dr. Neeley was hired in 2003. I don't know the cause of the firing but I always felt that it might have something to do with the fact that Dr. Neeley was completely apolitical. Robert was a definite Republican who had worked as an education adviser to both Governors Bush and Perry. Dr. Neeley was, in my view, a great Commissioner who didn't mind letting you know how she stood on anything, no matter what members of any political party or faction thought. And, I have no proof, but I sometimes thought that Mr. Scott would, on occasion, try to undermine her.

In 2008, the far right members recruited a candidate to run against my friend Pat Hardy. But they still hadn't learned their lesson about common candidate names and she defeated Barney Maddox by a huge margin. In 2010, almost every Republican incumbent received a primary opponent. Geraldine Miller had been on the board forever and had never had a primary challenger, but an unknown guy named George Clayton ran against her and won simply because she used her silly sounding nickname "Tincy" on the ballot. Don McLeroy was also defeated in the primary by Thomas Ratliff, who had good name recognition in the eastern part of the state because he was the son of former Lieutenant Governor Bill Ratliff, a supporter of mine. Cynthia Dunbar felt that she was too important for the State Board of Education so she ran for an open Congressional seat and was so far out there that she failed to get four percent of the primary vote. Bob Craig, my best friend on the board, had a primary opponent but had no problem winning re-election.

Except for one glaring negative (terrible candidate name), Ken Mercer's opponent in the 2010 primary was the perfect candidate. Tim Tuggey was a highly regarded San Antonio attorney and civic leader who was the law partner of Tom Loeffler, a former Republican congressman. Like Chase Untermeyer and Bob Craig, he was probably over qualified for the position he was seeking. Almost everybody who was anybody in the San Antonio Republican business, political, and legal communities including B.J. "Red" McCombs, Tom Loeffler, and HEB President Charles Butt, got behind Tim's candidacy. Money was no problem and Mr. McCombs even did a radio commercial for Tim that played all day every day on several local stations. Right after Tim announced, he called me for my support and also asked to meet with me at a coffee shop in downtown Fredericksburg. I was impressed with Tim's knowledge about the issues and agreed to do all I could to help but, when our meeting drew to a close, I had to tell him the bad news which was that there was no possible way that a candidate named Tuggey could beat one named Mercer in a State Board of Education primary race. I wish that I had been wrong but I was right. Mercer ended up with 69% of the vote to Tuggey's 31% even though Tuggey was far more qualified.

In 2012, Gail Lowe lost her seat in the primary and Tincy Miller won her's back after letting voters know that George Clayton was rumored to be gay. Poor George finished third in a field of four candidates. Both Tincy and David Bradley retired from the board in 2018 which means that Pat Hardy, who I recruited to run in 2002, is now the senior member of the State Board of Education. Only two other members, Barbara Cargill and Democrat Lawrence Allen, are remnants from my days on the board. When I was a colleague of Lawrence, he was currently the principal of Jesse H. Jones High School in Houston, where I had taught history and coached basketball in the mid 1960's.

When I left the board in 2006, I was 67 years old so it was time to retire anyway. I had already sacrificed financially by being a board member although I had continued to work part-time as a sales representative for a magazine in the Texas Hill Country that featured mostly multi-million dollar ranch properties for sale. Jo had retired from her job with the Admiral Nimitz Foundation and we were both already collecting Social Security. And, because our investments were doing well, plus Jo's German heritage as a cautious spender, we had no financial problems. There is an old joke in the German Texas Hill Country that copper wire was invented in Fredericksburg -- "Two Germans pulling on a penny". I've never pulled on a penny myself and there is no German blood in my Scots-Irish veins as far as I know. But I will admit to bending down to pick up a penny off the street every now and then.

In spite of all the controversies, most involving members of my own political party, I have few regrets. I made lots of good friends from Texas Education Agency staff, textbook publisher representatives, teacher organizations, charter school holders, state legislators, and just plain citizens interested in improving public education in Texas. In most cases, I never knew what their political affiliation was because I didn't care. As my old friend and former Democrat SBOE member Will Davis loved to say --"I've never seen either an "R" or a "D" on the forehead of a student in a public school in this state". I exited the public square with nothing more than my head held high and a big old chair with the seal of the State of Texas imprinted on it.

CHAPTER **24**

My Nemisis, David Bradley

IF I HAD any regrets, one would be that I could have had a better relationship with some of my colleagues such as David Bradley. But, other than his like-minded far right followers, my relationship with David was about as good as anyone else's. He had a very abrasive and confrontational personality and he had almost nothing positive to say about public schools. Why he wanted to be on a board that dealt exclusively with public education I'll never know, but I never questioned his right to do so.

David, who reminded me of a school yard bully, was known to operate on the edge. He had been indicted, along with two other board members, for violating the open meetings law only to have the charges dropped when he agreed to a ninety minute ethics course that he satisfied along with all other board members including myself. He was criticized in an independent audit of the Permanent School Fund for his questionable relationship with the board's performance consultant (Russell Stein), an "informal" advisor who was closely associated with the consultant (Brian Borowski), and at least one manager of PSF funds. In addition, he had been accused by a female board member of physical threats against her which caused the Department of Public Safety to increase security at board meetings. Plus, it was widely reported in the Southeast Texas news media that he was not even a legal resident of the district which he served and that he had rented apartments in Beaumont to registered sex offenders, including at least one who was a convicted child molester.

I could go on and on about this guy. Since I had spent a good part of my teaching and coaching career in southeast Texas, I had several friends who were still in the school business there and knew that I was a member of the SBOE. I lost count of the number of phone calls that I received complaining about David's antics, mainly surrounding his alleged attempts to micromanage schools in the area. I even got one anonymous call from a charter school employee to report on frequent meetings and phone conversations that David and her boss were having while he was chair of the Planning committee that dealt with charter schools.

In 2004, Mr. Bradley got a very strong opponent in the Republican primary that I was largely responsible for recruiting in retaliation for his efforts against me in 2002. She was the wife of a well-known Beaumont businessman and had been very involved in civic endeavors in the area. But, within twenty-four hours, she dropped out of the race because of the verbal attacks that David had launched against her. So, as usual, he had no opposition in the primary and the general election was no problem for him in a Republican district that ran all the way to Fort Bend County, southwest of Houston. Unfortunately, his intimidation tactics had worked again.

I will admit to a case of "sour grapes" after I lost the election in 2006. My loss undoubtedly had a lot to do with the large infusion of money from James Leininger to my opponent's campaign and to endorsements that he got from conservatives who wrongly believed that I was opposed to school choice such as vouchers. I am convinced that this false information came from David Bradley and Terri Leo even though David was the one that opposed vouchers, not me. Some of my opponent's endorsements came from heads of conservative groups to which I had donated money in the past. But these people were so clueless about the powers of the SBOE that they didn't even know that a decision about vouchers was not one for the board to make.

Since there had always been talk about David not living the district that he served, I did some research of my own and discovered that the evidence showed beyond any doubt that David and his family lived in Jasper County, which was in a different SBOE district than where he claimed that he lived. So I wrote a letter, with attachments for proof, and sent it to Tom Maness, the Jefferson County (Beaumont) district attorney whose office I was told had jurisdiction over candidate/office holder matters. One of the documents attached was a record in the Jasper County Appraisal District office that showed that the Bradleys had purchased a home in Jasper County in late 2000, had been granted a homestead exemption for tax year 2001, and had continued to claim this exemption through the present year which was 2007.

Texas law covering residential homestead exemptions requires ownership of the property on January 1 of each year of the exemption and occupation of the property as a principal residence on January 1. This statement was on the "Application for Residential Homestead Exemption" that Mr. Bradley checked and signed when he applied for the exemption, thus acknowledging that his principal residence had been in Jasper County since at least January 1, 2001. This county was in SBOE District 8 while the Bradleys' were using David's office in Beaumont, which was in SBOE District 7, for voter registration and office holder purposes. This property was listed on Jefferson County records as commercial, not residential.

I also presented evidence from school officials in Buna that the Bradleys' son was registered in the schools there and was not paying tuition which is required for students living outside a school district. One of the school officials said that the Bradleys attended the same Buna church as he and that he was also aware of the location of the house where they lived. The Buna phone directory also listed a number in Ms. Bradley's name.

Residency requirements for SBOE candidates and members are covered under Texas Education Code, 7.103(b) which reads – "A person may not be elected from or serve in a district who is not a bona fide resident of the district with one year's continuous residence before election", and David had signed a homestead exemption acknowledging that he was the occupant of the home in Jasper County and that it was his principal residence on January 1 of each exemption year. It would be impossible to be a continuous resident for a year without living there on January 1.

Not only was David violating residency requirements for a board member, he and his wife were probably violating Texas law by claiming residence in a county in which they didn't reside when they registered to vote as well as when they voted. It also appeared that he had violated Texas law (Penal Code Sec. 37.10) by making a false entry in a governmental record when he listed the Beaumont address as his place of residence when he filed for re-election in 2002 and 2004. And, if he could somehow prove that his office in Beaumont was his legal residence, he would have been violating the law when he applied for the homestead exemption in Jasper County.

After mailing the letter, with supporting evidence, to the district attorney in Beaumont, I never heard back so I felt that he had thrown it in the trash. But, a few months later, I got a call from an attorney in the office of Attorney General Greg Abbott. The Jefferson County DA had referred the matter to the AG and the lawyer assigned to it had resigned (or been fired) and had left it on his desk unopened. The attorney that called, along with the help of a colleague, had examined my evidence and had determined that it was a case that could be successfully prosecuted. He asked if he could come to my home in Fredericksburg and discuss the case with me.

By the time that the two AG attorneys and an investigator arrived at my home, they had already investigated to some extent and had determined that there was enough evidence to present to a grand jury. They had already interviewed several of my sources and ensured me that most of them had agreed to testify if needed. The investigator had already tailed Mr. Bradley's movements for a few days and determined that he always left his office in Beaumont in the afternoon, traveled to his home near Buna, and returned to his office the following morning. As a result, they were convinced that David had lied on an official document when he gave his Beaumont office as his residence for voting and office holder purposes. They told me that there was no question in their minds that his legal residence was in Jasper County and that he had been serving illegally for several years as an SBOE member representing District 7.

The day before the grand jury convened, I traveled to Beaumont to testify. The next morning, several other people, none of whom I knew, were waiting to testify. I later learned that most of them were people who were residents of houses or apartments in or near David's office building in Beaumont who were there to testify that they had never seen evidence of him staying overnight at his office. Because grand jury proceedings are secret, I cannot reveal what was discussed but I left convinced that an indictment would be forthcoming. The AG attorneys even told me as much.

Boy was I wrong!!! I never heard another word about the case until 2010 when I ran into one of the attorneys outside a courtroom in Fredericksburg. When he recognized me, he profusely apologized but said that something happened that he was not authorized to discuss and that the statute of limitations had expired on the case. When I asked him if Attorney General Greg Abbott had quashed the case for political reasons, he simply repeated that he was not authorized to reply. I didn't care much for Abbott before and, even though I won't vote for a Democrat against him now that he is governor, I can't bring myself to vote for him either. He, like too many other politicians in both parties, is too much of an ideologue for my tastes.

Although I am not a big Donald Trump guy, at least he is not an ideologue. Sorry, but I can't say the same for some of my own party's politicians from Texas such as Abbott, Ted Cruz, Dan Patrick, Ken Paxton, Sid Miller, and (God forbid) Louie "Gomer" Gohmert. The last two are complete clowns and, if I lived in Louie's district, I would have to consider voting for the Democrat. I've always said that I am a "mainstream" Republican and a "mainline" Christian Protestant. I guess that means that I am a "country club" Republican who can't afford the membership dues and a Christian who has nothing against beer, bourbon, short pants, country music, and dancing.

In 2008, I received a call from Laura Ewing, a lady from the southern Houston suburbs who, like Pat Hardy, I knew from my association with the social studies teacher organization in the state. Laura was a leader in this group and was also the director of social studies in the Pearland Independent School District. She was a sharp, attractive lady who had some political experience as a city council member in the city of Friendswood and had called to get my advice about running against David Bradley for SBOE, District 7. I had no idea what her political affiliation was but I knew that, with her common name, she would have a good chance to win in the Republican primary but almost no chance to win as a Democrat in the general election. I advised her to run as a Republican but I guess she was a committed Democrat and decided otherwise. This was a mistake and she eventually lost an election that she could have probably won had she followed my advice.

During that election, David Bradley sank to a new low (if that was possible) when he accused Ms. Ewing of seeking to put a Muslim curriculum in Texas public schools. His "proof" was a photo of a group of Texas educators, which included Ms. Ewing, posing in front of the Taj Mahal in India. He failed to mention the fact that the trip to East and North Africa and India was to study Islamic history and culture and that the trip was sanctioned by Governor Rick Perry because he said it is a "state of Texas requirement that sixth-grade world cultures classes as well as high school level world geography and history classes teach about the impact of Christian, Jewish, and Islamic culture on contemporary society." Governor Perry was quoting from the state-wide social studies curriculum that David Bradley had voted to approve. (I promise – I am not making this up!!!) David Bradley was actually accusing his political opponent of supporting a curriculum requirement that he had voted to approve.

CHAPTER **25**

Looking for a Shoulder to Cry On

I KEPT UP with the goings on with the SBOE for a couple of years after I left but I eventually lost interest. But I didn't lose interest in the state of public education in Texas. For many years, Texas students had done well on the NAEP (National Assessment of Educational Progress) which is a comparison, by state, of educational achievement for various student sub-groups such as Anglo, Hispanic, and African-American. Texas students in each sub-group had traditionally finished at or near the top among the states at the third grade level. They had also done okay at the eighth grade level but had fallen to near the middle of the pack. But, in the few years that twelfth graders were tested, Texas students finished near the bottom. This indicated to me that something negative was happening in Texas schools as students progressed toward graduation. While education leaders in Texas were bragging about how well our students were doing after completing third grade, I was, to quote country music singer Charlie Pride, looking for " A Shoulder to Cry On". After all, we don't send our students out into the world after elementary or middle school. The final product of K-12 education is the high school graduate. As a member of the SBOE, I expressed my concerns about this on numerous occasions only to have them dismissed by the statement that

"NAEP results for high school students are not valid because older students don't try as hard on tests when they know the results don't affect them individually". This view assumes that Texas students are more prone not to try than high school students in other states since they almost always underperformed on NAEP exams. That hardly made sense to me.

You would think that a State Board of Education member would be interested, as I was, in the quality of students that our schools were sending out into the world after the completion of a K-12 education. But, unfortunately, that was not the case. Most members were more interested in re-election and advancing up the political ladder. As a result, ideology trumped almost everything else. And, unfortunately, it probably still does. What one's stance is on evolution, global warming, gay marriage, and any number of other tired social issues probably is still more important than preparing Texas students for a successful adult life. It still haunts me that I was never able to do much to change that mindset.

CHAPTER **26**

"Montgomery Hill Plantation"

FOR ALMOST ELEVEN years after I left the coaching profession, I was a full-time contract print advertising account executive (high sounding term for "salesman"). That changed shortly after taking my seat on the SBOE and, for the next several years, I continued to work, on mostly a part-time basis, in magazine advertising sales. But that type of work, because of the internet explosion, eventually dried up, and for the past four years, just to stay busy, I have worked about ten or twelve hours a week for The News Group (TNG), the nation's largest magazine distributor. I work completely on my own and never have to leave the city limits of Fredericksburg.

I thought that my controversial days were over when I left the SBOE. But, in 2011, I got embroiled in a dispute caused by the discovery of twenty-five human remains (mostly children) on a small island in the Richland-Chambers reservoir that had once been Montgomery family property that we had been forced to sell to the Tarrant County Water District thirty years before. A severe drought had caused the remains, and their wooden coffins, to wash up onto the island which, as a boy, I knew only as a small hill in the middle of my family's pasture. The water district hired an Austin company with trained archaeologists and anthropologists to examine the remains to determine whose they might be. They eventually determined that they were most likely those of share croppers or tenant farmers who were descendants of freed slaves who lived in the area after the end of the Civil War. The remains were transferred to a predominantly Black cemetery in Corsicana and a historical marker was placed there by the water district. The inscription on the marker described the remains as those of "share croppers" and 'tenant farmers" who lived in the area after the Civil War. But, for some reason, the island was suddenly named "Montgomery Hill" even though I, nor any of my relatives, could ever recall anybody referring to it as that. To us, it was simply a small hill in the middle of a cow pasture.

Since I hadn't lived or spent a lot of time in Navarro County for several decades, I was only slightly aware of all the drama taking place until my cousin Margaret Montgomery Thomas emailed me a picture of a second historical marker that had been placed at the grave site by the Navarro County Historical Commission. The inscription on this marker told a completely different story than the first one that had been placed there by the water district. Even though Margaret was a member of the historical commission, she couldn't recall a vote being taken at a meeting that approved the new marker. It seemed as though that the chairman had pretty much acted alone. His name was Bruce McManus (no relation to Adam McManus, as far as I know).

The only time that there was much publicity about this event was right after the remains were discovered and while a decision was being made as to what cemetery they should be moved to. But, in almost every story, Bruce McManus was quoted. It seemed as though he was not satisfied that the company hired by the water district had not come up with a more dramatic story for the history books. So he did his own study which included research on my great grandfather Prosper King Montgomery Jr. He also conducted interviews with several African American people who supposedly grew up the area near where the remains were found.

Mr. McManus is an ordinary citizen with a community college education who considers himself an amateur historian. In his research on my great grandfather, he discovered an 1860 census record showing ownership of several slaves in Carroll Parish, Louisiana, which lies a few miles upstream from Vicksburg, Mississippi, on the western banks of the Mississippi River. He also discovered a deed record from the Navarro County Courthouse which showed Prosper King had bought land along Chambers Creek in November of 1865, several months after the Civil War had ended and after the slaves had been freed in Texas. Had he done more serious research, he would have discovered that Grant's Union Army had overrun most of Carroll Parish in 1862, and that the slaves on the plantations there had sought refuge at Lake Providence where Grant made preparations for attacking Vicksburg. He also would have discovered that Prosper King Montgomery Jr. had abandoned his plantation, joined the Confederate army in Mississippi, and was later captured at the Battle of Vicksburg. He, like all other captives at Vicksburg who swore an oath to never again take up arms against the Union, was paroled and there is no record that he owned any slaves after his parole or that he ever set foot on Texas soil until after the Civil War.

As for Mr. McManus's interviews with the people in the area who could have been descendants of the folks whose remains were interred in the cemetery --- several of them claimed to have known about the graves before the lake was built but none of them could explain why they had not notified authorities at the time so that they could have been relocated as other graves in the area had been.

Long story short, Mr. McManus, like my former SBOE colleague Terri Leo, evidently enjoyed the spotlight and was not ready for the story to end when the water district erected the marker at the new grave site. That marker told a story that had been properly researched by professional historians, archaeologists, and anthropologists. He wanted one that would be more dramatic so he imagined a scene from "Gone With the Wind" and a place called "Montgomery Hill Plantation", complete with plenty of mistreated slaves and an owner with a bull whip who lived a very lavish lifestyle and sipped mint juleps every day at happy hour. As a result, the inscription on the marker that Mr. McManus was responsible for erecting was completely fallacious because there was never any evidence that my great grandfather ever owned a single slave while he owned property in Navarro County, Texas. It is true that he, and his father before him, owned slaves in Louisiana and Mississippi. I abhor the very idea of human slavery, and am not proud to be a descendant of slave owners. But I also didn't want history to record the false narrative that my ancestors defied federal law by owning slaves after the abolishment of slavery in the United States.

I never met Bruce McManus personally nor did I ever talk with him by phone. All our communications were by email. In my last email to him I asked to appear before the Navarro County Historical Commission to make my case for removing the false marker that he had erected. I never heard back from him and my cousin Margaret soon informed me that the marker had been removed even though there was no vote to do so by the historical commission. Several weeks later, Margaret emailed me a picture of a new marker that had been placed at the site that told almost the exact same story as the one that had been erected by the water district. I was pleased to have won my fight but I was, at the same time, upset that Bruce McManus's craving for the spotlight had caused Texas taxpayers to waste unnecessary dollars. What a waste to have two historical markers at the same site that tell almost identical stories!!

After that not so pleasant experience, my life has been free from controversy. Jo and I recently celebrated our forty-fifth anniversary with brunch at Hilltop, our favorite Hill Country restaurant. Although we both have dodged a few bullets, we are in reasonably good health. Our five kids, seven grandkids, and five great grandkids are scattered all over the country and we try to spend as much time as possible with them, but that never seems to be enough. Because of some good fortune, lucky investing, and Jo's German frugality, we are financially secure and our home just off the main square in Fredericksburg has been free and clear for several years. I guess you could say that we are "living the dream" but that, at our age, may be a bit of an overstatement.

DAN MONTGOMERY

Like my adopted grandfather and country poet, Whitney Maxwell Montgomery, I own a home but, unlike him, I don't have a "rose at the gate". I have two gates and both lead into my back yard. Maybe I'll buy a rose for each gate to honor my family heritage. And on both gates, if I can scrape up the funds, I will place identical historical markers (with no help from Texas taxpayers) with my Uncle Whit's poem inscribed:

I cannot boast of a broad estate,
But I own a home with a rose at the gate.

I hold the title, and I keep the keys,
And in and out I can go as I please.

My home is not grand, but I live content,
For no man sends me a bill for rent,

And no man comes with a brush and a pail
To paint a sign on my door, "For Sale".

I cannot boast of a broad estate,
But I own a home with a rose at the gate.

Most of our clan at grandson Will's wedding in Austin in 2017
(He's with the bow tie)

About the Author

DAN MONTGOMERY, A fourth generation Texan, is a native of Navarro County, a graduate of Fairfield High School, and holds two degrees from Sam Houston State Teachers College. He was a coach, teacher, and athletic director for more than thirty years at the high school, junior college, and university levels in Texas. Dan also served as an elected member of the Texas State Board of Education from 2001 until 2007. He and his wife Joan have five children, seven grandchildren, and five great grandchildren. They are retired and have lived in Fredericksburg, Texas since 1990.